"*Core Competencies in Cognitive-Behavioral Therapy* vividly brings to life all that excellent CBT can be: science and art, systematic and reflective, authoritative and collaborative, serious and playful. Cory Newman embodies all that he teaches, he is a master CBT therapist and educator, and as a reader I feel privileged to be learning from him."

–Willem Kuyken, Professor of Clinical Psychology, University of Exeter, United Kingdom

Core Competencies in Cognitive-Behavioral Therapy

Core Competencies in Psychotherapy Series

SERIES EDITOR
Len Sperry
Florida Atlantic University, Medical College of Wisconsin

Competency represents a paradigm shift in the training and practice of psychotherapy that is already challenging much of what is familiar and comfortable. This series addresses the core competencies common to highly effective psychotherapeutic practice, and includes individual volumes for the most commonly practiced approaches today: cognitive behavior, brief dynamic, and solution-focused therapies, and others.

VOLUMES IN THIS SERIES

Highly Effective Therapy: Developing Essential Clinical Competencies in Counseling and Psychotherapy
Len Sperry

Core Competencies in Counseling and Psychotherapy: Becoming a Highly Competent and Effective Therapist
Len Sperry

Core Competencies in the Solution-Focused and Strategic Therapies: Becoming a Highly Competent Solution-Focused and Strategic Therapist
Ellen K. Quick

Case Conceptualization: Mastering this Competency with Ease and Confidence
Len Sperry & Jonathan Sperry

Core Competencies in Cognitive-Behavioral Therapy: Becoming a Highly Effective and Competent Cognitive-Behavioral Therapist
Cory F. Newman

Core Competencies in Cognitive-Behavioral Therapy

Becoming a Highly Effective and Competent Cognitive-Behavioral Therapist

CORY F. NEWMAN

Routledge
Taylor & Francis Group

NEW YORK AND LONDON

First published 2013
by Routledge
711 Third Avenue, New York, NY 10017

Simultaneously published in the UK
by Routledge
27 Church Road, Hove, East Sussex BN3 2FA

Routledge is an imprint of the Taylor & Francis Group, an informa business
© 2013 Taylor & Francis, LLC

The right of Cory F. Newman to be identified as author of this work has been asserted by him in accordance with sections 77 and 78 of the Copyright, Designs and Patents Act 1988.

Library of Congress Cataloging in Publication Data

Newman, Cory Frank.
Core competencies in cognitive-behavioral therapy : becoming a highly effective and competent cognitive-behavioral therapist / Cory F. Newman.
p. cm.—(Core competencies in psychotherapy series)
Includes bibliographical references and index.
ISBN 978-0-415-64346-7 (hbk) ISBN 978-0-415-88751-9 (pbk.)
1. Cognitive therapy. 2. Psychotherapist and patient. I. Title.

RC489.C63N49   2012
616.89'1425—dc23

2012002419

ISBN: 978-0-415-64346-7 (hbk)
ISBN: 978-0-415-88751-9 (pbk)
ISBN: 978-0-203-10744-7 (ebk)

Typeset in Palatino
by Apex CoVantage, LLC

To Becky

CONTENTS

CONTENTS

AUTHOR BIOGRAPHY

Cory F. Newman, PhD, ABPP, is Director of the Center for Cognitive Therapy, and Professor of Psychology in Psychiatry at the University of Pennsylvania's Perelman School of Medicine. Dr. Newman is a Diplomate of the American Board of Professional Psychology, with a specialty in Behavioral Psychology, and a Founding Fellow of the Academy of Cognitive Therapy. Dr. Newman has been highly active as a therapist and supervisor throughout his career, continuously maintaining a full caseload at the Center for Cognitive Therapy and having supervised over 250 cognitive-behavioral therapists-in-training over the past two decades. Dr. Newman has served both as a protocol therapist and protocol supervisor in a number of large-scale psychotherapy outcome studies, including the Penn-Vanderbilt-Rush Treatment of Depression Projects. Dr. Newman is also an international lecturer, having presented scores of cognitive therapy workshops and seminars across the USA and Canada, as well as fourteen countries in Europe, South America, and Asia. Dr. Newman is the author of dozens of articles and chapters related to the therapeutic relationship, clinical supervision, and cognitive-behavioral therapy for a wide range of disorders. He has also previously co-authored four books, including being the lead author of *Bipolar Disorder: A Cognitive Therapy Approach.* Dr. Newman is a past recipient of both the Earl Bond Award for distinguished teaching and supervision of psychiatry residents at the University of Pennsylvania, and the Penn Psychotherapy Professorship Award for clinical expertise.

ACKNOWLEDGMENTS

I would like to extend my sincere thanks to Len Sperry, the editor of the series on *Core Competencies in Psychotherapy*, for inviting me to contribute this volume on cognitive-behavioral therapy, and for his support as the project developed. Likewise, I am grateful to Marta Moldvai at Routledge/Taylor & Francis for her timely and helpful assistance in bringing the manuscript to fruition. My long-standing colleagues at the Center for Cognitive Therapy at the University of Pennsylvania—including Rebecca Naugle Keiser, Russ Ramsay, Kevin Kuehlwein, Mary Anne Layden, Pat Furlan, Rita Ryan, Tom Treadwell, Krishna Kumar, Tina Inforzato, and others—deserve appreciation, both in terms of my respect for their work, and with regard to their extra efforts while I was away writing this book on sabbatical. By extension, I want to thank Mark Whisman for arranging for me to be a Visiting Professor at the University of Colorado at Boulder in the Department of Psychology and Neuroscience, and for helping make the experience easy, enjoyable, and conducive to writing. I also wish to express my admiration and thanks to my colleagues in the field of cognitive-behavioral therapy—many of whom I have cited in this volume—whose efforts as trainers, authors, master therapists, and researchers have advanced our field in immeasurably valuable ways, and whose writings have significantly informed this text. I especially want to mention Ruth Greenberg, Art Freeman, Robert Berchick, and the late Fred Wright, who were my original supervisors at the Center for Cognitive Therapy, and from whom I learned how to be a proficient cognitive-behavioral therapist. Finally, I owe a significant debt of gratitude to Aaron T. Beck, my mentor for so many years, who has provided the substance and the inspiration for this work, and the works of so many others.

Cory F. Newman

LIST OF BOXES, FORMS, AND FIGURES

FOREWORD

Over the years, I have had the privilege of attending many workshops conducted by Cory Newman, in several different countries. In his lectures, Cory Newman displays such a wonderful blend of science and clinical wisdom that many colleagues and I hoped he would eventually find the time to put all that into a new book. So I was very pleased to learn that he had completed this volume on competencies in cognitive-behavioral therapy (CBT), and honored when offered to write this foreword.

The issue of competencies in psychotherapy is certainly not new, but interest in the topic has soared as psychological therapies become increasingly accepted as part of basic public health services.

It has been a long way since the early days of Janet and Freud, when psychotherapy was an emerging field, dominated by intuition rather than by empirical research. It may seem hard to believe today, but the fact is that only sixty years ago outcome studies in psychotherapy were almost non-existent. In those days, views on the efficacy of psychological interventions were black-or-white. While some believed psychotherapy was the greatest invention of the century, others saw it as just another form of quackery. Those who favored an empirical approach to the problem, although clearly in the minority, succeeded in generating a strong current of research, mostly focused on treatment outcome.

The empirical approach was very successful, and there are now a considerable number of empirically-supported psychological interventions to treat most mental disorders. Behavior therapy, and later cognitive therapy, played a significant role in this historical movement. Generic orientations, such as those provided by Freud in his technical writings, were replaced by detailed treatment manuals. The fidelity and skill with which these manuals were implemented had to be assessed as well, giving birth to therapist's competence scales.

Inspired by medical investigation, one of the early assumptions in psychological treatment outcome research was that the procedure was the main factor behind therapeutic change. Clinical experience suggested, however, that the importance of the therapeutic alliance should not be underrated. But it took some time before empirical data could substantiate this claim. We now know that the therapeutic alliance is as important–if not more important- than technical procedures for bringing about psychological change.

Having established that psychotherapy works, and that therapists achieved change by both technical and interpersonal means, scientific scrutiny turned to the procedures that were used for the training of psychotherapists. And the rather awkward truth was that training was much more based on common sense and lore than on well-researched teaching procedures. Expert therapists would train a small number of candidates in intuitive ways that made a lot of sense, but had never been put to the test. This state of things was clearly insufficient for a form of treatment that aspired to scientific rigor.

And so, the problem had to be addressed empirically. Research proved experts were right. We now know that we do not train in vain: workshops and supervision dramatically improve therapeutic performance and enable the supervisee to attain higher levels of quality and fidelity in delivering psychological treatments.

The success of psychotherapy, and particularly of CBT, has led to the dissemination of these treatments to an unprecedented level. Perhaps the best example of this current trend is the *Improving Access to Therapy* program in the United Kingdom, involving the training of thousands of psychotherapists employed by the public health care system. Naturally, the scale of dissemination demanded increasing systematization of training, leading to growing interest in the topic of developing competencies. Also, CBT became a global enterprise, adding cross-cultural issues to the already complex business of training psychotherapists.

Cory Newman's career as a therapist and a supervisor developed as these events were taking place, putting him in an ideal position for writing this book. Having trained with an expert of the stature of Aaron 'Tim' Beck, he has witnessed the development of the field of CBT from the vantage point of the Center for Cognitive Therapy in Philadelphia. He has treated people with diverse psychological problems, an experience reflected in publications on substance abuse, bipolar disorders, personality disorders and other mental conditions. He has supervised therapists participating in several research protocols, and has conducted workshops on CBT in places as different as North America, Argentina, Hong Kong, Switzerland, France, Poland, Brazil, and Scandinavia.

This book is a wonderful summary of all the experience accrued after so many hours devoted to treating clients, teaching CBT and supervising novice and seasoned therapists, in diverse cultural settings.

Chapter 1 summarizes all the current models of competencies that strive to describe and classify the different skills—technical and interpersonal—that a psychotherapist must possess in order to provide good psychotherapy. Cory Newman then lists the values of CBT therapists. These are simply and elegantly formulated, in a manner that is characteristic of his teaching. At the end of each chapter the reader will find the equivalent of CBT's *capsule summaries*: a list of key points to remember.

Chapters 2 and 3 review the conceptual and scientific basis of CBT, an essential requirement of good conceptualization. A good understanding of the principles that promote change according to cognitive-behavioral models is indispensable for moving effectively from reading treatment manuals to implementing them effectively in the office. A list of essential readings will be of use for trainees in CBT.

Chapter 4 and 5 are dedicated to the therapeutic alliance. They provide nice examples of how the therapeutic relationship is built in the spirit of collaborative empiricism, while being alert to the client's stage of change, and his/her sensitivity to distress. An excerpt from a supervision session provides a clear example of the process.

Chapters 6, 7, 8 and 9 present a state-of-the-art, succinct overview of all the steps in CBT: building a conceptualization and an intervention plan, selecting and applying techniques (including a very useful list of do's and don'ts), monitoring treatment evolution and assessing treatment outcome, maintaining treatment gains and closing therapy.

Chapter 10 refers to the issues of cultural and ethical sensitivity. In modern multicultural societies, the ability to include cultural and gender issues in conceptualizations and in building a therapeutic alliance becomes an indispensable competency for every therapist.

Finally, chapter 11 provides wise advice for novice therapists on how to continually improve their skills, as well as useful metaphors for engaging clients in the therapeutic process. This section closes with a reference to the issue of therapists' self-reflection, providing a few examples in which skillful self-application of CBT techniques by the therapist allows him/her to overcome an *impasse* in treatment.

This volume will prove a valuable tool not only for trainers and trainees in CBT, but also for training programs in other forms of psychotherapy. But should you still hesitate about reading it, I suggest that you pay attention to the post-therapy "thank you" postcards sent by clients of the Center for Cognitive Therapy mentioned in Chapter 11. They reflect with great precision what CBT can achieve when performed by a talented, committed therapist like Cory Newman. Every therapist wants to know how to get postcards like that, and this book can be of great help in achieving that goal.

Eduardo Keegan
March 2012

PREFACE

It is widely established that cognitive-behavioral therapies (collectively subsumed under the acronym "CBT") represent a plethora of evidence-based treatments, and that the manuals that outline and describe these treatments go a long way toward ensuring that therapists will have clear, up-to-date roadmaps by which to deliver them reliably to clients. However, the specific competencies that therapists need in order to be highly effective agents of a cognitive-behavioral therapy are not always easy to specify or quantify in a meaningful way. For example, the Cognitive Therapy Scale (CTS; Young & Beck, 1980) is one of the most well-known and well-established measures of therapist competency in conducting CBT (Trepka, Rees, Shapiro, Hardy, & Barkham, 2004), spelling out 11 areas of therapist functioning that are supposed to be present in any given session (e.g., setting an agenda, collaborating with the client, focusing on key behaviors and cognitions, sharing feedback, assigning and reviewing homework). Although the CTS has been very useful in guiding practitioners toward adhering to the categorical requirements of conducting CBT, it has been somewhat difficult to achieve high levels of reliability in rating the *quality* of the therapist's activities. In other words, the field has been able to determine *when* therapists are delivering the important components of CBT, but it has had more trouble in evaluating *how well* therapists are conducting the treatment.

Along the same lines, when we evaluate how well therapists are conducting CBT, we must take into account their level of training and experience. The *developmental stage* of therapists' education in and practical applications of CBT informs us as to what level of competency we expect from them (Rodolfa, Bent, Eisman, Nelson, Rehm, & Ritchie, 2005). Although it will go beyond the scope of each of the chapters that follow to spell out the separate levels of competency required of distinct categories of therapists such as graduate level trainees, postdoctoral fellows, newly licensed practitioners, early-career supervisors, seasoned therapists and trainers, program directors, and the like, mention will be made at times of those competencies that are necessary from early in one's training, as distinguished from those that are more indicative of diligent practice over many years.

In spite of the important distinctions to be drawn between novice and more experienced therapists, there is good reason for beginning therapists to be hopeful about their competence. For example, there is evidence that having supervised training in CBT allows early-career therapists to have better success in treating clients with anxiety disorders than their peers who have not had such training (Howard, 1999). This is not to say that years of experience are not important in conducting competent CBT, as it may be that the fund of knowledge possessed by seasoned CBT practitioners is especially useful in treating clients who have had longstanding psychological problems, and/or whose problems have been refractory to earlier treatments (Wilson, 2007). Nevertheless, there are data to suggest that, "... even beginning clinicians can obtain good outcomes, with a strong therapeutic alliance, good preparation ... and strong supervision ..." (Ledley, Marx, & Heimberg, 2010, p. 7).

Related to the above, there is ample evidence that good relational skills are central to the effective delivery of therapy (Crits-Christoph, Gibbons, Hamilton, Ring-Kurtz, & Gallop, 2011; Norcross & Lambert, 2011; Safran & Muran, 2000). Combining interpersonal competencies with faithfully following the guidelines of an evidence-based treatment allows clinicians the best chance to help their clients. At the same time, there are additional, important competencies that may help maximize therapeutic outcomes that are not often emphasized in the literature, though perhaps they are discussed in competent clinical supervision. For example, one may hypothesize that it is advantageous if a therapist communicates concisely and clearly, as opposed to speaking in a manner that is less fluent and less easily followed by clients. Similarly, given the multitude of tasks that are typically part of structuring and conducting a CBT session, one may posit that being well-organized also correlates with providing competent therapy. Additionally, consistent with the psycho-educational model that is inherent in CBT, it is reasonable to suggest that the best CBT therapists possess qualities and utilize methods that are similar to those of the most effective teachers, such as those who make a life-long impression on their students. Just as some teachers are more "inspirational" and get more out of their students than others, so do competent therapists maximize what their clients obtain from therapy, including long-term maintenance of gains. Anecdotally, this quality involves being unfailingly encouraging, leading clients who had serious doubts about their ability to change to come to believe in themselves, and consequently to do much more of the work of therapy than they ever expected.

Going further still, given the cognitive demands of managing factual and conceptual data across many clients in a caseload, one might surmise that using methods to enhance one's memory is yet another route toward competency as a CBT therapist. Having a good sense of "timing" arguably is also important (i.e., it's not simply *what* you say, but *at what moment* you choose to say it), as is having affective and vocal "range" (i.e., it's not only *what* you say, but in what manner, and with what tone), as well as a facility in being in "synchrony" with the client's nonverbal communications, including facial expressions and body language (see Ramseyer & Tschacher, 2011). Related to these factors is the variable of *humor*, which plays a role in making therapy more memorable and engaging, but may also risk the unintended side-effect of making the client feel mocked unless the therapist's "irreverence" is communicated in a way that laughs *with* the client (see Linehan, 1993). When handled with sensitivity, therapeutic humor can improve the sense of collaboration between therapist and client; it can amusingly point out the absurdity of rigid, dysfunctional ways of thinking; and it can model a health-promoting coping skill for the client (Wright, Basco, & Thase, 2006). These are the sorts of variables that will be illustrated in the sample transcript material in this volume, along with the nuts and bolts of the well-established procedures. Where there is a dearth of empirical data on the subject, hypothesis generation will be the course to take.

It should be noted that the competencies mentioned above are not orthogonal; on the contrary, they probably interact synergistically. For example, the therapist who is adept at remembering important historical dates of relevance to the client (e.g., birthdays, anniversaries), and the names of significant others in the client's life probably also succeeds in improving the therapeutic relationship, as the client feels that he or she is being treated as an important individual, rather than as just another name on a crowded schedule. Similarly, a therapist who has a good sense of humor and a broad affective and verbal range will be capable of being playfully irreverent at such times when it is likely that the client will respond favorably, but will also know how to be somber if the client is not as responsive to kidding around. Likewise, a therapist who is acutely perceptive to the client's interpersonal style may ironically demonstrate empathy best of all by being *restrained* in his or her overt expressions of compassion when the client is asking for more practical sources of support (see Elliott, Bohart, Watson, & Greenberg, 2011). Similarly, a therapist who generally makes it a point to stick to the agenda in order to remain "on task" may choose to be more flexible with the focus of a given session when the client is especially vulnerable and needs more validation and overt gestures of concern. To make such distinctions means that the therapist is highly attuned to the mood of the moment, and competent at conceptualizing each client's needs, so as to match the intervention to the individual, which of course requires a broad repertoire of delivery. These are the sorts of multiple-competency interactions that are difficult to operationalize, but which can be modeled in supervision, and depicted in illustrative transcript material. The *substance* of the CBT interventions still needs to be there, but the *style* of delivery may be quite important as well, and this text endeavors to illustrate that aspect.

Along the same lines, the core competencies of CBT that are described in the following chapters are in no way orthogonal with the core competencies of other approaches to psychotherapy (see Sperry, 2010). While CBT may have its own nomenclature, priorities, and points of emphasis, competent cognitive-behavioral clinicians have much in common with their competent brethren from other theoretical orientations (see Castonguay & Beutler, 2006; Norcross & Goldfried, 2005). Nowhere is this more apparent than in the area of the therapeutic relationship, where the two chapters explicitly devoted to this topic cite as much data from the general literature as from authors identified specifically as CBT clinician-researchers. As one of the core values of CBT is a respect for empirical findings, it is not incongruous for a volume on CBT to reference solid, empirical evidence from whatever source. Similarly, the chapter on achieving cultural and ethical competency in CBT is also pertinent to the field of psychotherapy as a whole, as all mental health professionals face the challenges inherent in putting professionalism, skilled practice, and the well-being of clients ahead of personal biases, and as dramatic demographic changes in society require greater attention to, study of, and respect for the role that culture plays in therapy (Cardemil, Moreno, & Sanchez, 2011).

Another component of competency in CBT—one that has been given increasingly more attention in the literature—is therapist *self-application* of the model and methods of treatment (see Bennett-Levy & Thwaites, 2007). Therapists who endeavor to "practice what they preach" gain valuable experience in terms of the sheer repetition of the techniques in their everyday life, as well as increased empathy for the difficulties clients may face as they attempt to implement their self-help assignments. Aside from the benefits that the self-application of CBT will have on therapists' competence in conducting treatment, there is the added benefit that therapists will experience an improved mood state, hopefulness, and sense of self-efficacy. Improved self-care and quality of life are important considerations for those who undertake the challenging work of being in the helping professions, and CBT methods can be at the center of those efforts to help us become beneficiaries of our own treatments, and better self-help role-models for our clients.

This book intends to do more than simply reiterate the treatment methods that are already so comprehensively described in many CBT manuals, though of course such techniques will be referenced and highlighted as a matter of course. Rather, this book additionally endeavors to "read between the lines" of the treatment protocols, so that the more difficult-to-pin-down therapeutic methods and therapist attributes that bring the best of the manuals to life, and get the most out of the clients' participation and involvement, are posited and explained.

This text endeavors to explicate the principles of competent CBT across a range of clinical concerns and diagnostic areas. Similarly, this book does not focus on one particular client population (e.g., children, geriatric clients, developmentally delayed) nor does it single out a given modality of treatment delivery (e.g., individual, group, couples, family, inpatient). While acknowledging that the above categories are important to distinguish as they represent relevant differences in the way that CBT is conducted, this book intends to spell out the core competencies of CBT that may be applied across the board, and across one's professional career.

The forthcoming chapters, headlined as they are in order to emphasize key topics such as forming a therapeutic alliance, maintaining a therapeutic alliance, conceptualizing cases, and implementing interventions (to name a few), could give the mistaken impression that these are discrete, self-contained categories. To the contrary, the reader will see clinical examples portrayed in a chapter about the therapeutic relationship that easily could have been used in a chapter on case conceptualization, and vice versa, and sample transcript material depicting the application of interventions that could just as well have been presented in the case conceptualization chapter. Similarly, issues regarding the optimal handling of the therapeutic relationship will be readily apparent in the chapter that discusses termination and maintenance. Although each chapter will clearly emphasize the core features of its given topic, there will be no attempt to separate clinical concerns that naturally dovetail. Similar messages that are presented across chapters are not so much redundancies as they are implicit cross-references. In fact, one of the hallmarks of the competent delivery of CBT may be the therapist's ability to combine important components of the treatment in an apparently seamless, time-effective, comprehensive manner.

For example, it requires considerable competence in conceptualization to ask the right questions to subtly, gradually encourage clients to disclose significantly important thoughts, feelings, and other relevant information that they had been keeping secret out of a sense of shame. In doing so, therapists have to be particularly empathic, as they give clients the clear message that the latter will not be judged, abandoned, or otherwise harmed for disclosing something they think is a terrible reflection on themselves and their lives, but that is so important in order to conceptualize the case and formulate potentially powerful interventions. In this manner, highly competent CBT is "polyphonic"—clear, horizontal lines of empathy, case conceptualization, and interventions are played out in such a way that they go together harmoniously at any given point in time, or at least lead to satisfying resolutions after moments of anticipatory tension.

The competent CBT practitioner understands and values the principles of adhering to well-established, evidence-based treatments. At the same time, he or she recognizes that even the best treatment packages are still "general" approaches that are applied in the context of an individually crafted treatment. Further, treatment manuals—as products of a positive feedback loop of hypotheses and empirical tests—are works in progress, and therefore represent single points on the field's learning curves, which presumably are ever-rising. The good-faith use of CBT manuals in real-life clinical settings invariably leads to new questions and altered applications, some of which may be considered to be "deviations" from evidence-based practice, others of which may be seen as benign digressions from established tasks, and still others of which (through further study) may come to represent the next set of advances in the field.

In some respects, delivering a well-conceived, competent CBT session is somewhat analogous to performing an Olympic ice-skating routine. On ice, each participant must complete the "required elements" of jumps, spins, strength moves, footwork, and combinations thereof to complete the routine free of penalized omissions. More than this, however, each skater also brings his or her own artistry, interpretation, creativity, music, style, pacing, and personality to the program, all of which have a lot to say about the quality of the final result. In this regard, achieving competency in CBT is more than "doing what you're supposed to do" in terms of fidelity to the model. It also has to do with competencies that imbue each of the "required elements" with a greater likelihood of having a positive and lasting impact on clients.

At the risk of stating the obvious, therapists who conduct CBT competently may share common skills, knowledge, and attitudes, but they are not carbon copies of each other. Psychotherapy is a human endeavor (the recent promise of computer-assisted methods of therapy notwithstanding, see Wright, Wright, & Beck, 2004), and individual differences in communication and relational styles can result in observable differences between one competent CBT practitioner and another, even as they both faithfully enact the core procedures of the model. Studying, learning, and practicing evidence-based treatments such as CBT do *not* require a relinquishing of one's personal style. Arguably, the most effective examples of the delivery of CBT are by those who have been able to weave the strengths of their individual style elegantly into the organized, procedural features that comprise assessment and intervention in CBT. Naturally, this book will reflect the personal style of its author, even as it endeavors to elucidate the core competencies that are pertinent to any practitioner of cognitive-behavioral methods. Likewise, other volumes on CBT speak with the voices of their respective authors. With that in mind, readers of this text are encouraged to develop and nurture their *own* personal strengths in the conducting of CBT, while also working diligently to improve areas that do not come as naturally. The goal is for practitioners to combine the best of themselves with best practices, resulting in even more favorable outcomes for more clients.

1

Introducing the Clinical Competencies of Cognitive-Behavioral Therapy

"To show our simple skill, that is the true beginning of our end."

William Shakespeare (Midsummer Night's Dream)

To the "naked eye," the conducting of CBT in a competent manner often looks very straightforward and uncomplicated. However, it is actually not so easy to deliver CBT in the manner in which it was intended—that is to say, with accurate empathy, warmth, good listening skills, and clarity of communication *as a starting point*, combined with the organizational, conceptual, and technical skills that are well-tied to CBT theory and principles. Adding to the challenge, these methods are to be practiced with a considerable level of energy, as CBT therapists generally do not sit back passively, but rather actively direct the course of treatment while enthusiastically collaborating with clients in setting and pursuing therapeutic goals (Beck, Rush, Shaw, & Emery, 1979). Further, the competent practice of CBT requires clinicians to be knowledgeable about cross-cultural and

1

ethical issues, and to be highly motivated to use this knowledge to provide clients with the most appropriate care.

TOWARD AN UNDERSTANDING OF "CORE COMPETENCIES"

What comprises the knowledge base, the practice skills, and the attitudes (or value system) that are necessary for therapists to demonstrate "competency"? This chapter will provide an overview of several models of competency that are highly instructive in their own ways, yet show a natural overlap that indicates concurrent validity. Extending from this, the chapter will briefly describe the rating items of the Cognitive Therapy Scale (Young & Beck, 1980) as exemplars of what constitute competency from a CBT perspective per se. This will be followed by an explication of some of the most important attitudes or values that competent CBT practitioners maintain to maximize the use of their fund of knowledge, their technical know-how, and their capacity for collaborating positively with their clients.

The Core Competencies in Counseling and Psychotherapy (the Sperry model)

Sperry (2010) explains that the route to becoming a highly competent and effective therapist involves significantly more than just learning and practicing a set of technical skills. He argues that the term *competency* connotes an integration of knowledge, skills, and attitudes such that there is authenticity and congruency between the therapist's behaviors and intentions. Taking this position a step further, the author states that successfully combining these important factors allows therapists to meet professional standards, to advance the well-being of others (e.g., clients, clinical trainees), to develop greater levels of expertise and capability, and to utilize self-reflection skills that will result in an enhancement of all of the above.

Sperry (2010) identifies six *core* competencies comprised of 20 subcategories that he describes as *essential* competencies that cut across many different mental health professions and theoretical orientations. The current volume will follow Sperry's organizational model closely, with many of the upcoming chapter titles reflecting these core competencies, and the chapter subheadings approximating the essential competencies. The following serves as a template for the way in which the Sperry model is reviewed in the present text:

1. *Conceptual foundation.* This refers to applying a conceptual "roadmap" to understand client functioning and dysfunction, and to direct the process of therapy. The current text will describe the conceptual foundations of CBT in Chapter 2.

2. *Relationship building and maintenance.* Covered in Chapters 3 and 4, this core competency includes establishing a positive alliance with clients; assessing their readiness for change and fostering treatment-promoting factors; recognizing and dealing effectively with resistance; noticing and repairing alliance strains; and managing the problems traditionally described by the descriptors "transference" and "countertransference," in cognitive-behavioral terms.

3. *Intervention planning.* Described in Chapters 5 and 6, this core competency entails performing an integrative, initial assessment; specifying a *DSM*-based diagnosis; formulating a cognitive-behavioral case conceptualization; devising a well-directed cognitive-behavioral treatment plan; and writing a thorough report that covers the above.

4. *Intervention implementation.* Largely presented in Chapter 7, this core competency involves establishing and maintaining a treatment focus across sessions; applying CBT procedures and related homework assignments; and dealing effectively with factors that would otherwise interfere with the successful delivery of CBT.

5. *Intervention evaluation and termination.* Reviewed in Chapters 8 and 9, this core competency is exemplified by monitoring client progress and modifying treatment accordingly (including the utilization of supervision for this purpose); helping clients maintain their treatment gains; and preparing clients for a positive end to treatment.

6. *Culturally and ethically sensitive practice.* Addressed in Chapter 10, this core competency is reflected by the development of effective, cultural case formulations; planning, tailoring, and delivering culturally sensitive interventions; and making ethically sound and sensitive decisions.

The final chapter of this text (Chapter 11) does not explicate a core competency per se, but rather presents the factors that help CBT practitioners to attain (and retain) competency and expertise over time, as therapists and as supervisors.

The "Cube Model"

A useful heuristic called the "cube model" (Rodolfa et al., 2005) illustrates three hypothesized dimensions on which to gauge the degree to which therapists are meeting the standards of the profession. The first of these dimensions has been labeled the *foundational* competencies, representing the overarching qualities to which all therapists should aspire, irrespective of their theoretical orientation. These include a healthy awareness of and respect for ethical standards; the ability to relate to others in a sincere, caring manner; possessing good communication and interviewing skills; being sensitive to cultural issues in conducting therapy and supervision; having the ability to engage in self-reflection and self-correction; possessing a working knowledge of models of psychological dysfunction and wellness; and collaborating effectively with practitioners across related disciplines. The clinician who demonstrates foundational competencies is already well positioned to become a competent CBT practitioner even before starting CBT training per se.

The second dimension is known as the *functional* competencies, which are comprised of a more specific knowledge base and practice skill set. From the vantage point of CBT, the list of functional competencies would include the ability to convert raw, clinical data into a cognitive-behavioral case formulation; facility in conducting well-paced, well-organized, goal-directed therapy sessions; knowing how to engage clients in an active, collaborative process; possessing a wide repertoire of cognitive-behavioral techniques; being adept at teaching those techniques to clients and using homework to solidify the clients' learning; and conducting CBT supervision in a way that promotes the trainees' development as CBT clinicians while simultaneously attending to the proper care of their clients, and others.

The third dimension of the "cube" is the *developmental* axis, which takes into account the therapist's stage of training and experience in assessing his or her level of competency. As skill acquisition is a process, and as learning for one's entire career (and life) is an important value (see below), it makes sense to assess a CBT practitioner's level of effectiveness at different junctures, from the early days of being a practicum extern in graduate school to the later years of being a seasoned therapist,

4

supervisor, and perhaps a training director. This text will describe core elements of competency that apply across the span of one's career, though some skills will be identified as basic, whereas others will be highlighted as being more advanced.

The DPR Model

The "declarative–procedural–reflective (DPR)" model (Bennett-Levy, 2006) represents another heuristic through which to understand how therapists acquire competencies. *Declarative* knowledge has to do with the verbal propositional knowledge base for conducting CBT. This is comprised of information gleaned from readings and lectures in order to reach an abstract understanding of CBT theory and how CBT treatments may be delivered. This information may be interpersonal (e.g., having to do with the therapeutic relationship), conceptual (e.g., how psychopathology develops and is maintained), and/or technical (e.g., descriptions of therapeutic techniques such as guided discovery, activity scheduling, and rational responding). Declarative knowledge is acquired throughout one's career, but there is significant "front-loading" of this information early in one's graduate training, as a prelude and later as a companion to practicum experiences in which early-career therapists begin to learn *procedural* knowledge, which has to do with the practice of therapeutic methods, either in classroom workshops or more naturalistically with clients. Procedural knowledge is obtained, honed, and grown through actual *enactments* of the methods of therapy, based originally on declarative knowledge, but enhanced and developed through personal, hands-on experience. Over time, as therapists practice CBT with a greater number and variety of clients, they develop implicit rules and procedures that guide their actions in session, helping them to "decide with which client, at which point in time in therapy, with which kind of problem, it is most appropriate to use what kind of intervention, under what circumstances" (Bennett-Levy & Thwaites, 2007, p. 258).

The *reflective* system of learning pertains to the therapist's moment-by-moment awareness and evaluation of what is happening in the session, including the therapist's own thoughts, feelings, and actions. This area of learning comprises immediate awareness of a problem (e.g., the client's anger about a homework assignment), assessment of this problem (e.g., the homework assignment is triggering the client's beliefs and feelings of mistrust and vulnerability), and hypotheses and ideas about how to deal with the problem (e.g., to express concern for the client's feelings and communicate a desire to understand his or her thoughts rather than simply try to convince the client to do the homework). Being "reflective" means that therapists are attuned to their own experiences, the client's perceptions, and their interactions. The development of these skills, "can help to move therapists from being average to being sophisticated, flexible, and responsive practitioners" (Bennett-Levy & Thwaites, 2007, p. 258).

To illustrate the above, novice cognitive-behavioral therapists may go to great lengths to learn the principles of exposure methods in helping clients who suffer from maladaptive anxiety and avoidance. Through readings and lectures, they learn that clients who are able to face feared situations in a graded-task fashion, perhaps along with corresponding cognitive restructuring, can habituate to these otherwise arousal-provoking situations, increase their sense of self-efficacy, improve their mood, and expand their behavioral repertoires so as to enhance the quality of their lives. As these therapists gain clinical experience, they practice the methods of graded-exposure exercises with their anxious clients and become more adept at helping the clients to generate relevant hierarchies of avoided situations and to design corresponding homework assignments. However, it may require an even higher level of expertise to manage clients who have unexpectedly adverse reactions to these methods. For example, if a client responds to a basic relaxation induction with sobbing convulsions, the highly competent CBT clinician will need to:

- express more empathy than dismay at the client's unexpected, problematic response;
- quickly conceptualize the problem (e.g., the client has a profound fear of being mistreated if he or she lets down his or her guard by relaxing);
- proceed in such a manner that the client's reactions are validated and respected
- but not necessarily give the message that the intervention cannot work; and
- express a desire to understand and correct the problem, and move forward constructively.

It would be oversimplifying the stages of professional development to state categorically that beginner therapists achieve competence via the acquisition of declarative knowledge, early-career therapists become good practitioners through the repetition and mastery of procedural knowledge (based on a foundation of declarative knowledge), and experienced, master therapists demonstrate the height of competency via the facile use of reflective skills (to maximize the results of their use of declarative and procedural knowledge). In many respects, the three categories of declarative, procedural, and reflective knowledge are required at all stages of training and across one's career. We expect novice therapists to be adept at self-reflection as part of what makes them self-select for the field of mental healthcare. Similarly, we expect highly experienced therapists to receive continuing education via readings, workshops, and consultation and advanced supervision. Thus, it is important to examine declarative, procedural, and reflective knowledge sets as important, interactive factors across all time frames in a therapist's career, though the *degree* to which we expect therapists to acquire and master these skill sets respectively is somewhat dependent on their training status and level of experience.

MEASURING COMPETENCE IN CBT

The most widely used *general* measure of therapist adherence and competency in the field of CBT as a whole is the Cognitive Therapy Scale (CTS; Young & Beck, 1980), a measure that presents highly instructive guidelines on what procedures are reflective of competency in conducting any CBT session, regardless of the population being treated (Trepka, Rees, Shapiro, Hardy, & Barkham, 2004). A summary of the 11 categories of procedures described by the CTS is presented below:

1. *Setting an agenda.* When done most competently, the agenda is set early in the session, in collaboration with the client, and focuses on important, well-prioritized clinical targets. The session then follows the agenda faithfully, but also allows for flexibility if an unplanned but critical topic emerges.
2. *Feedback.* The competent CBT therapist elicits and responds to feedback from the client, both during the session (e.g., checking to see if the client has understood an important point), and at the end of the session to confirm a positive sense of closure, or otherwise to make repairs.
3. *Understanding.* Competent CBT practitioners understand the client's "internal reality," as evidenced by making comments that empathically show they are tuning in to what the client is feeling

and/or trying to communicate. They pay attention both to the client's verbal and nonverbal cues.

4. *Interpersonal effectiveness.* Competent cognitive-behavioral therapists are optimally warm and genuine, friendly within good boundaries, and exude a confidently professional demeanor while still being humble and approachable. They make every effort to encourage, support, and motivate their clients.

5. *Collaboration.* The competent CBT practitioner engages the client in such as way that they are both active participants in the process. When problems arise, the collaborative therapist does not engage in a power struggle or try to be "right," but rather tries to solve the problem together with the client.

6. *Pacing and efficient use of time.* Competent cognitive-behavioral therapists manage therapy time very well. They help the clients stay actively focused on the tasks and goals of treatment and generally tend to accomplish a lot in any given session, without going too fast or overwhelming the client.

7. *Guided discovery.* Therapists who are adept at guided discovery do not simply tell their clients what to think and what to do, but rather ask the sorts of thought-provoking questions that will help clients come to new realizations, or at least open their minds to ideas they had not yet considered.

8. *Focusing on key cognitions and behaviors.* A competently run CBT session is readily identified by the therapists calling the clients' attention to their own behaviors and thoughts (contents and processes) that are germane to their emotional distress, and that may serve as important targets for therapeutic change.

9. *Strategy for change.* This area of competence pertains to the CBT practitioner's use of a solid case conceptualization in the service of a treatment plan that will lead to meaningful improvements— or, if not, will provide useful data that will inform a revised treatment plan.

10. *Application of cognitive-behavioral techniques.* Competency in the application of CBT techniques is reflected in a broad repertoire; the degrees of clarity, fluency, and accuracy in the delivery of the techniques; and how well the therapist has prepared the client for and debriefed him or her about the technique.

11. *Homework.* No top-flight CBT session would be optimally complete without the therapist assigning well-targeted homework.

The best homework assignments are clearly explained, involve a good clinical rationale, and include the client's input into its design. Competent CBT clinicians make sure to review the results of the client's homework, and to give constructive feedback.

It is interesting to note that of the 11 rating categories on the CTS (above), three of them are explicitly about the therapeutic relationship (understanding; interpersonal effectiveness; collaboration), and another is implicitly so (feedback). This demonstrates the great value that CBT places on the therapeutic relationship in the competent delivery of the treatment.

THE VALUES, ATTITUDES, AND BELIEFS OF COMPETENT CBT THERAPISTS

Individuals as well as organized groups of individuals inherently maintain value systems, and the population of therapists is no exception (Falender & Shafranske, 2004). The fact that the mental health professions have formal codes of ethics attests to this reality. Cognitive-behavioral therapies, in addition to their identified methods and procedures of conceptualization and intervention, also represent a set of values and related beliefs. While it would be oversimplistic to imply that such values are absolute and static—to the contrary, the population of therapists who self-identify as practicing CBT is comprised of individuals with varying points of view who are capable of developing and changing over time, and who represent cultural milieus that span six continents—it is reasonable to present and expound on a list of what one might call the "values, attitudes, and beliefs" of the prototypical CBT clinician. Those listed and explained below are in no way meant to be exhaustive, set in stone, or universal, but rather serve as points of reflection, discussion, and even debate within the larger question of "What are the qualities of competent CBT therapists?"

1. *"Time is precious; I will use it well."*
   One of the elements of doing competent CBT is being a good manager of time, both in terms of the pacing of a given session, and with regard to the trajectory of learning opportunities presented to clients between and across sessions. An effective CBT therapist endeavors to make every session count, and to include

9

the highest priority agenda items whenever possible. The CBT therapist who values using time well also typically contributes significantly to the sessions having a sense of direction and purpose. Setting a clear agenda goes a long way toward accomplishing this end.

2. *"To be maximally proficient in CBT, it is best if I use it myself."*
There are a number of compelling reasons why it is a good idea for therapists who value the work they do with clients to use CBT for themselves. First, self-application of CBT methods by therapists affords them maximum familiarity with the methods, and will enhance their proficiency in presenting and explaining these techniques to their clients. Second, therapists can *personally benefit* from using CBT in their everyday lives. Therapists who take good care of themselves psychologically will be better role models for their clients in this regard. Third, CBT therapists who self-apply therapeutic techniques will be in an excellent position to understand the sticking points and difficulties involved in enacting such self-help techniques. Therefore, they will be more empathic and better prepared to do collaborative problem-solving with clients who profess that they cannot do their assignments. Fourth, there is something to be said for striving for "congruency" between one's professional and personal life. As one therapist put it, "I like to use CBT techniques on myself because that's what I tell my clients to do, and I don't want to be guilty of applying a double standard."

3. *"Two of my main goals are to teach my clients skills and to promote hopefulness."*
Although many specific, discrete techniques have been described in the CBT literature (see Chapter 7), one may say that the two overarching goals of CBT therapists are to teach clients to be more efficacious in helping themselves, and to be more hopeful and constructive in their outlook. What are the practical applications of this value? For one, if a given homework assignment neither teaches the client something new and useful nor improves his or her morale, it is time to re-evaluate the assignment, and to assess what went wrong. This is also the case in taking stock of a single session, or more broadly assessing how the course of treatment is progressing. If the clients are learning new psychological

skills and experiencing symptom improvement, the cognitive-behavioral therapist is on the right track.

4. *"Hypothesis generation and testing are far preferable to self-assured dogmatism."*
One of the reasons that CBT has a collaborative, "user-friendly" feel to it is that it is not an authoritarian approach to treatment. In CBT, therapists are trained to work in tandem with their clients, sharing their expertise in the psychological sciences with their clients while they in turn learn from their clients' expertise about their individual life experiences. Competent CBT clinicians teach their clients how to be empiricists—making hypotheses, collecting data, and then testing and revising hypotheses (Beck et al., 1979; Tee & Kazantzis, 2010). For example, competent therapists do *not* give their clients the message that says, "Your thoughts are all distorted, whereas I know precisely how your thoughts should be changed." Rather, the therapeutic message is more like, "The way you think seems to be part of your distress, so let's examine and evaluate your thoughts to see if there is a more constructive and beneficial way to view things." On a more global level, the valuing of hypothesis-testing and the eschewing of dogmatism are philosophical stances that have enabled the field of CBT to develop and grow over the decades. The well-trained CBT therapist does not believe that he or she has all the answers, nor does he or she think that the field has reached a sufficient amount of definitive conclusions. Rather, CBT—at the individual and collective levels—puts great stock in studying and improving the field's understanding of clinical problems and their treatment, to the point of being willing to make significant changes in the ways that assessment and interventions are conducted in light of new, well-supported empirical findings.

5. *"It is wise to strive to understand the logic embedded in the apparent illogic."*
While it is tempting for CBT practitioners to view the dysfunctional automatic thoughts of their clients as being necessarily "illogical," it is more empathic and conceptually more sophisticated to endeavor to discover the ways in which the automatic thoughts "make sense" to the clients. We may ask, "What is the logic in the clients' apparently illogical ways of thinking?" This is similar to the behavioral analytic query of, "What is the function of the dysfunction?"

6. *"I welcome being in the role of a 'student' for my entire career."*
Learning must continue throughout one's career, and the competent CBT therapist and supervisor welcome such ongoing opportunities to learn. Being a "student" for one's entire career means attending conferences and continuing education seminars, keeping up with the literature, and learning from one's own clients and supervisees. Competent CBT practitioners humbly embrace being in the role of students into perpetuity.

7. *"To have the trust and collaboration of a client is a privilege, not a right."*
Therapists, by virtue of their professional positions as healthcare givers, know that they maintain the lion's share of the responsibility in creating and maintaining an environment in which clients will have the best chance to thrive. Yes, the clients themselves have responsibilities—therapy cannot be done *to* them, but rather must be done in collaboration *with* them—but competent therapists accept that they will have to carry the load when their troubled clients have difficulty in participating optimally in the therapeutic process. Arguably, the mark of relationally competent therapists is not how nice and helpful they are in the context of smooth, easy alliances with clients, but how composed, caring, and professional they are in the face of clients who evince excessively negative reactions in spite of the therapists' genuine efforts to help. Competent therapists do not feel *entitled* to receive warmth and respect from clients, but rather are willing to *be* respectful and warm regardless of the clients' capacity to return the favor.

8. *"My eyes are not the only ones that see, and I must widen my lens."*
In order to best understand clients—and in doing so formulate more accurate case conceptualizations and improve the therapeutic relationship—CBT therapists need to be able to put themselves in their clients' places; to "walk a mile in their shoes." A good starting point is the realization that "understanding" requires active listening and a humble willingness to learn from the clients, and that providing *accurate* empathy will require therapists to be aware of (and work past) their own mental filters and personal biases that stem from the human limits of individual life experience. For example, a therapist who is male, Caucasian, single, upwardly mobile, and young may have to acknowledge that he cannot easily comprehend the range of emotions and

cognitions experienced by an older, female client of color who is having family problems and economic hardships. In this example, the competent CBT therapist has to expand the margins of his own viewpoints—indeed, he would do well to welcome this opportunity as one of the special benefits of being in a helping profession.

9. *"The right words matter; I believe in communicating with clients, colleagues, and trainees with kindness and clarity."*
The words of therapists and supervisors create potentially significant impact, and therefore must be weighed carefully. Therapists and supervisors are capable of having bad days like anyone else, but they must take great pains not to let their frustrations and preoccupations lead them to make imprudent remarks that may reflect badly on the ways they represent the profession, and that may have lasting, negative impact on those who hear. Competent therapists and supervisors are *careful communicators*, using words to provide their charges with useful (perhaps corrective) information, and or to boost their sense of self-efficacy. Toward this end, the competent therapist/supervisor has good self-awareness, as well as an appropriate filter between thought and utterance. Using tactful, well-crafted words can facilitate therapeutic messages that may otherwise be difficult to hear. The song lyric from the movie *Mary Poppins* that states, "A spoonful of sugar helps the medicine go down," is apropos to this matter.

10. *"As a therapist who understands the drawbacks of 'all-or-none' thinking, I believe in finding the 'happy medium' in helping clients solve their psychological problems."*
Therapists potentially have significant influence over their clients, and they must use this power wisely, judiciously, and with consistency. Part of this mandate is to weigh clinical decisions carefully, giving consideration to a wide range of possible viewpoints, methods, and goals that may best suit the clients, and taking a thoughtful, cautious approach in suggesting interventions. This means—among other things—generally eschewing unnecessary extremes in conducting therapy, and being mindful of the potential drawbacks or unintended consequences of a planned intervention before proceeding. CBT therapists often point out the hazards of clients' all-or-none thinking and behaviors, and therapists need

to be role models for the same sort of moderate approach that they endorse. Toward this end, therapists help their clients to weigh pros and cons, consider multiple options, and generally avoid taking unnecessary risks in dealing with the problems for which they seek help.

WHAT LIES AHEAD

Each of the chapters that follow could require entire books to explain their respective topics adequately. Indeed, this volume will cite many books that do just that—books on the conceptual model of CBT, the therapeutic relationship, case conceptualization, interventions, termination, cultural competency, supervision, and the like. Thus, there will necessarily and regrettably be omissions in a volume of this modest length. However, *Core Competencies in Cognitive-Behavioral Therapy* is written in such a way that the reader will comprehend the central methods, as well as the heart and the art of competent CBT. The upcoming chapters represent important components of CBT, which—if put together diligently by therapists who are motivated to excel—will afford their clients the valuable opportunity to obtain enduring relief from their emotional suffering.

KEY POINTS TO REMEMBER

- Achieving CBT competency requires an integration of knowledge, skills, and attitudes that meet the standards of the profession of psychotherapy; that benefit clients and trainees; and that improve over time with continuing education, practice, and self-reflection.
- Core competencies include understanding the conceptual foundations of CBT; building and maintaining a therapeutic relationship; planning, implementing, and evaluating CBT interventions; preparing clients for termination with the CBT self-help skills to prevent relapse; and engaging in culturally and ethically sensitive practice.

- The Cognitive Therapy Scale (Young & Beck, 1980) is the most widely used general measure of competency in CBT, specifying the key elements that comprise a well-conducted CBT session.
- There are a number of attitudes and values that are reflective of the competent practice of CBT, including the importance of using time well; the conceptual value in understanding the "logic" in the client's dysfunction; earning the client's trust as being a privilege; an acknowledgement of the benefits of therapist self-application of CBT self-help methods; and an open-minded approach to testing hypotheses and seeking new information, among others.

2

Understanding the Conceptual Basis of Cognitive-Behavioral Therapy

"Life is 10% what happens to you and 90% how you react to it."

Charles R. Swindoll

CBT is a well-researched, integrative amalgam of several historically important theoretical paradigms, most notably behavior therapy (e.g., operant reinforcement and classical conditioning principles); social-learning theory (e.g., the importance of interpersonal influences and modeling); and cognitive psychology and information processing (e.g., the ways in which people perceive, learn, remember, hypothesize, reach conclusions, and the limitations and biases inherent in these processes). To understand the conceptual basis of CBT, therapists should strive to read extensively about the history of the above models (e.g., the central works of theoreticians and researchers such as Albert Bandura, Aaron T. Beck, Albert Ellis, Hans Eysenck, Cyril Franks, George Kelly, Michael Mahoney, Isaac Marks, Donald Meichenbaum, Walter Mischel, Jack Rachman, Joseph Wolpe, among many others), along with more recent readings on new advancements in and variations of CBT. Although these are almost too numerous to review, some of the notables include books on such topics as resistance in CBT (e.g., Leahy, 2001), the development of dialectical-behavioral therapy

(DBT; Linehan, 1993), schema-focused therapy (SFT; Young, Klosko, & Weishaar, 2003), constructivism (Neimeyer & Mahoney, 1995), acceptance and commitment therapy (ACT; S. C. Hayes, Strosahl, & Wilson, 1999), mindfulness and other meta-cognitive approaches (Wells, 2009; Williams, Teasdale, & Segal, 2007), the cognitive behavioral analysis system of psychotherapy (CBASP; McCullough, 2000), functional analytic psychotherapy (FAP; Kohlenberg & Tsai, 1991), and interpersonal process in CBT (Gilbert & Leahy, 2007; Safran & Muran, 2000; Safran & Segal, 1990).

THE BASICS OF THE CBT MODEL

In cognitive-behavioral theory, psychological health is related to the functionality and adaptability of people's behavioral repertoires and thinking patterns, as well as their capacity for emotional self-regulation (often tied to physiological reactivity). In brief, the related behavioral piece involves the person's breadth of repertoire of behavioral skills for meeting the demands of a range of situations and settings, as well as how well the person learns from consequences (both for oneself and via the observation of others), including rewards, punishments, and an absence of stimuli. In terms of thinking patterns, the model holds that people do not learn solely as a result of consequences (e.g., reinforcement) and conditioning (i.e., learned associations), and they do not simply respond reflexively to stimuli, but rather they actively *construe* themselves, their world, and their future (the *cognitive triad*, A. T. Beck, 1976), and that these interpretations serve to mediate their responses to situations.

To illustrate, two clients may both evince high levels of social anxiety and avoidance. Neither person converses very much with others, and both tend to stay at home rather than engage in social activities. However, one of the clients demonstrates a paucity of social skills. He is a poor listener, he speaks quietly and inarticulately, and the feedback he has received from others has been frankly absent or negative. Clearly, his treatment will likely involve a concerted focus on social skills training. The other client, by contrast, listens well, can carry an interesting conversation, and is genuinely liked by others. How can she therefore be comparably socially anxious and avoidant as the skill-deficient male client? The answer lies in her subjective perceptions. She *believes* that she lacks social skills, she experiences anticipatory fears of saying something wrong and being socially humiliated, and she overlooks or discounts positive comments from others. Her problem is not a lack of behavioral skills, but rather of excessive inhibitions borne of negative assumptions. Her treatment would have a more marked cognitive focus than the other client. Competent CBT addresses the concerns of both of these clients by conceptualizing their respective problems and targeting interventions to their respective needs.

From a CBT perspective, what are the elements of *well* functioning? By and large, people who are more active, and who regularly engage in behaviors that they enjoy and that give them a sense of mastery, will tend to have better mood states overall than those who are less active and therefore have fewer ways in which to feel a sense of accomplishment. If they have been fortunate enough to be raised in an environment rich in positive reinforcers by people who are adaptive role models for bonding well with others, meeting life's responsibilities, and being adept learners, they will have an increased chance (compared to their less fortunate peers) of acquiring the range of constructive behaviors necessary to optimize success in navigating life's challenges. Similarly, people who are more capable of seeing the positive, hopeful sides of themselves, others, and the future (within normal limits)—again, perhaps in the context of a personal history involving role models with positive outlooks—and whose lives have not been unduly affected by unfortunate events, will possess a greater sense of self-efficacy and be less vulnerable to mood disorders, anxiety disorders, and other maladies of emotional health. Its name notwithstanding, CBT views emotionality as playing a critically important role in wellness, as demonstrated by persons who are skilled at emotional self-regulation, yet still possess a sufficient range of affect and a capacity for joy.

Understanding the CBT model entails having a detailed understanding of the ways in which clients' problematic behaviors and cognitions develop, manifest themselves, interact with each other, and are maintained. Cognitive-behavioral therapists teach clients ways in which to increase their adaptive behavioral repertoires (e.g., coping skills, communication skills, graded tasks), and to think more flexibly (e.g., fewer rigid, stereotyped ways of viewing situations), more objectively (e.g., less biased against themselves), more hopefully (e.g., less likely to experience despair), and with better problem-solving skills (i.e., not lapsing into helplessness in the face of stressors), taking into account the clients' learning histories that may have hindered the develop of these psychological skills. The next section highlights some of the characteristics of maladaptive behaviors and cognitions that CBT clinicians assess and target for intervention.

AREAS OF BEHAVIORAL ANALYSIS

CBT clinicians assess the functionality and adaptiveness of clients' behavioral patterns by evaluating them for certain problematic characteristics. The following is a representative (though nonexhaustive) sample of such characteristics, more thorough descriptions of which can be found in texts such as Antony and Roemer (2011), Hersen (2002), and O'Donohue (1998).

Behavioral Deficits

People who lack certain behavioral skills (relative to their normative peer group) may have had an impoverished learning environment, and/or may suffer from developmental neurobiological problems. In such cases, they will need more intensive, direct training in acquiring task-oriented or social skills. CBT can provide this when the natural environment is insufficient.

Undercontrolled Behaviors

These behaviors have also been described by words such as "impulsive," and "acting out," and are often associated with aggressive verbal and physical behaviors; dysregulated emotions (e.g., anger) that are disproportionate to the situation; overly spontaneous, poor decision-making; and addictive behaviors. In CBT, clients with these problems are taught to slow down their process of responding to internal and external stimuli, to learn to reduce their physiological arousal, and to methodically, systematically assess their situation and options before acting.

Overcontrolled Behaviors

Often associated with excessive inhibitory processes, these behaviors are commonly seen in cases of anxiety disorders, where people hold back from engaging in activities of which they are capable, and that could enhance the quality of their lives. Overcontrolled behaviors are particularly dysfunctional when clients prefer the temporary relief brought about by avoidance (i.e., negative reinforcement) over the long-range benefits of solving problems and feeling self-efficacious. Exposures and graded tasks are frequently part of CBT for this problem.

Overgeneralized Behaviors

Maladaptive behaviors are often identifiable by being cross-situationally pervasive, enacted by persons who have difficulty identifying important discriminative cues about what behaviors are appropriate in what situations. CBT addresses this problem by assisting clients in learning to make cross-situational distinctions, and to broaden their behavioral repertoires.

Difficult-to-Extinguish Behaviors

Behaviors that have been intermittently reinforced on a variable schedule, and/or those that represent "one-trial learning" (e.g., based on a highly traumatic experience) often prove very difficult to extinguish, even when they are not reinforced again for long periods of time. Typical interventions include providing healthy doses of positive reinforcement for behaviors that are incompatible with the problem behavior, and cognitive restructuring methods so as to modify the faulty beliefs that are maintaining the difficult-to-extinguish behavior (see below).

"LEVELS" OF COGNITION

In conceptualizing the manifestations and effects of clients' subjective interpretations, CBT practitioners examine both the content and the process of their clients' thoughts. The *content* of the clients' thinking can be assessed at varying levels, as follows:

- Automatic thoughts
- Intermediate beliefs (including "conditional assumptions")
- Core beliefs or maladaptive "schemas"

The division of these types of cognitions into discrete levels is not absolute, but they illustrate which types of thoughts tend to be more accessible to spontaneous self-awareness (higher levels), and which tend to be more difficult to change (lower levels).

Automatic Thoughts

At the "top" level, the term "automatic thoughts" (Beck, 1976; Beck et al., 1979) pertains to the running commentary going through people's minds at any given point in time. These thoughts are automatic in the sense

21

that they do not require deliberation or effort, but rather occur spontaneously, representing immediate reactions to what is happening in the client's sphere of experience at that moment, and/or their recollections, ruminations, and the like. These automatic thoughts can come and go so rapidly that people sometimes are not very aware they are experiencing them, and yet such thoughts can have a significant impact on their emotions. Examples might be, "This will never work," which may induce someone to quit trying to solve an otherwise manageable problem, and "How could I be so stupid?" which may make someone feel ashamed, even when she did not do anything wrong. Teaching clients to be aware of these automatic thoughts helps to reduce their potentially harmful impact, because the clients may then utilize strategic questions (e.g., "What are some other ways I can think about this situation?") to help modify their thoughts and therefore mitigate the emotional and behavioral consequences.

Intermediate Beliefs

At a deeper level of thought content we have intermediate beliefs, which are often in the form of general assumptions pertinent to the cognitive triad (i.e., regarding the self, others and the world, and the future), and "if–then" rules (also known as "conditional assumptions") that people implicitly follow. Although these intermediate beliefs typically are not part of the person's spontaneous running monologues in his or her mind (as are automatic thoughts), they have an impact on the types of automatic thoughts the person will be prone to have. In general, the more extreme the "if–then" statement, the less adaptive the assumption, and the more likely that it will give rise to dysfunctional automatic thoughts. One of the earliest attempts to identify and measure the maladaptive intermediate beliefs hypothesized to be implicated in clinical depression and anxiety disorders was the development of the Dysfunctional Attitudes Scale (DAS; Weissman & Beck, 1978). With this self-report questionnaire, clients were asked to endorse their degree of agreement (on a 7-point, Likert-type scale) with a wide range of beliefs, the extremes of which were hypothesized to be indicative of cognitive vulnerability to depression and anxiety. Items include, "People will think less of me if I make a mistake," "If I fail at work, then I am a failure as a person," and "I am nothing if a person I love does not love me."

There is evidence with unipolar depressive clients that changes in such negative assumptions are associated with positive outcome in treatment, as well as the reduction of symptomatic relapses in the future (M. Evans et al., 1992; Hollon, DeRubeis, & Seligman 1992; Parks & Hollon, 1988). Further, significant improvements in clients' mood during the course of CBT have been found to follow sessions in which they made measurable changes in cognitions such as the above (Tang, Beberman, DeRubeis, & Pham, 2005; Tang & DeRubeis, 1999).

Core Beliefs or Maladaptive "Schemas"

At a deeper level still, we have constructs known variously as "core beliefs" or "schemas," terms that have been used interchangeably in the literature, as the concept of *schema* often denotes the most basic, core dysfunctional beliefs that clients (particularly those with longstanding, cross-situational disturbance) accept as fundamental truths in their lives (Beck, Freeman, Davis, & Associates, 2004; Young et al., 2003). Rather than being conditional, schemas are hypothesized to be absolute. The individual with an *unlovability* schema (see Layden, Newman, Freeman, & Morse, 1993) does not simply maintain that, "I am lovable only if everyone loves me," but rather, "I am unlovable (period)." Similarly, a person with an *abandonment* schema does not hold that, "I will be left alone by people unless I'm truly important to them," but rather, "Everyone I care about is going to leave me."

An example of a measure intended to assess clients' schemas is the Young Schema Questionnaire (YSQ; see Schmidt, Joiner, Young, & Telch, 1995), which uses a self-report, Likert-type scale to identify which of its 15 factor-analyzed schemas clients load on most heavily. These schemas include "mistrust," "defectiveness," "abandonment," "entitlement," and others, and they are hypothesized to be most prevalent in clients with the most severe personality disorders (see Box 2.1 for a summary of schemas). A sample item is, "It is only a matter of time before someone betrays me" (mistrust schema). Another measure of deeper cognitive content, the Personality Beliefs Questionnaire (PBQ; Beck, Butler, Brown, Dahlsgaard, Newman, & Beck, 2001) is a self-report measure that also uses a Likert-type scale and comprises a clinically derived set of beliefs hypothesized to correspond to specific personality disorders. For example, the item, "If I ignore a problem, it will go away," is hypothesized

23

to reflect a part of the cognitive style of clients who meet the criteria for Avoidant Personality Disorder (*DSM-IV-TR;* American Psychiatric Association, 2000). Research on the PBQ indicates that clients with personality disorders preferentially endorse items theoretically linked to their specific diagnosis (Beck et al., 2001). Studies of serious mental health problems such as borderline personality disorder have looked at schema-level changes as indicative of the benefits of cognitive-behavioral approaches to treatment (e.g., Arntz, Klokman, & Sieswerda, 2005; Giesen-Bloo et al., 2006; Spinhoven, Bockting, Kremers, Schene, & Williams, 2007), and recent texts have focused on explicating the theoretical, empirical, and clinical bases of schema work across a wide range of specific disorders (Riso, du Toit, Stein, & Young, 2007; Young et al., 2003).

Box 2.1.
Sample Schemas (Core Areas of Negative Beliefs)

"I am unlovable, defective, a bad person." (schemas of unlovability/ defectiveness)

"Everyone always leaves me. I am all alone." (schemas of abandonment/social exclusion)

"I can't trust anyone. The world is dangerous." (schemas of mistrust/abuse/ vulnerability to harm)

"I am helpless, incompetent, dependent on others." (schemas of incompetence/dependence)

"I am empty inside. Nothing can fill that emotional void." (schema of emotional deprivation)

"I don't know who I am or what I want." (schemas of lack of individuation/ subjugation)

"My needs are so great that they must be met!" (schemas of entitlement/ insufficient limits)

"I need things to be just the way I want or I can't stand it!" (schema of unrelenting standards)

[adapted from Beck et al., 2004; Layden et al., 1993; Schmidt et al., 1995; Young et al., 2003]

MALADAPTIVE INFORMATION PROCESSING

Given that information is voluminous, how do people organize, categorize, filter, and pare down their observations to make them more manageable and understandable? Language acquisition and development play a key role in how people understand concepts and create mental categories to organize their experiences in an efficient way. Also, with life experience, people learn to make quick associations and assumptions about situations they encounter. This has the advantage of helping them to process information more efficiently, and to reach conclusions and make decisions without undue delay. Unfortunately, there are drawbacks as well. When people make rapid suppositions about a situation, they run the risk of being inaccurate—perhaps because the new situation is unlike the previous situations that served as the context for their earlier learning—resulting in emotional and behavioral responses that may not be adaptive in the new context. Negative consequences may result, with the individual experiencing hardship and suffering. This outcome leads to new learning, which itself may be flawed via faulty cognitive reasoning about the situation, leading the individual to adopt "lessons" that continue to be dysfunctional and cause emotional distress. In short, *errors* or *biases* in processing information play an important role in clients' emotional and behavioral problems. The following is a nonexhaustive list of logical errors in thinking *process:*

All-or-None (Black vs. White) Thinking

Most things in life exist on a spectrum or continuum, and this includes most examples of adaptive thinking. The danger in thinking in all-or-none, black vs. white terms is that it artificially limits people to only two choices, both of which may be extreme, statistically unlikely, and often less than functional. Thinking in this manner as a general rule makes a person more vulnerable to extreme emotions and decisions, and inhibits creative problem-solving.

Arbitrary Inference (Jumping to Conclusions)

This refers to the reaching of a conclusion without sufficient supporting evidence. An example is someone who expects to fail before even trying, and thus gives up prematurely.

Selective Abstraction (Seeing Things out of Context)

A person who engages in the cognitive process of selective abstraction tends to miss "the big picture," instead focusing on a particularly negative (and unrepresentative) aspect of the situation. An example is a young person who suffers from health anxiety and who interprets his temporarily increased heart rate after climbing stairs as a sign of a dangerous cardiac condition.

Mind-Reading

While it is not unusual for people to surmise what others might be thinking, those who engage in the cognitive error of "mind-reading" overestimate the accuracy of their assumptions, and generally risk interpersonal discord and ill feelings by habitually reading things into what others are saying or doing that are not necessarily true.

Catastrophizing (Magnification of the Negative)

When people catastrophize, they think about worst-case scenarios as if they are likely-case scenarios or only-case scenarios, and thus self-induce a great deal of distress over anticipated hardships and losses that may in fact be unlikely, highly preventable, and/or not so bad after all.

Disqualifying the Positive (Minimizing the Good, Hopeful Data)

People who demonstrate a depressive, pessimistic mindset give great weight to those facts that are unfavorable in some way, but dismiss or ignore facts that would otherwise suggest something positive or hopeful. This type of thinking represents a double-standard of sorts—negative data are seen as "real," but positive data are deemed irrelevant.

ADDITIONAL AREAS OF COGNITIVE VULNERABILITY

Related to the above shortlist of cognitive processing errors is a set of cognitive vulnerabilities that the empirical literature suggests are implicated as risk factors for (and/or accompanying manifestations of) emotional disorders, including suicidality. A brief set of descriptions is provided below:

Hopelessness and Helplessness

There is significant evidence that the depressive affect of clients is worsened if they believe they are unable to positively change their life situations (helplessness; see Alloy, Peterson, Abramson, & Seligman, 1984), and if their view of the future is dominated by the anticipation of loss and misery, with little or no chance for improvement (hopelessness; see Beck, Steer, Beck, & Newman, 1993). When clients evince these types of thinking, their risk for suicide increases, and therefore it becomes critically important for the CBT therapist to help the clients to consider the possibility that their lot may improve, especially if they learn and enact useful coping skills. In order to keep tabs on this area of cognitive vulnerability, CBT practitioners can ask clients to complete the Beck Hopelessness Scale (Beck, Weissman, Lester, & Trexler, 1974), along with the Beck Depression Inventory-II (Beck, Steer, & Brown, 1996).

Rigid Thinking Styles and Poor Problem-Solving

Healthy, adaptive thinking, like a healthy, capable body, tends to be flexible. Cognitive rigidity, often typified by highly generalized all-or-none thinking, often leads people to reject helpful suggestions, ignore new ideas, and to shun using ingenuity to solve important problems (Ellis, 2006). Depressed, suicidal clients often perceive more problems but generate fewer solutions than their counterparts (Beck, Wenzel, Riskind, Brown, & Steer, 2006; Weishaar, 1996), and are similarly less apt to practice the principles of "damage control," essentially allowing bad situations to get worse (see Schotte & Clum, 1987). Thus, CBT therapists teach clients the steps of constructive problem-solving (Nezu, Nezu, & Perri, 1989).

Poor Autobiographical Recall

Clients with mood disorders have been found to have deficits in specific memories about their personal histories (Evans, Williams, O'Loughlin, & Howells, 1992; Gibbs & Rude, 2004). Consequently, they have more difficulty in learning useful lessons from past experiences when compared with nondepressed persons, and they similarly fail to acknowledge the importance of previous *positive* experiences that might otherwise weigh against their sense of general dissatisfaction. In CBT, therapists help clients to think with a higher degree of specificity, and to perform exercises

27

to improve their memories (e.g., writing detailed accounts of important events in the past; keeping a detailed journal moving forward).

Perfectionism (of the "Morbid, Self-Punitive" Variety)

Another form of all-or-none thinking is seen in morbid perfectionism, where clients engage in excessive self-criticism if they do not meet the highest standards, thus effectively punishing themselves rather than encouraging their ambitions (Blatt, 1995; Hewitt, Flett, & Weber, 1994). Recently designed and tested self-report measures for assessing anxio-genic and depressogenic levels of perfectionism are the Evaluative Concerns Perfectionism Scale (ECPS) and the Self-Critical Perfectionism Scale (SCPS) (Wheeler, Blankstein, Antony, McCabe, & Bieling, 2011). Perfectionism interferes with self-acceptance, and with achieving satisfaction through "good enough" solutions to problems. Thus, cognitive-behavioral therapists encourage clients to devise multiple solutions to problems (not just the best one), to see the merits in learning from mistakes (rather than trying desperately to avoid them), and in valuing themselves both for their strengths and for their struggles.

SOCIALIZING CLIENTS INTO
THE BASICS OF THE CBT MODEL

One of the key, educational messages that CBT therapists give their new clients as they try to socialize them into the CBT model is, "It's not just the situation that matters; it's how you *think* about the situation." In the following monologue, the therapist explains the role of thinking in creating needless stress. Note the therapist's use of the word *we* and *our* (rather than *you*), which already begins to establish a sense of collaboration.

> "We all experience stress in life, but some of the stress is unnecessary, because it's of our own making. In other words, some stress is objective, in that most people—if they were put in the same situation—would agree that it's not a pleasant experience and they might be upset. However, a lot of stress is *subjective,* because it's mostly coming from our own interpretation of the situation, and perhaps a lot of other people wouldn't be as upset. And sometimes stress is *both* objective and subjective, in that we're truly going through a difficult situation, but we're unnecessarily *adding* to the problem by what we're thinking and doing about it. One

of the most important things we're going to do in CBT is become more adept at separating the objective stress from the subjective stress, learn to do excellent problem-solving to handle the objective stress, and learn to do something called 'rational responding' in order to lower the subjective stress. Those are two central skills we're going to practice, and the result is going to be a big improvement in your mood and outlook."

The competent CBT practitioner also educates clients about the importance of their behavioral habits in determining such important factors as their health, their moods, their self-esteem, their impact on others, their degree of success in life, and the consequences they incur. For example:

"Another important aspect of your treatment will be an examination of what you do with your time, how you handle problems, how you interact with others, and which aspects of all of these work for you, versus those which do not work as well. By doing this, we can make planned improvements in your behaviors, and help you become more effective in getting more of what you want out of life. What are your thoughts about this? Does it make sense to you? Do you have some ideas about where you would like to start?"

CBT clinicians endeavor to teach their clients to think like social scientists about themselves. There is something very empowering about "collecting data" on oneself, and this is the sort of skill that competent CBT practitioners inculcate in their clients. When clients learn to self-monitor their moods, behaviors, cognitions, and other processes in their lives, they achieve multiple gains, including greater objectivity, improved observational skills, reduced impulsivity, and an ability to see the "bigger picture" (looking at data over time and across situations).

HOW DOES THEORY TRANSLATE INTO TREATMENT?

Dobson and Dobson (2009) present a thorough overview of the field of CBT research, noting the evidence in support of the efficacy of cognitive-behavioral approaches across a plethora of clinical problems. However, they add that we are still trying to understand the active ingredients of CBT, and to improve our understanding of how treatment creates clinically significant results in ways that transcend "symptom reduction" and "diagnostic remission," such as in enhancing clients' self-esteem, improving their functioning in their important life roles (e.g., as a student, employee, citizen, parent, love partner), and facilitating general health.

Dobson and Dobson (2009) cite the work of Barlow, Allen, and Choate (2004), who have hypothesized three main principles by which CBT produces most of its benefits for clients with mood disorders, anxiety disorders, and other clinical problems such as eating disorders. "These include: (1) altering the cognitive appraisals that precede emotional disturbance, (2) preventing the avoidance of negative emotional experiences, and (3) encouraging actions not associated with the dysfunctional emotion" (Dobson & Dobson, 2009, p. 242). These factors are highly visible in the therapy manuals across the CBT spectrum, including the procedures of cognitive restructuring (a mainstay in most CBT manuals), experiential exposure (such as seen in CBT manuals for anxiety disorders and post-traumatic stress disorder, as well as the exercises of acceptance and commitment therapy; see Hayes et al., 1999), behavioral activation (Martell, Dimidjian, & Herman-Dunn, 2010), "opposite action" (see the DBT methods of Linehan, 1993), behavioral experiments (Bennett-Levy et al., 2004), and others. Dobson and Dobson (2009) add that the evidence-based benefits of the therapeutic relationship also need to be more explicitly woven into the treatment procedures of cognitive-behavioral therapies, a sentiment echoed by other prominent theoreticians and researchers in the field (e.g., Gilbert & Leahy, 2007). Further, the authors state that while treatment manuals serve important functions, it is a measure of therapist competency to "be able to move beyond manualized practice, to a case-conceptualized and flexible use of the cognitive-behavioral approach to treatment" (Dobson & Dobson, 2009, p. 242). The chapters that follow will focus on such important factors as the therapeutic relationship, and case conceptualization.

KEY POINTS TO REMEMBER

- CBT as practiced today is an evidence-based hybrid of behavior therapy, social-learning theory, and cognitive psychology. Though there are many variants of CBT that emphasize their own special points of focus, they share robust, common empirical principles.

- From a CBT perspective, psychological wellness is comprised of a number of characteristics and capabilities, including a person's possessing: (1) a broad behavioral repertoire that can be used effectively to solve problems, to relate well to others, and to respond in differential ways that will be positively reinforced across many different situations; (2) cognitive flexibility, objectivity, astute observational skills, and hopefulness, along with a sense of self-efficacy; and (3) good emotional self-regulation, while still possessing an appropriate range of affect and a capacity for joy.
- Categories of problematic behavioral patterns that CBT clinicians assess and target include clients' behavioral deficits, undercontrolled behaviors, overcontrolled behaviors, overgeneralized behaviors, and difficult-to-extinguish behaviors.
- The three main "levels" of clients' thinking that CBT clinicians assess and modify include (in "descending" order) automatic thoughts, intermediate beliefs, and schemas. Negative schemas represent fundamental viewpoints of the self, the world, and the future that adversely affect clients across many aspects of their functioning. Schemas are identified by labels such as "unlovability," "abandonment," "mistrust," "incompetence," "entitlement," "unrelenting standards," and others.
- Categories of problematic cognitive patterns that CBT clinicians assess and target include clients' all-or-none thinking, catastrophizing, disqualifying the positive, and others.
- Other empirically based areas of clients' cognitive vulnerability include hopelessness and helplessness, cognitive rigidity and poor problem-solving, poor autobiographical recall, and morbid, punitive perfectionism.
- Cognitive-behavioral therapists educate their clients about the CBT model, thus giving them a conceptual basis for understanding treatment, and thus beginning to empower them.

3

Forming an Effective Therapeutic Alliance

"Remember that everyone you meet is afraid of something,
loves something, and has lost something."

H. Jackson Brown, Jr.

Competent CBT clinicians are very mindful of the importance of being warm, genuine, and supportive, not only because these are important qualities and components of effective therapy in their own right, but also because they also enhance the more technical aspects of CBT. In the absence of competent interpersonal behavior, therapists who practice CBT would quickly find that their methods would fail to carry as much positive impact, and the clients would be less inclined to be active participants in the therapeutic process. Understanding and learning the skills of CBT can be perceived by many clients as hard work, which is especially difficult to enact when they are feeling worn down, anxious, underconfident, and perhaps hopeless. Having a CBT therapist who is supportive, encouraging, nonthreatening, and facilitative of the work of therapy is a vitally important part of the process.

The early, seminal publications on Beckian cognitive therapy were very clear in their assertion that a positive working relationship between therapist and client was essential for the process of treatment to be most helpful (Beck, 1976; Beck et al., 1979). Similarly, a landmark text on the practice of behavior therapy (Goldfried & Davison, 1976) described warmth and empathy as central skills of the therapist, adding that, "Any behavior therapist who maintains that principles of learning and social influence are all one needs to know in order to bring about behavior change is out of contact with clinical reality" (p. 55). Where CBT differs from other therapeutic orientations is in its assertion that a positive therapeutic alliance is a necessary but *not* sufficient condition for the competent delivery of the treatment (unlike in Rogerian, humanistic traditions where an accepting therapeutic relationship is seen as necessary *and* sufficient), and in not needing to address the therapeutic relationship as an overt topic in therapy if it is working consistently well and posing no complications (unlike psychoanalytic approaches, in which the therapeutic relationship is necessarily a key component for conceptualization and change as a rule). As we will see, competent CBT clinicians recognize the importance of conceptualizing and solving *problems* in the therapeutic relationship, and they do not shy away from this vitally important task (see Chapter 4).

Cognitive-behavioral therapists value the concept of working together with their clients as a team in order to identify, understand, and solve the client's psychological concerns. This relational competency in CBT is known as "collaborative empiricism," in which therapists enhance their working alliance with clients by teaching them the skills to look as objectively and constructively as possible at the data that comprise their lives (Beck et al., 1979; Tee & Kazantzis, 2010). In doing so, therapists reinforce a positive relational bond by helping clients feel more empowered to help themselves, and more hopeful about their prospects for improvement. This chapter highlights how CBT therapists create a positive connection with their clients while concurrently introducing them to the methods of CBT. Further, the chapter will explain how competent practitioners of CBT collaborate with their clients in establishing appropriate goals, and how they elicit feedback to communicate respect for the clients' opinions and input in the process of CBT. Later, the chapter will describe the concept of "distress sensitivity," which represents a high level of interpersonal competency. Case examples throughout the chapter will illustrate all of the above, including the actions of a competent CBT *supervisor* in helping a trainee to attend to the therapeutic relationship most effectively.

ESTABLISHING A POSITIVE CONNECTION
WITH THE CLIENT

What is the best way for CBT practitioners to establish a positive working relationship with clients right at the outset? The novice therapist correctly assumes that it is important to be friendly, and to be a good listener. To be sure, these are important interpersonal skills that facilitate the formation of a bond between people. However, therapists who are more highly experienced and/or proficient in CBT know that there is more to it than that. The competent therapist makes it a point to try to inspire the client's hope for psychological improvement and confidence in the process of CBT, right from the first session. How is this accomplished? One way is for the therapists to show they are willing to *work* to help their clients. For example, therapists who have access to preliminary clinical information about their new clients (e.g., pre-therapy questionnaires, intake report, documentation from the clients' previous practitioners), demonstrate that they have done their homework by familiarizing themselves with these important data, and therefore becoming conversant regarding the clients' history and current concerns. Such clinicians show that they are ready and eager to understand their clients accurately, and to help them make progress starting *today*. The following is a sample dialogue between a competent CBT clinician and his client (named "Chessie") at the start of the first therapy session following her intake evaluation with a different clinician:

Therapist: Hello and welcome. I'm happy to meet you.

Chessie: Thank you. (Pauses and looks down.) I'm not sure how we're supposed to start.

Therapist: Well, I would be happy to tell you what an agenda for a typical opening session might look like, and then I would be happy to get your feedback on that, because you may have some high-priority things you want to discuss today and I want to make sure you have the opportunity to tell me.

Chessie: I'm not sure what I want to talk about. What do you think we should talk about?

Therapist: (Already silently conceptualizing the client's response, hypothesizing that the client may have some anxieties about being in treatment, may be prone to defer to other people's opinions, and may have difficulty self-monitoring her most important thoughts and feelings.) I read the report from your appointment with the assessment clinician, and I thought I would summarize what I know about you, and check in with you to see if you think I understand the basics of how you're doing and what brings you here. So that's one agenda item. Another agenda item is to start talking about your goals for therapy. In other words, what would you like for us to be able to accomplish here, so that when you leave, you'll know that you are in better shape than when you first came in, and you'll have confidence that you have the coping skills to weather further stressors that occur in life? Of course, another agenda item is for me to explain a little bit about cognitive-behavioral therapy to you, so that you have a sense of what to expect by working with me. What are your thoughts about what I'm saying so far? Is there anything that you would want to change, or add to our list?

Chessie: Something happened yesterday that upset me, and I was hoping to talk about it today.

Therapist: For sure, let's add that to our list. I would like to learn about what's going on right now in your life that is causing you difficulties, and maybe we can begin to do some problem-solving, if you believe that's appropriate. Anything else you would like to add?

Chessie: Could you start by telling me what you learned about me from my intake session?

Therapist: I would be more than happy to summarize what I know about you. Please let me know if my summary is on target.

Notice that the therapist includes an overt allusion to the *agenda* right at the beginning. Far from being an impersonal "list of things," the agenda is part of establishing a solid therapeutic relationship in CBT, as it conveys the message, "We are going to talk about the things that matter a great deal to you so that you get the most out of each session, including this one." This is a caring communication in its own right. The competent CBT practitioner imbues each structural or interventional method with a sense of care, collaboration, and hope. At the same time, discussing an agenda sends the message that therapy will involve a plan and a direction. Not only is this approach consistent with the proactive spirit of CBT, there is also evidence that agreeing on goals and tasks early in treatment is associated with better therapeutic alliances, and improved outcomes (Webb, DeRubeis, Amsterdam, Shelton, Hollon, & Dimidjian, 2011). In general, it is difficult (and perhaps unnecessary) to examine the therapeutic relationship and instrumental treatment methods as orthogonal variables. In a Special Issue of the journal *Psychotherapy* on the topic of *Evidence-Based Psychotherapy Relationships*, Norcross and Lambert (2011) describe a "deep synergy between treatment methods and the therapeutic relationship" (p. 5), and they summarize empirical evidence suggesting a reciprocal interaction between these factors. They add that, "…what one does and how one does it are complementary and inseparable," and that, "…the value of a treatment method is inextricably bound to the relational context in which it is applied" (p. 5).

Chessie's therapist continues with the following summary from the client's intake report:

Therapist: What I learned from reading the intake report is that you have experienced a number of episodes of depression in your life, usually triggered by some major stressors or losses—such as right now, because your mother passed away about three months ago, and I'm very sorry to hear that—and that you have managed to be quite functional in spite of everything. For example, you were able to complete your college education even after you were injured by a car while riding your bike on campus, you were able to stay focused on your job even when your apartment complex had a fire that forced you to move, and you were able to establish a new relationship even after your fiancé broke off your engagement, and so on. So it's clear that you have excellent coping skills and a lot of resiliency. However, you have suffered a lot, and now your mother has passed away, and that just hurts terribly. (Noticing that the client is misty-eyed.) This is difficult to hear, isn't it? I'm so sorry. How are you right now? What's going through your mind?

Chessie: (Tearful.) That's my life in a nutshell. I do my best, and horrible things keep happening that set me back. I don't know if I can rebound this time.

Although the client is expressing doubts, it is also clear that the therapist has successfully summarized the client's history, and is attuned to some of the issues pertinent to the client's emotional distress. By having a good working knowledge of the client's intake report, the therapist has already demonstrated high motivation to understand and help the client, starting immediately. Now it is important for the therapist to inspire a little bit of confidence and hope in the client as well. The therapist continues along the following vein:

Therapist: Most importantly, this office will be a place where you can feel free to talk about your grief. I want to know what your mother meant to you, and I hope you will feel comfortable enough to talk about her. Also, in looking at your life history, I see that you have some significant psychological *strengths.* Maybe one of our goals in therapy could be to identify and build on your strengths so as to help you from this point forward. What are your thoughts about this goal?

In sum, in the interest of establishing rapport and a good working relationship with the client, the therapist above has already done the following:

- Made the therapy session a safe place for Chessie to express herself freely.
- Expressed an appreciation for the client's sense of profound loss.
- Demonstrated that he has prepared well for this session by studying the assessment report, thus showing the client that he is already invested in the process of helping her.
- Commented on his views of the client's *strengths.*
- Begun to link the interpersonal aspects of CBT (e.g., accurate empathy, collaboration) with the functional, procedural aspects of CBT (e.g., utilizing an agenda, and establishing goals).

ASSESSING CLIENT READINESS AND FOSTERING TREATMENT-PROMOTING FACTORS

Competent therapists understand that not all clients enter therapy with the same sense of purpose and direction. There is a full spectrum of levels of client readiness for change, from those at one end who are mandated for treatment and would rather be almost anyplace else but the therapist's office, to those at the other end who have already made significant therapeutic changes in their lives, and are looking for professional assistance in maintaining the gains so as to prevent relapse and everything in between. Competent therapists are aware of the "stages of change" model of Prochaska, DiClemente, and Norcross (1992), which describes the importance of "meeting the clients where they are" in their level of motivation for change in order to establish an agreeable working agenda. For example, when clients are at the "pre-contemplative" stage, in which they do not perceive a problem and are not considering making changes, it does little good for the therapist to eagerly present an aggressive treatment plan. Similarly, when clients are at the "contemplative" stage, in which they are mulling over the idea that perhaps they might change in some way, at some point down the road, it may be an exercise in poor timing for the therapist to assign ambitious homework assignments before learning more about why the client is on the fence, and hesitant to proceed.

As there are data showing that many clients terminate therapy before they have a chance to receive a sufficient "dose" of an evidence-based treatment—as when they do not come back after the first session (Barrett, Chua, Crits-Christoph, Gibbons, & Thompson, 2008)—it is important for CBT therapists to be aware of and sensitive to the misgivings that clients may have as they commence therapy. Competent CBT clinicians understand that there is no guarantee that a new client will return for further sessions, therefore they craft the first session in such a way that that clients will understand that their opinions, intentions, and goals will be respected. Therapists may spend more time discussing the client's options, rather than diving into interventions, and they may place more emphasis on using the client's stated concerns as data in socializing him or her into the CBT model (see transcript below). Competent cognitive-behavioral therapists are also aware of when clients are at the more advanced stages of change, such as "preparation," "action," and "maintenance," where it may be more appropriate and helpful to initiate a bolder treatment plan promptly. By virtue of their being directive, competent CBT clinicians can do this very readily, as will be described in later chapters.

In the case of Chessie, the therapist would work together with the client to establish a short list of topics and goals, perhaps with the client's grief over the loss of her mother getting the most attention at first. However, the importance of collaboration in goal-setting is illustrated in the following dialogue, in which the client says something that the therapist did not necessarily expect, but would need to take into account now.

Chessie: (Tearful.) I don't know how much I can bear to talk about my mother anymore. I've been crying to my friends for weeks about this, and it makes me feel so wrung out. I'm afraid that if I keep going on like this I won't be able to function at all.

Therapist: I see. I understand. I'm glad to hear that you have a support system of friends to talk to, but I'm sorry to hear that you feel weakened by talking and crying so much about your mother. I would be happy to talk about whatever you think would make you stronger.

Chessie: That's another thing. You said that I have strengths, but that's not the way I feel. I feel so weak, and I don't know what I'm going to do without my mother.

Therapist: I appreciate your telling me that. It helps me understand you better. The reason I came to the conclusion that you had a lot of coping skills is that your history shows that you seem to rebound better than expected from some pretty difficult life events. I still think that counts for something, but right now I'm more concerned about hearing *your* perceptions of yourself. It sounds like you view yourself as "weak," and that you minimize or even discount your strengths. If you agree, that may be one of the issues we discuss in CBT. The research shows that people who are clinically depressed tend to have overly negative views of themselves, their lives, and their futures, and I wonder if your underestimation of your strengths is part of that.

Chessie: I just have so much going on…things I haven't even told you about yet. I'm not sure I have enough energy left to deal with it all.

Therapist: I hear you Chessie. I will do my best not to underestimate the stress in your life. We're going to use this treatment to take a fair, objective look at your life, including the hardships and the hopes, your vulnerabilities and your coping skills. We're going to look at all of it in a way that does justice to your life situation, and that puts us on a track to help you recover from your depression in spite of everything that is difficult in your life.

The following transcript material depicts the interpersonally genuine and supportive manner in which this competent cognitive-behavioral therapist presents Chessie with important information about what she can expect in treatment.

Therapist: In CBT, we are going to work on some coping skills you can use to help yourself manage stressful emotional reactions and to solve problems. I will be happy to show you how to apply these skills, and to give you encouragement and support along the way.

Chessie: What sort of coping skills are we talking about here? I have to tell you that I have been trying my best to cope, but I don't know what more I can do.

Therapist: I have no doubt that you have been doing all that you can do to cope. In fact, it would be very helpful if you could tell me all about how you have been trying to manage your problems, so that we can put our ideas together. Sometimes it just takes a little change, here and there, to get more out of your efforts.

Chessie: That sounds fine, but what coping skills are we talking about?

Therapist: Well, I can give you the big picture right now. We'll get into the finer details as we go along. For now, I can tell you that we'll work on such coping skills as learning to think more objectively and constructively, overcoming fatigue and low motivation through planning daily activities, having more self-control over extreme emotions and behavioral impulses, relaxing yourself in health-promoting ways, and using better communication skills with the important people in your life, among other skills.

Chessie: It sounds good, but I've been depressed for a long time, and I don't know how much that can change. I don't know if I'm going to be able to do this kind of therapy. It seems like a lot of work, and I just don't have any energy right now.

Therapist: You're right that doing CBT involves a lot of work, and at first it may seem difficult. It just involves you and I putting together a sensible plan, based on your individual needs, and then doing the work. My job is to understand what you're going through, to tailor the treatment to your goals, and to give you encouragement every step of the way.

Chessie: But what if I can't do the work? What if I fail this therapy?

Therapist: I'm on your team. Whatever we accomplish in therapy, we're going to do it together. And by the way, there are more than just the two possible outcomes of *total success* or *failure.* There is every reason to believe that you can experience a *moderate* amount of success, even if you start out feeling the way you do—tired and doubtful. Once you learn the ropes and start making progress, your energy will pick up, and then you can do better still. It just takes a little practice and patience, but we'll get there.

Chessie: I'm just worried that you're going to find out that I can't change, even in CBT.

41

Therapist: Well, we could start learning about CBT right now, by taking what you just said, and trying to look at it more objectively and constructively, rather than just believing all the pessimistic things you're saying to yourself.

Chessie: I'm not sure what you mean.

Therapist: Let me explain. Our actual *situation* right now is that this is your first CBT session, and we're just getting started. However, your *thoughts* are already racing ahead to worst-case scenarios of failing therapy. This is an example of depressive thinking, because you're engaging in what we call "jumping to conclusions" and "catastrophizing." When you think like that, what effect do you think it has on your mood and motivation?

Chessie: It makes me want to give up before I even start.

Therapist: And that's a very unfortunate outcome! I would like to propose that *neither of us* should give up on you. We should *see for ourselves* how things go before judging. We should give you the benefit of the doubt, rather than just look ahead and *assume* that you cannot succeed. If we can start with that idea, then we're already making some good changes in the way that you think.

As one may glean from the above, the therapist is not simply trying to explain some of the basics of CBT in the abstract, but is already applying them to Chessie's concerns personally. At the same time, he is additionally attempting to provide some hope so as to boost Chessie's morale. The above example also shows that the competent therapist offers empathy for Chessie's negative state of mind, but not at the expense of taking the hope out of the therapeutic endeavor. The implicit message from therapist to client is as follows: "I care about how you are feeling; nevertheless, we have to work together to assess and modify the *thoughts* that are behind those feelings, because they may be making you feel worse, unnecessarily." In the process, the therapist also begins to educate Chessie about the cognitive-behavioral model.

At the end of the first session, clients are likely to have a positive feeling about treatment (and about the therapist) if they have a sense that their therapist is going to make an investment in them, that they are going to learn something useful from their therapist, and that they have found a trusted professional in whom they can make their own investment (e.g., of time, energy, emotion, and money). The competent CBT therapist's bedrock "to-do" list in the first session includes the following:

- establishing rapport through good listening and caring words,
- discussing the client's goals for treatment and establishing a sense of collaboration in pursuing these goals,
- beginning the process of teaching clients about the model of CBT and how it applies to their particular concerns, and
- capping off the meeting with a homework assignment that sends the message, "We are already moving forward."

As there is evidence that early success in therapy—in terms of learning self-help skills and experiencing a reduction in symptoms—can serve as a boon to the therapeutic relationship (Feeley, DeRubeis, & Gelfand, 1999; Strunk, Brotman, & DeRubeis, 2010), being task-focused is eminently compatible with establishing a positive therapeutic relationship. In fact, borrowing from the adage that "nothing succeeds like success," one may hypothesize that building a positive therapeutic relationship and building the client's CBT self-help skills create a positive feedback loop that reinforces each variable (Crits-Christoph et al., 2011; Newman, 2007).

FEEDBACK

Near the completion of a first session, therapists should summarize the session and ask the client for feedback. This sets the standard for future sessions, as well as giving both the therapist and client the chance to reflect on their feelings and opinions about their first meeting. Here is how the hypothetical first session with Chessie may have concluded:

Therapist: Chessie, thank you for being so open with me today. We've only just met, but you're putting a lot of faith in me by sharing so much, and I appreciate it. How did this session go for you, compared to how you were envisioning that it might go?

Chessie: I really didn't know what to expect. I was worried I might just fall apart.

Therapist: How do you actually feel right now?

Chessie: A little better, surprisingly.

Therapist: I'm glad to hear that and I'm glad you came in today. What are the main take-home points from today's session?

Chessie: That maybe I'm feeling weak, but that doesn't mean that I *am* weak. Maybe I can miss my mother without feeling helpless without her.

Therapist: That's a good summary. I agree with what you're saying. I would add that you helped me to grasp just how important your mother was to you, and how difficult a decision it was for you to come to therapy. I appreciate the courage it took for you to come today.

Chessie: Oh, here's something else. I think the homework assignment of taking stock of some of my personal strengths is an interesting one. When you first brought it up, I didn't think I could do it, but I already have some ideas about what I'm going to write.

Therapist: I'm looking forward to talking about it. (Pauses to smile in response to Chessie's comment, then resumes.) Was there anything about this session today that you didn't like, or that you would like me to change in the next session?

Chessie: (Thinks about it.) No. Just don't expect *too* much from me.

Therapist: Are you feeling some pressure from me to be a "super coper" right away?

Chessie: (Chuckles.) Something like that!

Therapist: Well, please let me know if you feel too much pressure from me, and I will try to dial it back just a little. I want to help you get the most out of treatment, but I also want us to pace ourselves and not overextend. I think we can find a happy medium.

Chessie: Yeah, not "all or none," right?

Therapist: Exactly. Well put.

As the dialogues between Chessie and her therapist suggest, the first session (or any session early in treatment) provides ample opportunities for a therapist to create a sense of bonding with the client, while simultaneously formulating some therapeutic goals, as well as the preliminary means by which to pursue those goals.

DISTRESS SENSITIVITY

A concept known as "distress sensitivity" has been described by Gilbert (2007). This area of interpersonal competency refers to the therapist's "antennae" for the client's mood, based on carefully and caringly observing the client's posture, facial expressions and eye contact, tone of voice (and *changes* in tone of voice), as well the contents of what the client is saying. This is a competency that can be developed by making it a point to be attentive to clients, to be motivated to understand—even admitting,

"I don't understand, but I really want to, so could you explain it to me again?"—and to practice by watching oneself do therapy in video-recordings. In the following example, a therapist who viewed her previous session with "Kal" addresses what she thought was her failure to empathize adequately.

Therapist: I want to thank you again for being willing to have our session video-recorded last time. I watched it during the week, and I learned some things that I think I missed the first time around, and I want to share my thoughts with you.

Kal: (Perking up and showing interest; very happy to hear that her therapist took the time and found her important enough to watch the video.) What did you miss?

Therapist: When you talked about your memory of leaving school, your voice trailed off, and I think your eyes were glistening. Then you switched topics, and I just went right along with the new topic. I think I may have failed to realize just how much of a sense of loss you experienced when you left school. When I saw the recording, the emotional impact really hit me. I feel terrible about the fact that your family problems led to your abandoning your academic goals. Would you like to talk more about that today as part of our agenda?

Kal: (Becoming misty-eyed.) Thank you for saying that. (Pause.) I'm not sure what I can say about it, and I'm not even sure I can talk about it. (Pause.) You're right. It's very painful to think about, but it's true. I don't want to be resentful of my family, but then all I do is blame myself for never going back to school. (Cries.)

Therapist: I am so sorry Kal. (Leans closer and hands her a tissue.) If you want to talk about it, just let me know. If not, I will respect your wishes. I want to know how you're feeling, and I want to be responsive.

The therapist in the above example is making it clear not only that she cares about the client, but that she is highly motivated to be even better at listening and understanding. Additionally, the therapist is currently respecting "where the client is" at the moment. Although the therapist is already thinking, "Perhaps at some point we can do some problem-solving about Kal's returning to finish her college degree," she is not prepared to push that agenda at this sensitive time, when it may be best simply to "bear witness" to Kal's emotional pain.

One of the questions that new therapists will sometimes ask in supervision is, "What if I notice my client's distress, and I invite the client to talk about it, but the client doesn't want to?" The following dialogue represents the competent CBT supervisor's attempt to help the trainee navigate this problem in the therapeutic relationship.

Supervisor: I see your point. You want to be able to acknowledge the client's emotional pain in order to create a sense of bonding with her, but at the same time you want to respect her wishes when she says that she doesn't want to talk about it.

Trainee: And I'm also concerned that if I don't press the issue of her obvious emotional suffering, then I am just supporting her experiential avoidance, which is not good, but if I *do* press the issue, she may leave therapy altogether, and that's not good either!

Supervisor: This might be a good opportunity for you to "use yourself" in treatment. That means that you nicely disclose what is going on for you in the therapeutic relationship.

Trainee: What would that look like in practice?

Supervisor: Let's do a little role-play exercise. I'll be you—the therapist—and you can play the role of your client. You can start by telling me that you don't want to talk about the issue, using words that you think she would use.

Trainee: Actually, she is more likely to cry, and then just say that everything is "fine" and she doesn't want to talk about it.

Supervisor: Okay, in that case we'll act as if you have just been weepy, and I will start the role-play by trying to address that. So let's start. (Taking the role of the therapist, and leaning a little toward the trainee, who is playing the role of the client.) "I'm so sorry if this topic is upsetting to you. I wonder what it going through your mind right now."

Trainee (as the client): "It's fine. I really don't want to get into it. It's fine."

Supervisor (as the trainee): "I can really feel your sadness right now. I'm so sorry."

Trainee (as the client): "Please, let's just go on. Please. I'll be fine."

Supervisor (as the trainee): (Pauses to think, and then speaks softly.) "I really want to help you. I think there are two ways I can help you right now, but the two ways don't fit together, and so I'm in a little bit of a quandary. On the one hand, I can help you by respecting your wishes and by respecting your privacy, and that means moving on to the next topic. On the other hand, I can help you by noticing your pain, and understanding your pain better by helping you explore it, such as by looking at what's on your mind. I'm not sure which way to go right now. Can you help me (trying to sound appropriately playful)?"

Trainee (as the client): "Please, it's too much. I just can't talk about it right now."

Supervisor (as the trainee): "Okay, I understand. I will respect your wishes for privacy. I just wanted you to know that I noticed your emotional pain, and I don't ever want to ignore it. We can move on, as you wish, but I want you to know that I really feel for you right now, and I would welcome any chance to learn and understand more about what's happening for you, as soon as you feel up to talking about it with me." (Coming out of the role.) What is the main learning point that you are taking from this role-play?

Trainee: I guess it's that I need to be genuine about my conflict about how to handle the situation, but in the end I have to respect the client's wishes.

Supervisor: That's on target. What else? What other message do you need to send to the client about your clinical judgment, and about your connection to her?

Trainee: I have to let her know that my goal is to help her, and if that means bypassing an important topic because she is pleading with me to do so, then that's what we'll do, but I can't ignore her expressions of sadness and emotional pain and pretend that it didn't happen. And I have to say that in a very gentle, non-confrontational way.

Supervisor: Beautiful! That's it. You're sending the message that you care about her, that you want to collaborate with her, that you are well aware of her emotional reaction, *and* that you are open and eager to talk about it whenever she would like. You're validating her in every way, including giving her an open invitation to talk about difficult material when she decides that she wants to. And you're being compassionate and kind. Well done.

Trainee: But it all starts with my noticing that she is upset in the first place.

Supervisor: You bet. That was a good example of "distress sensitivity" on your part.

The above dialogue demonstrates competency on the parts of both the supervisor and the trainee, as they work hard to create a therapeutic environment that will be acceptable to the client. They effectively use a role-playing exercise to practice the advanced relational technique of the trainee's "using herself" (see Chapter 4) to address the issue of "avoiding the upsetting topic or not" in a way that is most empathic.

KEY POINTS TO REMEMBER

- CBT values the therapeutic relationship as indispensible to the process of treatment. Aside from offering support, warmth, and hope, CBT clinicians also join with their clients in a process called "collaborative empiricism," in which they work together to objectively understand the client's life and to make agreed-upon, constructive changes.
- Competent therapists establish a positive connection with clients by investing energy in them right away, showing that they have done their "homework" in preparing for the session, and striving to give the client something tangible to work on from the very first meeting. This begins the process of empowering the client, and creating a sense of hope.
- Competent therapists know how to combine the procedural/technical aspects of CBT with its relational components. CBT is best delivered with tact, respect, and accurate empathy.
- Clients enter treatment in various stages of readiness for change. Competent CBT practitioners "meet the clients where they are" by collaborating on the establishment of goals, and pacing the treatment in accordance with the client's level of motivation.
- Competent CBT practitioners ask for their clients' feedback, showing that they respect their clients' opinions, welcome their input, want to make sure that they have benefited in some way from the session(s), and are willing to make adjustments.

- Therapists who evince a high level of "distress sensitivity" are capable of expert levels of relational competence, in that they are able to make accurate adjustments in their expressions of empathy and in their utilization of CBT techniques based on detecting subtle changes in the clients' verbal and nonverbal signs of emotional distress.

4

Maintaining an Effective Therapeutic Alliance

*"If you want others to be happy, practice compassion.
If you want to be happy, practice compassion."*

The Dalai Lama

The course of the therapeutic relationship sometimes does not run smoothly. For example, therapist and client may find that they disagree about the goals of therapy. The client may then feel misunderstood, and/or pressured into discussing matters he or she would rather avoid. Sometimes either the client or therapist (or both) experience frustration about the pace of treatment and/or the client's progress. When tensions arise in the therapeutic relationship, they may be subtle, as when one or both parties detect some vague discomfort in their interactions. At other times their relational stress may be abundantly apparent, such as when therapist and client disagree vocally. Episodes of strain in the therapeutic relationship are informative—at times critical—moments in the course of treatment. Depending on how competently the therapist manages such difficulties, and how responsive the client is to the therapist's attempts to make repairs, problems in the therapeutic relationship can result in such disparate outcomes as the premature termination of treatment, or conversely a significant corrective experience that bolsters the client's sense of hope and progress (Safran, Muran, Samstag, & Stevens, 2001; Strauss et al., 2006). Sperry (2010) has described difficulties in maintaining a healthy, productive therapeutic relationship as broadly falling under three categories of "treatment interfering factors": (1) client resistance and ambivalence, (2) transference–countertransference enactments, and (3) alliance ruptures. This chapter will examine these phenomena from a CBT perspective.

RESISTANCE AND AMBIVALENCE

The term *resistance* refers to those aspects of client functioning that maintain the status quo in their psychological life, even though they may otherwise profess a desire and intention to change. Historically, CBT clinicians and psychoanalytically trained therapists had highly contrasting views on the nature of resistance. For example, CBT therapists equated resistance with the client's *behavioral noncompliance* with the treatment plan and/or homework assignments (see Kazantzis, Deane, Ronan, & L'Abate, 2005), thus representing a hindrance to treatment, whereas psychoanalytic therapists conceptualized client resistance as a natural and expected reflection of the latter's internal conflicts. Thus, interpretations of client resistance were considered a necessary part of the therapeutic process. More recently, the gap has narrowed somewhat, with CBT therapists noting that resistance indeed may reflect such factors as ambivalence (i.e., conflicting emotions); longstanding maladaptive beliefs (i.e., not just behavioral deficits and/or environmental contingencies that reward stasis and punish change); and interpersonal factors, including clinician errors (Leahy, 2001).

Although CBT clinicians value being directive and time-effective, and thus work diligently to promote positive changes in their clients, they must also be perceptive of and empathic about the clients' misgivings about change if they are to be truly competent. Although it is customary for clients to state that they wish to experience an alleviation of their emotional suffering (e.g., symptoms of depression and anxiety), they may simultaneously be frightened of change. The clients may acknowledge that their long-standing patterns of functioning are not working well, but they may firmly believe that trying to change their standard modes of operation would actually make their condition *worse*. Given the apparent choice between "bad versus worse," the logical choice is to choose "bad," which means remaining the same! The empathic CBT practitioner understands this, empathizes with the clients about their dilemma, and immediately works on ways to show the clients that there are more than just the two choices of "bad versus worse"—there is also the choice known as "better." However, competent CBT clinicians recognize that it is not so easy for clients to accept this premise, and that the entire therapeutic enterprise asks a great deal from the clients. As Newman (2002) explains, we as therapists must appreciate that we are expecting clients to:

1. *Trust* a therapist they really don't know well.
2. *Work* at learning new coping skills, even though they may feel fatigued, depleted, and beaten down by life.
3. *Become* someone who is "new and improved," even while they are having trouble identifying a sense of who they are right now.
4. *Listen to and understand* the myriad, complex things that their therapists are telling them, while paying less attention to the habitual, automatic thoughts they tell themselves.
5. *Commit* to a process of therapy that is difficult yet not guaranteed to help.
6. *Explore* new ideas and ways of functioning, even though the familiarity and predictability of the clients' current ways of being may offer them their only reliable sense of "safety."
7. *Have hope* that their lives will improve, even though they may be terrified of being let down by life once again.

Competent, empathic therapists realize that these are demanding requirements, and that clients will need to be guided gently through this process, with a lot of leeway given for their missteps, backtracking, and other forms of "resistance." In order to assist clients in navigating the perceived uncertainties and perils of therapy, Newman (1994) recommends that CBT therapists make every effort to be accepting and tolerant of the clients' difficulties, and to try to conceptualize the resistance in cognitive-behavioral terms by pondering questions such as:

1. What is the *function* of the client's resistance?
2. How does the client's current resistance fit into his/her *historical* pattern?
3. What *beliefs* does the client maintain that may be promoting the resistance?
4. What *consequences* does the client fear if she or he engages more fully in treatment?
5. How might the client be *misunderstanding* or *misinterpreting* the therapist's intentions and related therapeutic suggestions?

6. What skills does the client lack that may account for his/her difficulties in collaborating optimally with the cognitive-behavioral treatment?
7. What factors in the client's environment may be providing him or her with insufficient positive reinforcement for change (and perhaps even *punishes* change)?
8. How shall I update and revise the case conceptualization to improve my understanding of the client, and his/her resistance?

By asking the above questions, the competent CBT therapist not only stands to gain a more accurate conceptualization of the problem, but also an improved sense of accurate empathy for the client's plight, rather than feeling exasperated and discouraged by the client's resistance. In order to help the clients feel better about managing the demands of treatment (and thus reduce resistance), competent CBT therapists can do some or all of the following:

1. Provide the clients with choices and an active say in the treatment plan.
2. Review the pros and cons of change, and the pros and cons of the status quo.
3. Be willing to compromise, such as in scaling back the treatment goals, being less time-urgent, and being accepting when the client says "no" to an intervention.
4. Nevertheless, demonstrate a benevolent commitment to change, such as being prepared to resume more active CBT methods when the client feels more inclined to engage.
5. Avoid implying that the client "does not really want to change," which has an accusatory tone, and instead discuss the client's *ambivalence* about change.
6. Increase the use of open-ended questioning, and decrease the use of directives.
7. Encourage clients to be active participants in designing their homework assignments, give them positive reinforcement for their efforts in doing them, and make a genuinely caring attempt to understand the clients' difficulties if they do not do the homework.
8. Continue to communicate hopefulness about the clients' capacity for positive change, even when the clients express self-reproach and discouragement about their prospects.

CBT practitioners do not always expect that resistance will necessarily play a significant role in treatment, as some clients do not experience excessive fears of change or demonstrate related noncompliance with the treatment plan. However, when resistance does occur, competent CBT clinicians try to conceptualize the clients' negative beliefs and related fears and ambivalence about change, provide empathy for their clients' reactions, and correct or otherwise alter their interventions in ways that will elicit greater client collaboration.

TRANSFERENCE AND COUNTERTRANSFERENCE FROM A CBT PERSPECTIVE

Many clients experience interpersonal difficulties in their everyday life. Some of these problems may be due to unfortunate circumstances (e.g., the client currently has an abusive parent, spouse, employer), and some may be a result of the clients' own maladaptive interpersonal beliefs and behaviors (e.g., being unduly mistrustful, expressing inappropriate and disproportionate anger), as well as combinations of the above. The idiosyncratic and/or problematic interpersonal patterns of clients—especially those who meet diagnostic criteria for personality disorders—are likely to emerge in the therapeutic relationship (see Gilbert & Leahy, 2007; Safran & Muran, 2000; Safran & Segal, 1990), and the competent cognitive-behavioral therapist will be prepared to assess and address these problems in a constructive manner.

In general, CBT therapists do not view terms such as "transference" and "countertransference" as necessarily being the sole province of psychoanalytic theory. However, they *use* the terms somewhat differently in that CBT does not require an interpretation of transference as part of therapy, and does not construe the concepts of transference and countertransference necessarily to be about unresolved, unconscious processes. In CBT, clinicians view transference in terms of the client's *overgeneralized interpersonal beliefs,* and countertransference in terms of the therapist's cognitive, emotional, and behavioral responses to the client, which may be less a reflection on the therapist's individual personality and history than a normative response to the particular client in question. Thus, rather than seeing countertransference as being a window into the psyche of the therapist, the CBT theorist is more likely to view counterteransference as being reflective of the client's problematic psychological impact on others, therapists included—information which itself is very useful for the case conceptualization and the treatment plan.

The case of "Delia" provides an example of the power of a client's interpersonal beliefs in the context of the therapeutic relationship, and their impact on her therapist. Delia, a 35-year-old, single, Caucasian, heterosexual woman who met criteria for borderline personality disorder worked with her male CBT clinician for 6 months, during which time they generally had excellent rapport. Delia genuinely liked her therapist, and was very engaged in the process of treatment with relatively few complications, until the session in which the therapist came back from his "time off" sporting a brand new wedding ring. Delia seemed perturbed, and frequently looked at her therapist's left hand. Finally, the therapist inquired about Delia's reaction, at first hypothesizing that Delia was upset that he had never shared the personal information of his pending marriage, or that perhaps she felt some jealousy or sense of loss. He gently asked Delia what was on her mind, whereupon she surprised him by exclaiming, "I thought you were gay!"

As the two of them discussed the matter further, Delia explained that "All the straight men I've ever known have been total pigs...but you have been so nice." Delia's realization that her "nice" male therapist was actually heterosexual created tremendous cognitive dissonance within her, pitting Delia's mistrust schema against her actual real-life experiences in interacting with her therapist. Unfortunately, rather than concluding that "Maybe some straight men are caring," Delia began to doubt her actual experiences of interacting positively with her therapist, and changed her perception of her therapist to fit her longstanding, mistrustful beliefs (that had been based on her subjective experiences with *other* heterosexual men). The therapeutic relationship took a negative turn, as Delia became much more guarded, hinting that she "might have to find another therapist." For his part, Delia's therapist at first was quite dismayed, thinking (in the form of a rhetorical question), "After all this time of our good therapeutic relationship, and all the evidence of my honest commitment to help her, Delia now decides that she is going to mistrust me because of her overgeneralized, negative views of straight men?"

The therapist's "countertransferential" reaction was arguably a normative response to being mistrusted in spite of being trustworthy. However, in order to respond competently as a *therapist*, he would have to rise above a mere "normative" response, and instead be therapeutic, which means understanding and having compassion for Delia's reaction, and being willing to put his own feelings of indignation aside so as to attend better to Delia's feelings, and to make repairs. This would involve providing a large dose of empathy based on an understanding of Delia's mistrust schema, gradually transitioning into a discussion of Delia's beliefs about male–female relationships, and how these played a role in dramatically changing her views and feelings toward her therapist (and perhaps toward other reasonably trustworthy heterosexual men in her life as well).

When clients tend to have troubled relationships, perhaps characterized and exacerbated by their dysfunctional interpersonal beliefs, the other persons sometimes respond with a fight-or-flight reaction—either battling with the clients in some way, or trying to reduce or avoid contact with them. These problematic interpersonal scenarios can trigger clients' schemas of unlovability, abandonment, mistrust, dependency, and vulnerability to harm. By contrast, competent therapists make every effort *not* to respond in a manner indicative of fight-or-flight, even when clients express disapproval and anger. To remain calm and thoughtful in the face of client complaints, accusations, and/or stony silences, CBT therapists need to be highly motivated to empathically understand the client's reactions, to express this understanding, to conceptualize the problem, and to work to find a solution that seems supportive.

COMPETENT MANAGEMENT OF STRAINS AND RUPTURES IN THE THERAPEUTIC RELATIONSHIP

The importance of the therapist's competency in managing strains or ruptures in the therapeutic relationship cannot be overstated. The sense of being rejected by one's own therapist can have a demoralizing effect on clients who may already be feeling hopeless, and may discourage them from seeking treatment in the future. By contrast, the experience of directly addressing and solving a problem with a therapist can be a highly positive learning experience, giving hope to clients that interpersonal issues *can* be worked out. A study by Strauss et al. (2006), which studied the relationship between the therapeutic alliance and diagnostic outcomes for a population of clients receiving a year of CBT for avoidant and obsessive-compulsive personality disorders, lends support to this hypothesis. Here, the authors found that clients had the best outcomes when they experienced a strain in the therapeutic relationship that was well-managed and resolved. On the other hand, the worst outcomes (including premature terminations) occurred when there were problems in the therapeutic re-lationship that were not resolved. Such findings suggest that moments of tension or conflict between client and therapist represent critical cross-roads for the course of treatment. Therapists who succeed in maintaining a calm, caring, involved demeanor even during times of strife also serve as valuable role-models for affective self-regulation, communication skills, and interpersonal maturity.

What methods must the competent CBT clinician utilize and strive to master in order to accomplish the above? One of these is the ability to *conceptualize* what is happening in the here-and-now, in light of the cli-ent's personal history and related beliefs, and in the context of the ongoing therapeutic relationship. For example, competent therapists do not simply *react* to a client's angry outburst, they *study* what is happening. Even if at first the therapists are caught off-guard and otherwise do not know what to make of the alliance strain, they do not succumb to helplessness and hopelessness, instead telling themselves that "It's all data." They try gen-tly to explore what is transpiring in the therapeutic relationship, such as by inviting the clients to share their thoughts, and by offering their own thoughts about how they as therapists are trying to be helpful. The over-arching message that competent therapists send to their clients is, "I see that you are distressed, I care that you are distressed, I want to understand what just happened between you and me, and I want to work it out."

Competent therapists not only think about how to conceptualize the client's reactions, they also factor themselves into the interpersonal equation by studying their own possible contribution to the relational difficulty. Hardy, Cahill, and Barkham (2007) describe several aspects of therapist functioning that can be detrimental to the therapeutic relation-ship, including making critical, moralistic comments, being rigid (i.e., not very collaborative), appearing bored, and attempting to use techniques repeatedly when the clients have already found them to be less than use-ful. Additionally, therapists fail to instill confidence in their clients when they allow for prolonged silences at times when the clients are looking for input, and by expressing a sense of helplessness rather than determina-tion to look for ways to understand the clients and to solve problems. In other words, even when therapists are at a loss as to what to do next, it is ill advised for them to simply throw up their hands and say, "I don't know what to do to help you." Rather, they need to acknowledge that they and their clients *together* have their work cut out for them, but they are going to persevere and continue to explore ways to make positive changes.

Another problem in the therapeutic relationship occurs when therapists engage in a misapplication of a technique, such as when they insist on correcting the client's "maladaptive" thinking instead of looking for evidence that the client's thoughts merit some validation, especially with regard to a real problem in the therapeutic relationship. In the following example, the therapist misuses a CBT technique (identifying automatic thoughts) to pathologize the client's reaction, leading to an increase in ill feelings in the therapeutic relationship. The therapist in this example of poor relational skills also becomes defensive. This is followed by a more appropriate, competent use of the technique, and a better relational style.

Poor Use of a Technique,
Thus Harming the Therapeutic Relationship

Therapist: I want to let you know that I will be relocating in about three months, and so I will not be able to continue seeing you beyond that point.

Client: I don't think I'm going to be ready to finish therapy in three months. I wish I had known sooner, so I could have started with someone else. This is pretty upsetting.

Therapist: Let's look at your automatic thoughts about this. Are you assuming that you can't make improvements in less than three months? Are you jumping to conclusions?

Client: I'm saying that it's upsetting if I work with one person, and then I have to switch to someone new. I wish I had known about your plans to leave before we got started.

Therapist: I'm giving you three months notice, which is more than enough. You knew that CBT was a time-effective treatment when you started, and that therapy is sometimes no more than three or four months anyway.

Client: All I'm saying is that it's difficult for me to have to make a change of therapists.

Therapist: Are you assuming that you will have to start again at "square one?"

Client: I didn't say that. You're mind-reading, and *that's* a cognitive distortion.

Therapist: I'm just hypothesizing, and there is no reason to get angry.

[Therapist and client continue to engage in a counterproductive dialogue.]

Appropriate, Competent Use of the Technique, Thus Facilitating the Therapeutic Relationship

Therapist: I want to let you know that I will be re-locating in about three months, and so I will not be able to continue seeing you beyond that point.

Client: I don't think I'm going to be ready to finish therapy in three months. I wish I had known sooner, so I could have started with someone else. This is pretty upsetting.

Therapist: I'm really sorry. I wasn't sure that I would be leaving when we first started working together, and I made the assumption that we would have enough time anyway. I guess what you're saying is that I could have told you about the possibility of my leaving anyway, even if I wasn't sure. I wish I had done that. It would have been fairer to you.

Client: I don't think three months time is enough for me.

Therapist: I can hear that you're upset about this, and I'm truly sorry. I guess I underestimated how this might impact you. What are some of your thoughts right now about how my leaving will affect your treatment and your well being?

Client: I'm thinking that I'm going to have to start over again with someone else and I'm not going to be as comfortable, and they're not going to know as much about me as you, and it's going to be a setback.

Therapist: I agree with you that it would be more ideal if we could continue to work together, especially after becoming familiar and comfortable with each other. It will require an adjustment to switch to someone new, that's for sure. But I also hear you saying things like, "It will be a setback." Can we do some problem-solving so that we can prepare you—and prepare a new therapist—so that making a change to the new therapist would not necessarily have to be a setback? Maybe there is another way to look at that. Maybe you and I can make a treatment plan for the next 12 sessions that will be as helpful to you as possible, and I can also do some things to help you and a new therapist become familiar with each other even before I leave, so that the two of you could hit the ground running. What do you think about that?

In the above example, the competent therapist owns her part of the problem, and does not become defensive. She addresses the client's automatic thoughts about experiencing a "setback," but she also validates his concerns, and offers to do some problem-solving to improve the situation for him. A very important lesson is as follows: In general, *competent therapists do not use CBT techniques as a way to put the entire burden of a therapeutic relationship problem onto the client*. Instead, competent CBT practitioners place more emphasis on providing the client with validation, in demonstrating motivation to repair the alliance strain or rupture, and in taking active steps to share the responsibility for doing so.

THERAPIST SELF-AWARENESS AND THE THERAPEUTIC RELATIONSHIP

It is important for therapists to recognize when they harbor negative feelings towards clients, as these may have an adverse impact on the therapeutic relationship if they are simply ignored, whereas addressing and working on these feelings can result in more positive outcomes (Safran, Muran, & Eubanks-Carter, 2011). This finding emphasizes an important skill that competent CBT therapists must develop to repair problems in the therapeutic relationship—namely, *self-awareness* and a related willingness to apply CBT methods on themselves reflectively in order to function optimally. For example, a therapist-in-training who is able to self-assess that she is on the verge of engaging in a power struggle with a client (e.g., over the client's refusal to do therapy homework) may consequently counteract her initial inclination to press the matter in a way that might risk seriously damaging their ability to continue therapy. Instead, this competent therapist-in-training may be able to do the following mental calculus, quickly and silently:

> "I'm having worrisome thoughts about getting negative feedback from my supervisor if I don't include homework in the treatment. I'm too caught up in fearing that I am *failing* if I let the client have her way and avoid the assignments. I'm also annoyed because I'm taking it personally that the client is implying that therapy homework is 'harmful,' as if I'm a cruel person who just wants to boss around a client for no good reason. That's why I'm starting to sound a little bit defensive, and that's not therapeutic. I need to step back and *listen* to the client's concerns. After I *reflect* on her arguments against the homework, maybe I can conceptualize the problem sufficiently so that I can give her an accurately empathic reply. I will report all of this in supervision. These sorts of difficulties are

61

part of doing therapy, and they don't signify that I am failing. I have confidence that my supervisor will understand and confirm this. Just relax, study what's going on, and first try to preserve the therapeutic relationship. There are other positive things we can accomplish in therapy even if we can't come to an agreement on the homework at this time."

Here is how a hypothetical dialogue between the therapist above and her client ("Mina") might sound. Bear in mind that the therapist's chief goal is the maintenance of the therapeutic relationship. Coming to an agreement about homework is of secondary importance at this moment. After all, a client who angrily bolts from therapy will not be doing homework anyway.

Mina: It [the homework] is just going to make me cry. I don't want to write about what I'm doing wrong and how I'm thinking wrong. I don't want to just remind myself about how badly I'm messing things up in my life. I'm tired of always being blamed for things. I'm tired of being the one who has to change (cries).

Therapist: [Thinking that the client is making some extremely negative interpretations about homework, but understanding that she feels vulnerable.] I think you and I are in agreement about a number of things. We agree that it's not helpful if you just get blamed for things, and that it's not necessary to do things if it's only going to hurt you and not help you. I guess I didn't realize that you viewed the homework that way.

Mina: [With angry tears.] Well how else am I supposed to view the homework? You're asking me to write down my *distorted* thinking. My pain is real. I already feel like a failure and nobody cares how I feel.

Therapist: When you put it that way, yes, I can see how my suggestions might come across as not caring how you feel, and I truly apologize if that is how I sounded. I do care about how you feel, and the last thing in the world that I want is to blame you and make you feel worse. I know you're pain is real. There is no doubt in my mind.

Mina: So why do I have to do this assignment that just makes me doubt my own perceptions?

Therapist: Actually, unless we come to an agreement that a homework assignment—or any intervention for that matter—has more advantages than disadvantages for you, we should hold off and not do it. We have to both see the potential benefits.

Mina: Well I don't see the benefits of this homework so I'm not going to do it.
Therapist: I hear you.
Mina: So now you probably think I'm just being difficult.
Therapist: I think you're feeling vulnerable, but you're bravely standing up for yourself.
Mina: (Glances up.) So where do we go from here?
Therapist: We could talk about the next thing on our agenda. I think you mentioned something about an upcoming meeting that you're worrying about. I also have something else I could mention, but only if you are on board. Without implying that you should *do* the therapy homework, I am nonetheless interested in spelling out the *rationale* for the homework, and to highlight the intended benefits for you. It would be something that you could file away in your memory and maybe at some point we could revisit the issue.
Mina: Let's talk about the meeting instead.
Therapist: Okay, let's do that.

The vignette above demonstrates the high priority the therapist places on preserving the therapeutic relationship. It should not be taken to imply that the concept of homework in particular and the general notion of addressing clients' avoidance behaviors and their maintaining beliefs are abandoned. Rather, it is an issue of *timing*. The competent therapist does not *force* the issue of the client's negative beliefs about homework at this point in time, reasoning to herself that if she and her client can solidify their sense of collaboration, and if the therapist can use this incident to understand the client better (i.e., build on the case conceptualization), there will be other (perhaps more favorable) opportunities to re-visit the issue of homework and related beliefs down the road. At such time there will be better congruity between the therapist's intervention and the client's expectations and sense of preparedness, thus facilitating a sense of collaboration and shared purpose (Horvath, Del Re, Flückiger, & Symonds, 2011).

Additionally, the therapist's responses focus on the client's well-being. Even though she may be feeling unjustly accused of wrong-doing by the client, and even though she may be worried about what her supervisor will say if homework is omitted, the self-aware therapist is able to put those concerns on the back burner while she attends to the more immediate needs of the client. Being self-aware means that therapists notice their own potential adverse reactions, they rationally respond to themselves so as to regulate their affect, they remain confident in their skills, and they utilize a repertoire of comments that are simultaneously self-respecting and respectful of the client.

Competent CBT therapists communicate in a manner that is both clear and polite. They are able to give constructive feedback to their clients in a thoughtful, hope-inducing, well-mannered way. When a therapeutic alliance rupture occurs, highly effective CBT therapists do not become argumentative, or hopeless and passive. Instead, they do their best to understand what caused the damage to the relationship, to express a desire to resolve the problem, and to move forward with a renewed sense of collaborative purpose and optimism. The following are some brief comments that therapists can make in order to set a positive tone:

> "I think there are a number of things we agree on. Let's focus on those too."

> "I would like to work this out. Let's talk and try to come to a better understanding."

> "I probably need to listen more carefully to what you're saying. I intend to do that."

> "We've done some good work together leading up to today, and that makes me feel confident that we can deal with the misunderstanding we're having now."

> "Even though we're not seeing eye to eye right now I want to tell you that I am very motivated to try to help you. That hasn't changed one bit."

When competent cognitive-behavioral therapists notice a problem in connecting with clients, they take stock of their thoughts, feelings, and behaviors in an attempt to understand what is amiss, and to make changes in themselves that might positively affect an otherwise problematic interaction (or general trend) in the therapeutic relationship. Most often this is done silently, in that therapists self-assess and make adjustments based on what is happening in the immediacy of the moment with clients, without announcing this to the clients. Additionally, therapists may self-reflect on the changes in attitude and behavior that they wish to bring to the next session, in the hope of improving the tenor of the therapeutic relationship. At other times, however, highly competent therapists may wish to "use themselves" in session by openly verbalizing (in a tactful, well-reasoned manner) what is "going on" for them, in the hope of overtly discussing the problems in the therapeutic relationship, and how to solve them (Layden et al., 1993).

In the following monologue, a therapist addresses an alliance strain with the client by openly modeling her own approach to using CBT, in-vivo. She says to her client,

> "I have to admit that I was having some automatic thoughts about having 'ruined all of our work together' by being too insistent on the exposure intervention in spite of your stated misgivings. I started feeling very guilty, and a little bit hopeless about getting things back on track again— but then I did some rational responding, saying to myself that there is a lot of evidence that we have made good faith efforts to find common ground, and to help you participate in techniques that feel positive and safe for you, and I believe we can do this again. So now I feel a little more hopeful about working out our current differences so we can move forward constructively. That's my CBT on myself! What do you think about that? Am I doing it right? (smiles warmly)."

The therapist above who described her own automatic thoughts to her client was engaging in a strategic self-disclosure that was therapeutic by virtue of its being directly relevant to the client and to their working relationship. It was tactful, playfully self-effacing, and hopeful in its content.

THE CASE OF "HENRY"

The case below provides an example of a problematic therapeutic relationship in CBT, in which the therapist perceived the client to be somewhat resistant to acknowledging the relevance of CBT methods, even though he appeared to be making progress, and in which the therapist typically had the sense that the client was angry with him, though the reason was not apparent. The therapist had to demonstrate a high level of competence in maintaining the therapeutic relationship in order to work through these problems, and to continue to provide the client with a treatment that otherwise seemed to be helping.

Henry was a 25-year-old single, straight, Caucasian, male, medical student who presented for treatment with depressive symptoms that he stated were interfering with his academic and clinical performance. Although he specifically sought CBT as his treatment, Henry often discussed (at length) his views about the biochemical etiology of his depression, sometimes to the exclusion of other agenda items that his cognitive-behavioral therapist thought would represent a better use of their time (e.g., how to cope with and modify his rampant, self-critical thoughts). In spite of his status as a medical student, Henry described himself as the "black sheep" of his family, at times bitterly reflecting on how his older brother was "revered," and how their father was especially critical of Henry. Henry's vocal quality in addressing the therapist often seemed to have an irritated "edge," and the therapist mused to himself that whenever he met with Henry he himself felt "like the black sheep of therapists!" This dark joke to himself was a sign of something important that the therapist was experiencing in his interactions with Henry, and it would play a role in his case conceptualization before long.

In response to the therapist's probing about Henry's beliefs about his personal worth, both in his own estimation and as a reflection of family interactions, Henry described a particularly galling memory in which he worked extremely hard to overcome his difficulties in math, enduring his older brother's snide remarks as he "tutored" Henry at the father's request. Henry studied long hours on his own and ultimately received an "A" on the final exam, only to hear his father extol the virtues of the older brother for being a "miracle worker" in supposedly helping Henry learn math. To Henry, this was a sentinel moment in his upbringing, telling him that he would never get credit from his father or brother for his accomplishments, no matter what he did. Instead, the brother would be praised, even if he did not deserve it.

Over the course of treatment, the therapist perceived that Henry was making progress as indicated by his scores on the Beck inventories, his increased behavioral activation, and his spontaneous expressions of confidence in his work on the wards. The therapist genuinely admired Henry for his accomplishments, and told him so. Unfortunately, Henry steadfastly maintained that he was not getting well, and that "therapy was not working." At first, the therapist tried to make sense of this in terms of Henry's habitual, long-standing pessimistic thinking style. However, a hypothesis occurred to him when Henry mentioned his brother's upcoming 30th birthday party. The therapist, who was also 30 years old, wondered if he somehow reminded Henry of his dreaded older brother who bogusly took all the credit for Henry's success in math. It was only a short leap for the therapist then to hypothesize further that Henry might worry that the therapist would "take all the credit" for Henry's improvement in therapy too, hence...Henry's assertion that he was not getting any better, when so many variables indicated otherwise! This might also account for why Henry generally seemed to exhibit a hostile tone toward the therapist.

As a provider of CBT, the therapist was not necessarily primed to make such a hypothesis, but the facts of the case seemed to warrant its consideration. Further, as a CBT practitioner, the therapist did not believe it was necessary to make an overt transference interpretation. Rather, he decided to try to use his updated case conceptualization to inform his behavior in session so as to provide Henry with as much data as possible to go against his "overgeneralized interpersonal beliefs." The therapist determined that even if Henry was his customarily curt self, the therapist was *not* going to be reserved and cautious in response. Instead, the therapist would be very open about his positive regard for Henry, in a manner that was the opposite of the feedback the client would actually receive from his brother or father, and perhaps contrasting from what he might subjectively expect from the therapist as well. This method reflects the competent CBT therapist's knowledge, skills, and attitudes in changing problematic patterns in the therapeutic relationship, so that the clients' negative expectations are not fulfilled, and new, healthier beliefs about relationships can begin to be formed (Safran & Muran, 2000; Safran & Segal, 1990).

In the following session, Henry mentioned how his depression was not remitting, how he was once again giving strong consideration to leaving CBT and instead beginning a trial of antidepressant medication, and then he nonchalantly reviewed his successes of the week as a medical student. The following is a paraphrased version of what the therapist said next.

> "Henry, I just want to tell you that I am very sorry that you are not experiencing relief from your depressive symptoms. I strongly support anything you might choose to do to get the help you need. If you want to keep working in CBT, I am committed to finding a way to be of service to you. If you want to consider medication, I totally support that option too. I respect your judgment. I also want you to know that I admire the fact that you are functioning so effectively in your work at the hospital in spite of your mood problems. I think it speaks well of your inherent coping skills. I know that you're going to be successful in your career as a physician, because you've got the knowledge, the talent, and the resilience to do it, no matter how you feel. But I would be so happy for you if you were also able to achieve a higher quality of life in terms of your emotions. That's what I wish for you. If I can be part of that, I would be

very happy. If you want to go in another direction for treatment, I will respect your decision, and my door will still always remain open for you to have further sessions, if you think they would be beneficial."

The therapist's comments above were intended to serve several purposes, including, (1) changing the interpersonal tenor of the session from cautious and tense to warmer and more open; (2) giving Henry direct evidence against the idea that the therapist was looking to "grab the glory" for Henry's improvements in treatment; (3) showing overt respect and positive regard, no matter how Henry felt about CBT or his therapist; and (4) in doing the above, hopefully repair the ongoing strain in the therapeutic relationship, reduce Henry's resistance to fully embracing the methods of CBT, and provide a corrective experience with a male who otherwise could be mistaken for a hostile older brother! The therapist noticed that Henry did indeed warm up a bit, he remained in CBT for two more months, his condition continued to improve, and the therapist never explicitly addressed the hypothesis that led to the intervention above.

KEY POINTS TO REMEMBER

- From a CBT perspective, *resistance* is not necessarily always a salient factor in treatment. However, when clients fear or have ambivalence about change, maintain faulty beliefs about therapy itself (e.g., about being "controlled" by the therapist), underutilize the self-help methods being taught to them in therapy, or disagree with their therapist's conceptualization and/or interventions (which may in fact be in error), resistance then becomes an important variable to understand and manage in CBT.
- Competent CBT clinicians do not state that their resistant clients "really do not want to change." Instead, they empathize with the clients' concerns, conceptualize the problem, and consider their own potential contributions to the clients' resistance.
- From a CBT standpoint, *transference* is understood in terms of the clients' longstanding interpersonal problems and related

beliefs, their tendency to perceive others in an overgeneralized manner, and their idiosyncratic, rigid ways of interacting with others, including their therapist.

- In CBT, *countertransference* is not necessarily about the therapist's interpersonal issues, but more commonly reflects his or her emotional, cognitive, and behavioral reactions to the interpersonal dysfunction of a given client—reactions which may be normative, and at the same time informative about the client's problems in relating.

- Competent CBT practitioners are aware when there is a strain or rupture in the therapeutic relationship, and they strive to repair such rifts in the alliance so as to provide clients with positive experiences in working out interpersonal problems successfully.

- Self-awareness and self-application of CBT methods by therapists themselves can help them to be more empathic and understanding in the face of problems in the therapeutic relationship, thus increasing the chances of being able to make constructive and instructive repairs with their clients.

- Highly competent CBT therapists know how to describe openly (to clients) how they are using CBT methods on themselves so as to solve problems in the therapeutic relationship.

5

Performing an Integrative Cognitive-Behavioral Therapy Assessment

"Where observation is concerned, chance favours only the prepared mind."

Louis Pasteur

In the early days of CBT when the field emphasized behavioral factors more so than cognitive, an initial assessment of the client's presenting problems focused mainly on the unique learning history and current life situation of the client, including the etiological factors that led to the client's developing maladaptive behavioral patterns, and the environmental contingencies that were maintaining these problematic patterns (Bellack & Hersen, 1977; Haynes, 1978). The goal was to formulate a *functional analysis* of the client's behavioral difficulties, typified by identifying current situational *antecedents* (e.g., environmental stimuli); the client's associated *behaviors* (which could also include his or her physiological responses, emotions, and thoughts), and the resulting *consequences*, the so-called "A-B-Cs" of assessment.

Let us consider the hypothetical case of a young man named "Joey" (whose assessment and treatment we will follow in the following chapters). Joey sought treatment for "stress and high anxiety." A functional analysis might find that the current *antecedents* involved Joey being told that his company would be undergoing a restructuring, with potentially significant implications for his job. Joey's *behaviors* (broadly construed to include multiple aspects of his experience) included fear of a change in or the loss of his job, high physiological arousal and associated anxiety, and increased use of alcohol. The *consequences* might be a temporary reduction in Joey's bodily arousal and anxiety (as a result of the depressive effects of alcohol) that would negatively reinforce and therefore tend to increase his use of alcohol, but lead to an increase in his dysphoria, an impairment of his functioning in his job, and a worsening of his actual job status, thus strengthening the original antecedent situation. The result might be a vicious cycle in which Joey would exacerbate his objective situation via maladaptive coping behaviors, leading to more anxiety, more drinking, and an ever-worsening condition.

A functional analysis would also take into account Joey's learning *history* in order to formulate hypotheses about how his problems developed. A CBT therapist asking Joey about his familial, social, and educational backgrounds would learn that the client grew up in an unstable household in which both parents suffered from chemical addictions, and in which Joey himself was alternately physically abused and neglected. Joey was able to succeed in school with the help of a mentor, and later obtained gainful employment, but he always had a foreboding sense that disaster could happen at any time, and tended to ruminate on worst-case scenarios. When his anxiety would be heightened by transitions and/or uncertainty in his life (e.g., graduation, a change in his job responsibilities), Joey would rely on the main "coping" behavior he had witnessed and modeled while growing up—drinking alcohol. This behavior would lower his anxiety temporarily, but would serve as a hindrance to his functioning at his best, leading to additional consequences and an increasing sense of gloom and doom. Thus, Joey's maladaptive behaviors, formed long ago, would be maintained until the present, and would be triggered and worsened by situations that he associated with his unstable upbringing.

As the field of CBT shifted to place more emphasis on the client's subjective perceptions, a functional analysis came to place more weight on other aspects of the client's "behaviors," including the client's automatic thoughts and implicit beliefs. Thus, an initial evaluation of Joey would also focus on his cognitive responses to his current life situation, and his general beliefs about himself, his life, and his future—the "cognitive triad" (Beck et al., 1979). The therapist conducting the assessment would discover that Joey harbored self-reproachful thoughts about his anxiety, accusing himself of "not having [his] act together," that he viewed his life as consisting of "one unexpected disaster after another," and that he feared that his future would involve personal collapse and financial destitution, all of which exacerbated his anxiety and dysphoria.

In addition to CBT's evolution from a more heavily behavioral approach to a more balanced cognitive-behavioral approach, a shift occurred as a result of the general field of psychotherapy's increasing reliance on formal diagnosis, as promulgated by the publication of the *DSM-III* (American Psychiatric Association, 1980). Although many in the field of CBT preferred the idiographic approach to assessment (as exemplified by the functional analysis) to the more nomothetic approach of formal diagnosis, contextual factors (e.g., insurance companies' requirements of an official *DSM*-based diagnosis in order to financially reimburse treatment) put pressure on CBT practitioners to apply their treatments in ways that would differentially address diagnosed psychiatric disorders. In addition to this practical factor, two theoretical factors also encouraged CBT clinicians to become more focused on general diagnoses. One was the CBT ethic of clearly specifying clinical procedures so that they could be subjected to empirical testing and replication. Thus, the manualization of CBT treatments for different *DSM*-based diagnostic categories began to flourish. The second factor was a retrospective acknowledgement of the empirical finding that actuarial predictions of clinical course, treatment, and outcome (of the sort that could be made by categorizing clients by diagnosis) were often better than an individual clinical expert's judgment (see Meehl, 1954), though the author noted that each type of prediction (actuarial vs. individual) had its merits and valid uses. In the end, the field of CBT did not abandon its roots of doing individualized functional analyses. Rather, it *combined* the use of idiographic assessment methods of examining the individual client's learning history, including etiological and maintaining factors of his or her psychological problems, with nomothetic assessment procedures such as formal diagnostic interviewing.

This chapter will summarize the basic procedures of such an *integrative* initial assessment, in which both an individualized cognitive-behavioral evaluation and a formal diagnosis are among the goals. We will also review other important aspects of Joey's initial assessment, such as his mental status examination and risk assessment. Further, we will see how the CBT clinician's data collection at this initial meeting sets the stage for a more comprehensive cognitive-behavioral case conceptualization, which will be described in more detail in Chapter 6.

THE INITIAL INTAKE INTERVIEW: IDIOGRAPHIC AND NOMOTHETIC COMPONENTS

The following is a sample, introductory comment that competent therapists can offer to clients at the start of the intake interview to ease them into the process:

> "I would like to tell you how we're going to structure this session, so that you will know what to expect. This appointment is called an *assessment,* because it is more about trying to understand what is bringing you into treatment than in jumping in and providing therapy. I want to be able to get a good understanding of who you are and what is going on in your life before I make any assumptions about what the best course of action will be to help you. Does that sound sensible and reasonable?"

[If the client is agreeable, the therapist may continue with the following]:

> "Our session today will have three main parts. One part involves some questionnaires that I would like you to complete. You already began doing that earlier, when you filled out these mood inventories in the waiting room (therapist glances at them), which tell me that you're experiencing a lot of depressive and anxiety symptoms. Thank you for taking the time to complete these questionnaires. The second part, which we will begin right now, is what most people expect when they come to a first-time appointment. It's where I ask you questions such as, 'What problems bring you here today, how long have they been going on, and what would you like to change and improve in your life?' My goal is to try to learn as much about you and your life as possible, though I realize that I can't get the whole picture in one meeting. The third part is a formal, structured interview, where I will ask you questions about various symptoms you may have experienced, representing different diagnostic areas. For example, I will ask you questions about mood disorders and suicide risk, anxiety problems, alcohol and other substance use, eating issues, health concerns, personality issues, and other related things. We will certainly cover more areas than you expected—and more than may

be relevant for you—because we want to make sure we don't miss anything, so I appreciate your being patient with this process. As you may have gathered, by talking about issues such as suicidal thoughts and substance use, we'll be doing what is called a 'risk assessment,' because the top priority in treatment is to make sure that you are safe from potential harm. As a result of all this questioning, we hope to have a good sense of your concerns and your goals."

Competent clinicians who have a good deal of experience in performing initial evaluations usually have a customary routine, and therefore can model a state of ease and relaxation by calmly going through the various sets of questions. They typically have a good idea of how long the evaluation will last, and how much leeway they have to probe certain matters in more depth if there is evidence that the clients have an area of concern that warrants additional questioning. Therapists-in-training who are just learning to conduct intake evaluations will need to go out of their way to prepare themselves in advance of their sessions by making sure their offices are client-ready (e.g., free and unoccupied, reasonably tidy, absent of conspicuous information about other clients), and by having all of their necessary assessment forms at their quick and easy disposal (see Ledley et al., 2010 for more extensive information on the parameters of professional behavior for new therapists).

One of the elements of competency in meeting with a client for the initial assessment is in knowing how to keep the flow of the questioning moving forward smoothly, without seeming to rush clients or cut them off mid-sentence. Therapists will need to use their judgment about when to pursue certain matters in greater-than-anticipated breadth and depth, such as the client's heightened suicidality. To be alert to such situations, it means that the competent therapist needs to be listening carefully to the client's comments, rather than thinking ahead to asking the next pre-determined question on the list. Even novice therapists can become highly adept at pacing if they do initial assessments on a regular basis.

Idiographic, Open-Ended Questioning

Following the orientation to the intake described above, the CBT clinician can proceed with a series of standard, open-ended questions, toward the goal of obtaining data with which to construct a functional analysis. As noted in the sample dialogue below, the therapist specifically asks the client to report on his thoughts, emotions, physical symptoms, and actions that are pertinent to the problematic antecedent situations:

Therapist: What are your concerns that bring you to therapy?

Joey: I'm having a lot of stress in my life. Really high anxiety, to the point of feeling like I'm getting panic attacks. I'm also not my usual self in that I can't get myself going. I'm like a slug, not doing much, keeping to myself, not talking to people. (Big sigh.)

Therapist: Sorry to hear that, Joey. What is all the high stress about? [Looking for the antecedent conditions, or "precipitants" to the activation of Joey's current problems.]

Joey: It's my work, mainly. Like I wrote on my forms, I'm a middle manager for [a major pharmaceutical company] and they're about to undergo a major restructuring. It's almost certainly going to affect my job. I feel like my job security is nil. It's preying on my mind.

Therapist: [Summarizing one of Joey's main cognitive reactions, and searching for more.] So one of the thoughts that runs through your mind in response to this stressful situation is, "My job security is nil," is that right? (Joey nods yes.) What are some other thoughts that are preying on your mind?

Joey: I imagine all sorts of worst-case scenarios. That's something I do all the time anyway, even when things are going okay. But when something's really going on, I just go over the top. I start thinking that I'm going to lose my job, and that I'm going to become destitute. I know that people lose their jobs all the time, and they survive and move on, but I've got major problems with anxiety. What if I can't get my act together and I just collapse? What if I can't support myself anymore?

Therapist: [Looking to assess Joey's emotions and physiological reactions to both the antecedent situation and his own resultant cognitions.] When you start asking yourself those negative "What if?" questions, what sorts of emotions do you experience?

Joey: So much anxiety that I just want to shut down. I can't enjoy anything. I'm too upset.

Therapist: Anything else?

Joey: I get really bummed out. I'm not myself anymore. I mean, even though I'm usually anxious anyway, at least I can face people and at least I can get things done. But right now I can't even do that. I've lost interest in things. I feel so weighed down by everything.

Therapist: How does your body react? What are some of your physical symptoms?

Joey: The main thing is that my stomach acts up. I'm always running to the bathroom. It's really embarrassing and uncomfortable. I've always had this problem when I feel stressed.

Therapist: Anything else?

Joey: Just other things that are embarrassing too, like sweating too much. I also get these heart palpitations, like I'm having a panic attack. I'm just way too tense in general.

Therapist: [Doing some preliminary diagnostic assessment, in light of Joey's comment]: Do these "panic attacks" come on very suddenly, getting very intense very quickly, as if they're coming "out of the blue?"

Joey: No, it's pretty much there most of the day. I'm all revved up with no place to go. And they're not out of the blue. I know what's going on.

Therapist: So you have a good idea what's happening. What *is* happening?

Joey: I'm torturing myself with all these worst-case scenarios, to the point where I just feel awful. I don't know how to shut it off. Sometimes I think it's all useless, and that I just have no prayer.

Therapist [Looking to assess more of Joey's behaviors]: What effect does all of this stress have on what you actually *do*?

Joey: I keep to myself. I don't want people seeing me fall apart.

Therapist: What does that look like in your everyday life?

Joey: I don't go to meetings at work. I stay in my cubicle. I don't socialize as much. Well, I still hang out with my best friend Jack Daniels (laughs loudly). Actually, Jack Daniels isn't my best friend, it's my medication (laughs even louder).

Therapist: Are you saying that you drink hard liquor when you feel anxious?

Joey: Not really, I'm just kidding around. I drink, but it's not out of control.

Therapist: [Makes a mental note for later in the assessment when they do structured diagnostic interviewing in the "alcohol and other drugs" module.] What are some of the *consequences* of the ways you react to your job stress?

Joey: What do you mean?

Therapist: What happens as a result of avoiding people, and not going to meetings, and drinking, and thinking so much about worst-case scenarios?

Joey: I guess I just get worse, and nothing gets solved. That's why I'm so worried about falling apart.

As the interview progresses, the therapist would also ask Joey about his personal history, which is vital in understanding Joey's key learning experiences that have shaped his self-image, belief systems, emotional responses, coping repertoire, development of personal strengths, and extent of resources (e.g., familial, social, educational, financial). Some of the questions may touch on areas that Joey did not intend to disclose, but that may be quite relevant to treatment nonetheless. These include inquiries about past sexual abuse and/or other trauma, history of mental health issues and suicide in Joey's family, and legal involvements (previous and ongoing), among other important but highly sensitive matters.

While this information can be obtained face to face in an interview, it may be advantageous for the clinician to produce a written questionnaire for new clients to complete, perhaps in advance of their first appointment, which will allow them sufficient time to reflect and report on a wide range of life events and memories. Clinicians who conduct the initial assessments can make use of the clients' responses on these questionnaires to guide some of their questioning in the face-to-face meeting, as well as to provide extra detail when writing up the report. It is also useful to solicit the signed consent of a prospective client to obtain records from previous therapist(s), which assists in continuity of treatment, and in obtaining a more longitudinal view of the client's psychological concerns and care.

The kinds of answers that clients provide to the clinician's open-ended assessment questions will be revealing not only in terms of content, but also in the *manner* in which they respond. Some clients will be very verbose, and others will offer a few words, if that. Some clients will be able to report their history of personal difficulties in a clear, comprehensive way, whereas others may profess to have forgotten important psychological landmarks in their lives, and/or may otherwise be inconsistent autohistorians. Some clients will discuss their problems with high affect (e.g., crying, physical agitation, expressions of anger), while others seem flat and detached, while others demonstrate moods that appear incongruous with their words (e.g., a client who frequently laughs while discussing the beatings she and her sisters used to receive). Some clients will be specific about what they want from therapy (e.g., "I want to be able to manage my anxiety so I can go back to school"), others will be more vague (e.g., "I just want to feel better"), and some will profess to want nothing at all (e.g., the client who is mandated for treatment, but does not want to be there).

All of these differences in response style are important parts of the therapist's initial assessment of the client, some of which are reflected in

78

the Mental Status Examination (MSE). The MSE provides a format for assessing the client's psychiatric status by describing his or her level of functioning during the interview (see McIntyre, Norton, & McIntyre, 2009), and may alert the clinician to more serious problems than the client is reporting, such as may occur in cases of psychosis and/or organic brain disorders. Typically, the clinician will use a checklist to indicate various levels of client dysfunction (if any) in a number of areas, such as:

- Physical appearance (e.g., Is the client poorly groomed; inappropriately dressed?)
- Attitude toward the clinician (e.g., Is the client guarded; uncooperative; belligerent?)
- Motor activity (e.g., Is the client highly agitated; or showing gross retardation?)
- Affect/mood (e.g., Is the client's mood labile; flat; incongruent with speech and behavior?)
- Speech (e.g., Is the client's speech slurred; hard to understand; delayed?)
- Thought content (e.g., Does the client show signs of delusional thinking?)
- Orientation (e.g., Is the client alert; oriented to person, place, and time? How much impairment is there in each of these areas?)
- Memory (e.g., Does the client show deficits in short-term or long-term memory?)
- Attention/concentration (e.g., Is the client highly distractible; showing difficulty in focusing on the interviewer's questions?)
- Judgment/insight (e.g., Is the client showing lack of awareness of his or her illness; lack of awareness of the impact of his or her behavior on others?)
- Reliability (e.g., Is the client a poor historian; providing inconsistent information?)

A sample MSE checklist is presented later in this chapter in the context of the full intake report for our client "Joey" (see Form 5.1, later). As we can see, Joey's mental status at the time of his intake was largely unremarkable in the sense of his not demonstrating any marked impairments in functioning. He was alert, communicative, cooperative, and demonstrated no suicidal or homicidal ideation. However, Joey's mood was anxious and dysphoric; his voice tended to get loud at times (when he was "laughing off" sensitive issues such as his dysfunctional upbringing and his current drinking); and he may have been minimizing certain problems, perhaps reflecting some embarrassment and/or limits in self-reflection.

Structured Diagnostic Interviewing:
The Nomothetic Approach

An initial evaluation customarily involves at least one portion of the session devoted to a formal interview such as the Structured Clinical Interview for the *Diagnostic and Statistical Manual-IV-TR* (SCID; First, Spitzer, Gibbon, & Williams, 2002). Although obtaining an initial *DSM*-based diagnosis is an important first step in terms of understanding the areas of psychological distress in the clients' lives that may be classified by nosological categories, it is a means to an end—rather than an end in itself—in doing an individualized assessment. For example, although the term *Major Depression* is an important diagnostic category that has assisted mental health professionals in conducting research and developing effective treatments, it is actually a highly heterogeneous concept, and there may be great contrasts between one clinically depressed client and another (see Whisman, 2008). For example, although Joey met *DSM-IV-TR* criteria for major depression, he had a comorbid diagnosis of generalized anxiety disorder that was of more primary clinical concern, as well as a subclinical problem with excessive alcohol use that threatened to exacerbate his dysphoria. These additional problems would set Joey apart from other depressed clients who did not have these issues, or who had other comorbid concerns. Further, a *DSM-IV-TR* diagnosis alone does not tell us about the contextual factors in Joey's life that may better explain the etiology and maintenance of his problems with anxiety, depression, and alcohol use. Thus, a formal diagnostic interview should be viewed as a useful starting point in developing a case conceptualization (see Chapter 6), but much more personalized information about a client such as Joey is needed to gain a clearer picture of his clinical issues and needs (see Form 5.1, later).

Aside from the SCID, additional questionnaires may be administered to gain more information about the client. There are many psychometrically sound measures that the clinician may use depending on the client's presenting problems, and the competent CBT therapist is mindful of the literature on such instruments, and/or tries to obtain them when necessary for particular cases (e.g., Antony, Orsillo, & Roemer,

2001; Nezu, Ronan, Meadows, & McClure, 2000). Professional networking among CBT clinicians is an excellent way to be informed about the wide range of relevant assessment tools that are extant in the field. For example, two of the major internet *listservs* for CBT are hosted by www.abct.org and www.academyofct.org, where it is common for participants to ask their colleagues at large if anyone can recommend an empirically based measure for a given clinical problem. This sort of consultation is part of being a competent therapist. A short sample of such client self-report questionnaires includes the Beck Anxiety Inventory (BAI; Beck, Epstein, Brown, & Steer, 1988), the Beck Depression Inventory-II (BDI-II; Beck et al., 1996), the Beck Hopelessness Scale (BHS; Beck et al.,1974), the Outcome Questionnaire-45 (OQ-45; Lambert, Morton, Hatfield, Harmon, Hamilton, & Reid, 2004), the Patient Health Questionnaire (PHQ-9; Kroenke, Spitzer, & Williams, 2001), the Personality Beliefs Questionnaire (PBQ; Beck et al., 2001), the State-Trait Anger Expression Inventory-2 (STAXI-2; Spielberger, 1999), the State-Trait Anxiety Inventory (STAI; Spielberger, 1983), the Yale–Brown Obsessive-Compulsive Scale (Y–BOCS; Goodman et al., 1989), and the Young Mania Rating Scale (YMRS; R. C. Young, Biggs, Ziegler, & Meyer, 1978), among numerous others. A glance at Joey's intake report in Form 5.1 (later) shows that his self-reported responses on the BDI-II were moderately elevated, but his responses on the BAI were severely elevated, indicating very high anxiety.

Utilizing self-report questionnaires as part of the intake serves several useful purposes. First, they provide the clinician with data that may help guide the formal evaluation, such as a given client's responses on her BDI-II alerting the clinician that the client is experiencing severe, depressive symptoms along with suicidal ideation. When this happens, relatively more time and care can be taken in doing a risk assessment, in fleshing out the details of the client's mood symptoms across a broader diagnostic spectrum (e.g., Is there a comorbid personality disorder?), and in probing his or her history for earlier signs of serious symptoms and their treatment. Second, self-report questionnaires may provide clients with a subjectively "safer" way of acknowledging problems, thus enabling them to be more self-disclosing than they might be if their only option was to acknowledge their difficulties face to face with the clinician.

Third, by providing the intake clinician with a source of data that goes beyond the interview, self-report questionnaires allow for a reliability check of sorts. For example, does the client appear to be cheery, engaging, animated, and often answering questions with a giggle, and yet complete her self-report questionnaires in a manner that endorses high symptoms of anxiety and depression? If so, this incongruity between what the client reports on paper and what she demonstrates behaviorally and interpersonally is extremely important information for the case conceptualization (see Chapter 6).

RISK ASSESSMENT

Although reference to the client's risk for suicide or homicide typically is part of the MSE, these topics will require additional, more specific questioning if there are indicators that the client poses a danger to himself or herself or to others. Interview-based questionnaires such as the Beck Scale for Suicide Ideation (BSSI; Beck, Brown, & Steer, 1997) provide an extremely thorough basis on which to assess the client's risk for suicide. Whether a clinician uses a formal assessment instrument or not, questioning regarding suicidality and homicidality must be handled with great sensitivity. When there is reason to believe that the client or others may be in danger, the competent therapist encourages the client to provide as much detail as possible. Therapists may introduce this section of the intake evaluation in the following way, so as to elicit the client's maximum collaboration with a minimum of stigma.

> "The next part of our meeting is called a 'risk assessment,' which we routinely do with every new client because the top priority is to be aware of anything that could be harmful for you or others around you. Some of these questions will fit your situation, and some won't, but I will go over all of them just the same, just to be sure and to be safe. Here are the main categories of questions: risk for hurting yourself, risk for hurting others, risk of being hurt by someone in your home life or personal life, and risk to you because of the use of chemicals such as alcohol, controlled substances, or street drugs. Those are serious topics, and I greatly appreciate your answering the upcoming questions as accurately as you can. Thanks. Do you have any questions before we begin?"

It should be noted that the issue of the client's use of, abuse of, or dependence on alcohol or other drugs can also be covered in great detail as part of the SCID. However, the topics of homicidality and domestic violence need to be initiated by the person conducting the assessment (outside of the formal use of the SCID) if these topics are to receive the attention they may need. For example, the intake therapist may ask:

"Are you experiencing any violence at home or in a personal relationship? If so, can you tell me more about that? What effect is that having your mood? What have you done to try to cope with this situation? Have the police or other authorities been involved?"

The therapist may go on to ask:

"Are you under such stress that you have been thinking about harming someone else, maybe even killing that person?"

If the client indicates feelings of homicidality, the therapist will need to ask highly specific questions, similar to those that are asked in cases of client suicidality (see below), in order to assess the seriousness of the situation, to determine if the ethical "duty to warn" should be enacted (see APA, 2002), and to arrange for the proper level of supervised care for the client (and for the protection of his or her intended victim).

When there is reason to believe that the client has a history of suicidality, or present ideation and/or intent, it is customary for the initial evaluator to ask questions such as:

- How *often* do you experience thoughts of suicide?
- Do you have a *plan* to hurt yourself?
- Do you have a *method* in mind, and is the method *available* to you?
- How much of a sense of *control* do you have over making a suicide attempt?
- Have you told anyone? If you are keeping it to yourself, is it because you don't want anyone to stop you?
- Have you made any arrangements in anticipation of dying, such as making a will or giving things away, or otherwise getting your affairs in order?
- Do you expect that you will try to commit suicide (again) in the future?

In addition to the above, which are general questions that may be asked regardless of the theoretical orientation of the clinician doing the assessment, there are additional questions that a CBT-oriented therapist may ask as well, so as to get a better sense of the client's thoughts about life and death. For example, one of the questions on the BSSI is, "Do your reasons for living outweigh your reasons for dying, or do your reasons for dying outweigh your reasons for living, or is it about even?" The clinician may then follow-up to flesh out more of the client's subjective views about his or her "reasons" for living or dying. Similarly, the clinician can inquire about dysfunctional beliefs that the client may maintain that may contribute to his or her suicidality (see Ellis & Newman, 1996; Newman, 2005), including:

- "My problems are too great, and the only way to solve or escape them is to kill myself."
- "I am a burden to others, and I can alleviate this burden only if I kill myself."
- "The only way to escape from my emotional pain is to end my life."
- "I hate myself and I deserve to die."

Questions about the client's homicidal thinking can also be pursued with the level of specificity more commonly associated with the assessment of suicide risk. The clients' responses will have major implications for the appropriate disposition of the case, and for the level of urgency in getting the clients the care they need as quickly as possible. Our hypothetical client Joey does not exhibit suicidal ideation at the time of the intake, and he has no reported history of either suicidality or homicidality, though he "joked" about wanting to kill his father when he was a kid. His most significant area of risk has to do with his drinking, which seems to have the potential to worsen his overall functioning, to cause more real life consequences, and to become a fully fledged diagnosable problem in its own right if not curbed at present.

WRAPPING UP THE INTAKE SESSION WITH THE CLIENT

Competent therapists are studiously able to follow a standardized assessment protocol all the while being relaxed, warm, accepting, attentive, and a good listener. They typically end the intake on a positive note by offering words of encouragement and thanks, such as:

"Well, that was a long meeting, and I want to thank you for persevering through all of these questions, many of which I suspect may have been difficult and painful to try to answer. It takes a lot of work and motivation to begin therapy, and I think you're off to a very good start. You have given me a lot of useful information already, and I know you will provide more as you begin to have your regular therapy sessions. Before we wrap up, do you have any questions for *me*? I want to be as helpful in answering your questions as you have been in answering mine."

Clients sometimes are curious about the clinician's findings at the end of the intake assessment, and they may ask direct questions such as:

- "What do you think is wrong with me?"
- "What is my diagnosis?"
- "Do you think I can be helped?"
- "Should I really be coming here for help?"

For beginning therapists, it may be sufficient simply to offer an empathic summary of what the client has reported, and to confirm that all the information the client has provided in the intake will be integrated into a report that will be reviewed by a supervisor. The trainee can add that it may be premature to give a diagnosis, but that the client will have a right to see his or her chart, and perhaps it will be possible for the client to review the provisional diagnosis in the presence of a clinician (e.g., the client's assigned therapist) at a later date. Ledley et al. (2010) make the important point that some states in the USA and provinces in Canada actually prohibit nonlicensed clinicians from communicating formal diagnoses to clients. Thus, discretion is the better part of valor when clients ask a trainee for an official diagnosis. In response to the other questions listed above, it is appropriate for a novice therapist to respond as follows:

"I appreciate your concerns, and I think your questions are reasonable, but it may be too soon for me to answer as specifically as you would like. You have given me a very good idea about the distress you have been experiencing, and the issues that you are facing in your life. I am going to take all the information you have given me, consult with my supervisor, and write a report that will go to the person who will see you for therapy. If you have any concerns or doubts about whether or not this is the right place for you to receive treatment, I would be happy to give you the phone number for my supervisor, and perhaps the director of the clinic. Regardless of what the next step is, I am glad you have taken this important first step in seeking help."

More experienced, fully licensed therapists may opt to give clients feedback immediately at the end of the initial evaluation, including diagnostic information and a preliminary case conceptualization (also see Chapter 6). However, at this early stage it may be best to keep the information simple, concise, clear, and hopeful. Ledley and her colleagues (2010) recommend giving clients a summary of their strengths, a list of their stated problems, the diagnoses that are consistent with those problems, a brief case formulation, and treatment options. They add that the feedback should be a two-way street, and that the clients' questions should be welcomed, even if they cannot always be answered as definitively as the clients might like.

WRITING THE REPORT

The competent therapist promptly writes a thorough report that covers all of the major areas of concern, while at the same time humbly recognizing that the report is just a starting point, and that much more information is still to be gathered. For example, the clinician writing the report may note in several places that further questioning is needed to explore a given matter, or that a certain diagnosis is "provisional," or needs to be "ruled out" pending further observation and/or the receipt of records from the client's other practitioners.

While there is no single template for an initial intake report that represents the standard for the field, there are characteristics that thoroughly, effectively written CBT assessment reports have in common. Form 5.1 illustrates the competent CBT clinician's initial intake report (labeled "Integrative Evaluation Summary") for our client Joey, which includes the following major headings:

1. Client's identifying information.
2. Client's chief complaints and symptoms.
3. History of the client's problems and precipitating events.
4. Treatment history (including hospitalizations, suicidality, medications).
5. Relevant family and personal history (e.g., school, work, relationships).
6. Medical history.
7. Client's history of alcohol & other substance use/abuse/dependence (including the present).
8. Mental status during the interview
9. *DSM-IV* 5-axis diagnosis
10. Treatment recommendations / Goal list / Brief case formulation

Form 5.1

INTEGRATIVE EVALUATION SUMMARY

Client's Name: _"Joey"_   Interviewer's Name: _Dr. N._

Sex: M ●   Birth Date (MMDDYY)   Age: 32   Evaluation Date (MMDDYY)
     F ○

Beck Depression Inventory II:	18	(mild to moderate symptoms)
Beck Anxiety Inventory:	36	(moderate to severe symptoms)
Beck Hopelessness Scale:	6	(within normal limits but slightly elevated)
Beck Scale for Suicide Ideation – Current:	0	(no reported suicidal ideation at present)
Beck Scale for Suicide Ideation – Worst:	0	(no reported suicidal ideation in the past)

I. Client's Identifying Information

Joey is a 32 year-old, single Caucasian male who self-identifies as "Irish-American." He lives alone in a local apartment and works as a middle manager for a major pharmaceutical company. He is a college graduate, he has never been married, and currently he is not in a romantic relationship. He is seeking treatment on the recommendation of his friend and neighbor, who told him that she had once been a client and found that her anxiety problems were helped significantly. He appeared for his appointment on time, appropriately groomed and dressed for the setting.

II. Client's Chief Complaints and Symptoms

Joey states that he is experiencing "high stress" over his employment situation. More specifically, he cites having "panic attacks," though the symptoms do not appear to be the sudden, intense spikes of physiological arousal associated with frank panic attacks. Instead, it appears that Joey is experiencing high levels of anxiety, which worsen when he ruminates about an uncertain future. Joey also experiences depressive symptoms, though he did not use the term "depressed" or "sad" during the interview. Instead, Joey spoke of being "weighed down," "bummed out," and "not [his] usual upbeat self." A summary of specific symptoms include:

Emotional: anxious, worried, anhedonic, dysphoric
Physiological: excessive sweating, heart palpitations, gastro-intestinal distress, muscle tension
Behavioral: agitation alternating with lethargy, frequent sighing, less talkative
Cognitive: Ruminative expectations of the worst, typified by comments such as,
"I have no prayer."
"My job security is nil."
"What if I can't support myself anymore?"
"What if I can't get my act together and I just collapse?"

III. History of the Client's Problems and Precipitating Events

Joey states that his current difficulties were "a direct result" of learning (approximately a month ago) that his company will be undergoing a "restructuring" in the coming months, leading him to expect that he will either lose his job altogether, or have to work in a department that will be "outside [his] comfort zone." He is also worried that he may have to re-locate in order to keep working in the same company, a proposition he dislikes and would probably decline. Joey notes that he has gone through similar periods of heightened distress in the past, mostly surrounding life transitions and/or uncertainty, such as when his two older brothers left the family home, and when he graduated from high school and college. However, Joey self-identifies as a "worrier" under any conditions. He first remembers being "panicky" when he was a young child, but he thought it was normal because "anybody would have a panic attack if they had to live in *my* house" (he laughed loudly as he said this).

IV. Treatment History (including hospitalizations, suicidality, medications)

Joey immediately made the point that this was the first time he had ever "needed to go see a shrink." He denies any suicidal ideation, intentions, or actions in the present and in the past. The same is true of homicidality, though he joked, "Unless you count my wishing my father was dead whenever he beat me" (laughing loudly once again). Joey has never been hospitalized for a psychological problem, has never seen a counselor, and admits that he rarely sees either a doctor or a dentist. He is not on any medication, though he loudly laughed about "Jack Daniels" being his "medication." (Then he quickly said that he was "just joking.")

V. Relevant Family and Personal History (e.g., school, work, relationships)

Joey grew up locally, the youngest of three boys. He lived in a working class neighborhood and attended public schools all the way through until high school graduation, though he notes that all his neighborhood friends went to Catholic schools. He reports that both of his parents had problems with alcohol and other substances (e.g., his father also abused amphetamines and his mother also abused pain medications), and that his home life was "off the charts awful." He recalls being beaten by his father, and adds that he was often left alone without adequate supervision or even food. His older brothers often stayed at other people's houses, and Joey remembers nights that he spent alone in his house, fearful of who might "break in." Joey said, "I was like that kid in the movie, 'Home Alone,' but it wasn't funny." Joey liked his brother Bob, but Bob went into the military and "basically disappeared." Joey found out through the internet where his brother

Bob now resides, but he is hesitant to re-establish contact, as he expects that Bob would not care to interact with anyone in the family anymore. Joey noted that he had a "mentor" in high school (not a "counselor," he was quick to add), and this teacher helped him to have more confidence. With the mentor's help, Joey was able to get high enough grades and sufficient funding to attend college, and to become emancipated from his parents. Joey graduated on time and went on to have a number of jobs, the latest of which is his position at the pharmaceutical company. Joey states that he has "many friends," including old college buddies, "drinking buddies," and "a bunch of really nice neighbors." One of Joey's worries at present is that he will lose his job, no longer be able to afford his apartment, and will have to move to a different locale, away from many of the people he likes the most. Joey reports that he has "dated off and on, but never anything serious." He did not state much more about his social life, and seemed particularly fidgety when asked about it.

VI. Medical History

Joey reports an apparently unremarkable medical history, with no major illnesses or surgeries. However, he notes that he was beaten a number of times by his father when he was a schoolboy, and never received any medical care. He states that his only significant injury was a broken arm when he was "horsing around" at a party in college. Currently, Joey states that he "rarely" goes to see a doctor or a dentist, but that he "feels just fine."

Family Physician's Name: (Joey states that he does not have a physician at present).

VII. Client's History of Alcohol & Other Substance Use/Abuse/ Dependence (including the present)

Joey began drinking when he was in high school, starting with beer but then adding hard liquor starting in college. He denies ever having had a black-out, or serious consequences from drinking (e.g., never having had a "drinking while intoxicated" citation), though it is possible that his broken arm in college may have been alcohol-related. He acknowledges "binge drinking" with his friends on "special occasions" (such as going to a football game), but downplays any overall problem or concern. Joey stated that he self-medicates with whisky, but then quickly stated that he was "just joking." He denies the use of any other controlled or illicit substance "beyond experimentation," and adds that he hasn't smoked cigarettes in over five years. Based on Joey's response style, he may be under-reporting, but this will need to be assessed over time.

VIII. Mental Status During the Interview

Appearance	● Well groomed	○ Disheveled	○ Bizarre	○ Inappropriate
Attitude	● Cooperative	○ Guarded	○ Suspicious	○ Uncooperative
	○ Belligerent			
Motor Activity	○ Calm	○ Hyperactive	● Agitated	○ Tremors/Tick
	○ Marked slowness			
Affect	● Appropriate	○ Labile	○ Expansive	● Incongruous
	○ Flat			
Mood	○ Euthymic	● Depressed	● Anxious	○ Euphoric
	○ Irritable			
Speech	○ Normal	○ Delayed	○ Soft	● Loud
	○ Slurred			
Thought Process	● Intact	○ Circumstantial	○ Loose Assoc	○ Tangential
	○ Flight of Ideas			
Thought Content	● Normal	○ Delusions	○ Hallucinations	
Orientation	● Intact	○ Time disorientation	○ Place disorientation	
	○ Person disorientation			
Memory	● Intact	○ Immediate loss	○ Short-term loss	
	○ Long-term loss			
Attention	● Intact	○ Distractible (mild)	○ Distractible (significant)	
Judgment	● Intact	○ Minimal deficit	○ Moderate deficit	
	○ Severe deficit			
Insight	○ Intact	● Minimal deficit	○ Moderate deficit	
	○ Severe deficit			
Suicide Ideation	● No ○ Yes	Plans: ● No ○ Yes	Intent: ● No ○ Yes	
Homicidal Ideation	● No ○ Yes	Plans: ● No ○ Yes	Intent: ● No ○ Yes	
Patient Reliability	○ High	● Moderate	○ Low	

IX. DSM-IV 5-Axis Diagnosis

Axis I: Clinical Disorders ordered by Severity and/or Functional Impairment

	DSM-IV Code	Description
Primary:	300.02	Generalized Anxiety Disorder
Secondary:	296.21	Major Depressive Episode, single episode, mild
Tertiary:		

Axis II: Personality or Developmental Disorders

	DSM-IV Code	Description
Primary:	None.	

Axis III: General Medical Conditions (as reported by the patient)

	DSM-IV Code	Description
	None.	

Axis IV: Psychosocial and Environmental Problems

Check

O Problems with primary support group   *Specify*:

O Problems related to social environment.   *Specify*:

O Education problems   *Specify*:

● Occupational problems   *Specify*: <u>Upcoming restructuring in his company with resultant job uncertainty.</u>

O Housing problems   *Specify*:

● Economic problems   *Specify*: <u>Anticipated hardship if he loses his job.</u>

● Problems with access to health care services   *Specify*: <u>Has not been to a doctor or dentist in many years.</u>

O Problems related to interaction with the legal system/crime   *Specify*:

● Other psychosocial and environmental problems   *Specify*: <u>Living alone, estranged from family.</u>

Axis V: Global Assessment of Functioning (GAF) Scale

Current	Highest in Past Year
70	80

Additional considerations pertinent to the diagnosis:

Joey does not report any past episodes of clinical depression, thus the current diagnosis designates a "single episode." However, this report may be somewhat unreliable owing to the client's apparent propensity for downplaying his symptoms, joking about his difficult upbringing, and clear discomfort in meeting with a mental health care professional. Joey had an extremely adverse upbringing, but does not demonstrate signs of post-traumatic stress disorder such as flashbacks. Still, he seems to engage in experiential avoidance. Thus, other signs of post-traumatic stress should be monitored. Although he describes his anxiety with terms such as "panic attacks," the diagnosis of Generalized Anxiety Disorder seems more appropriate given his steady anxiety and ruminations related to an ongoing stressor at work and its anticipated difficulties, as well as his general worries about money, life changes, uncertainty, appointments with healthcare professionals, and perhaps dating as well. Joey's use of alcohol, as he describes it in the intake, does not rise to the level of "abuse" or "dependence," but drinking seems to be his chief method of coping. Given this, and given his family history, the therapist needs to watch and assess this area of Joey's functioning very carefully to determine if he meets criteria for a diagnosis. In any event, Joey's drinking habits should be on the therapeutic agenda, and reducing his consumption should be a treatment goal.

X. Treatment Recommendations / Goal List / Brief Case Formulation

● Individual Therapy   ○ No Treatment Recommendation   ○ Pharmacotherapy

○ Other: ○ Group Therapy   ○ Couples or Family Therapy

○ Refer to: _____

Goals for therapy

1. Reduce catastrophic, ruminative thinking.
2. Improve problem-solving (e.g., with regard to his job situation)
3. Reduce the use of alcohol.
4. Improve general coping skills.
5. Increase Joey's social activities (and assess more about this part of his life).
6. (Perhaps) address Joey's painful experiences growing up with his family.
7. (Perhaps) address Joey's ambivalence about reconnecting with one of his brothers.
8. Address any anxieties or fears that Joey may have about doctors and dentists, and perhaps help him to make appointments for regular check-ups.

Brief, preliminary case formulation

Joey attributes his increased anxiety in the here and now to the upcoming changes at work that he expects will adversely affect his career and financial security, and he also cites his family history of abuse and neglect, in which he learned that disaster could occur at any time, no matter what he would do. Thus, Joey's sense of helplessness and hopelessness is elevated, and he feels both vulnerable to negative outcomes and powerless to prevent them. At the same time, Joey under-estimates his personal strengths, as well as the deleterious effects of his drinking on his functioning. His tendency toward catastrophic, ruminative thinking will need to be modified so that he engages in more active problem-solving to deal with his current situation more effectively, and to reduce the chances of actual negative consequences in his life. Joey will also benefit from social skills training, without the crutch of alcohol (which is worsening his symptoms in the long run). Joey's dysphoria may be linked somewhat to loneliness, as he is estranged from his family of origin, and reports no history of meaningful personal relationships.

Cory F. Newman, Ph.D.   MM/DD/YYYY

_____

Interviewer's Signature   Date

Good reports also note and explain the client's scores on evidence-based inventories (self-report; interview-based), and make reference to any complications in the assessment that may make the overall findings tentative, pending further assessment over the course of treatment. Although it may not be necessary to write up a fully formulated case conceptualization on the basis of the first meeting, therapists may choose to include a brief case conceptualization that will serve as a foundation for further data-gathering and hypothesis-testing. Later, during the course of treatment, the CBT clinician will likely opt to construct a more comprehensive case conceptualization (see Chapter 6), a topic to which we turn our attention to now.

KEY POINTS TO REMEMBER

- In CBT, an initial assessment involves both an idiographic approach to understanding the development and maintenance of the client's unique presenting concerns, as well as the nomothetic approach of determining whether the client's symptoms meet criteria for *DSM*-based diagnoses.
- A functional analysis of the client's problems includes an examination of key situations, the client's responses (in terms of behaviors, emotions, physiology, and cognitions), and the consequences of these responses, both in the present and in the context of the client's learning history.
- Competent CBT clinicians orient the client to the assessment in such a way as to create as much of a sense of comfort and safety a possible, as well as to help the client know what to expect in the interview.
- Competent CBT clinicians conduct well-organized, well-paced initial assessments that maximize the amount of clinical information that is obtained, all the while establishing rapport with the client.
- Thorough initial assessments include a mental status examination (that includes not only *what* the client's responses are, but *how* he or she is responding), and a risk assessment (e.g., evaluating the client's problems with alcohol and

other substance use, domestic victimization, suicidality, and homicidality).
- At the conclusion of the initial assessment, competent CBT clinicians promptly write up an intake report that includes such information as the client's presenting problems, specific symptoms (emotional, physiological, behavioral, cognitive), precipitating, predisposing, and perpetuating factors, mental health and medical histories, family and social history, *DSM*-based diagnoses, treatment goals, and a preliminary cognitive-behavioral case conceptualization that will become clearer and more thorough as treatment begins and more information comes to light. The tone of the report is objective and professional.

6

Developing a CBT Case Conceptualization and Intervention Plan

"I have striven not to laugh at human actions, not to weep at them, nor to hate them, but to understand them."

Baruch Spinoza

Case conceptualization is a vital link in the connection between the initial diagnostic assessment and the treatment plan. While a diagnosis and/or problem list is an important starting point in understanding the client's psychological difficulties, they do not provide an explanatory model for the development and the maintenance of the client's problems. Further, although diagnostic labels are appropriate in terms of highlighting clusters of related symptoms, and in grouping clients within a useful taxonomy that reflects what they have in common with others who meet criteria for the same diagnosis, such labels do little to spell out *individual differences*. For the clinician to understand a given client—a person who has a unique learning history and current set of life circumstances, who may present with numerous and complicated symptoms that cross diagnostic boundaries, and who possesses methods of coping (for better or worse) that are not exactly the same as anyone else's—case conceptualization is required. Although therapy manuals that detail CBT for specific disorders are extremely valuable as teaching tools and as a means to conduct their respective treatments reliably and with fidelity (and consequently as clinical research tools), they must be applied with flexibility in order to be maximally responsive to each client (Persons, 2008; Roth & Pilling, 2007). This requires a method for organizing the psychological data from clients' lives in such a way that useful hypotheses may be posited and tested about their functioning and dysfunction—hypotheses that then suggest possible interventions that may be implemented and evaluated. This chapter will outline and describe the development of a CBT case conceptualization, highlighting how competent CBT clinicians start with an initial intake report (such as Joey's, in Chapter 5) and progress to a more complete formulation of the case along with a treatment plan.

As we have seen in the previous chapter, the initial, integrative assessment has resulted in Joey's provisional *DSM-IV-TR* diagnosis of generalized anxiety disorder, and a mild, single episode (perhaps recurrent) major depressive episode. The report also notes Joey's drinking, highlighting the need to address this problem in treatment, and suggesting the possibility that Joey may meet diagnostic criteria for an alcohol-related disorder, pending the collection of further data. (In upcoming chapters, we will also see how Joey's therapist considers further revising the diagnosis to include such problems as social anxiety disorder, and avoidant personality disorder as well.)

The initial, integrative assessment also begins the process of suggesting a preliminary case formulation, such that we gain a glimpse into Joey's world and the factors that have led him to choose to begin CBT. It is *preliminary* in the sense that the therapist surmises that more information will emerge as therapy progresses, and that these data will be incorporated into the case conceptualization, including an updating of the diagnosis (if applicable). Such information may come from any number of sources, including:

1. Records from past and concurrent treatment(s).
2. Joey's responses to structured interviews (perhaps administered periodically), such as the Hamilton Depression Rating Scale (Williams, 1988).
3. Joey's responses to empirically based self-report measures, such the BDI-II (Beck et al., 1996), that he may complete on a regular basis (e.g., prior to each session).

4. Disclosures from key people in the Joey's life (if he is willing to involve others).
5. Disclosures from Joey himself, as he comes to trust the therapist and to take more risks in mentioning things that he had previously withheld.
6. Discoveries that emerge when the work of therapy helps Joey make conceptual linkages or generate hypotheses he had not considered previously.
7. Hypotheses that may be formulated as a result of the way that Joey manages the process of therapy itself, including the therapeutic relationship.

It is therefore no wonder that the case conceptualization has been described as a "crucible" through which so much information is combined and synthesized, including broad theoretical concepts; idiographic information on a given client (including the client's personal theories about his or her problems); the client's environmental and cultural context; the therapist's observations of the client in the light of the former's knowledge of the research literature; and the resultant description of the client's problems and treatment goals in cognitive-behavioral terms—from which the treatment plan follows (Eells, 2011; Kuyken, 2006).

FACTORS THAT COMPRISE A CBT
CASE CONCEPTUALIZATION

As noted, case conceptualization (as a vitally important part of CBT) has its roots in the functional analysis of clients' behavior that was so central to the early work of clinical behavior therapists, who endeavored to stay close to the data, and who avoided the broad, abstract theorizing that they associated with psychoanalysis. Over time, as CBT began to incorporate more inferential concepts such as clients' beliefs and schemas, case conceptualization became more of an acknowledged mixture of science and art (Kuyken, Padesky, & Dudley, 2009), in which therapists had to observe and collect objective data, while also formulating tentative hypotheses regarding factors that organize the data, so that "the dots are connected." However, CBT practitioners do not reify their hypotheses; they test and modify them, consistent with an approach that values an empirical approach to assessment and treatment. Similarly, competent CBT therapists are not content with case conceptualizations that simply identify problems (e.g., having diagnostic utility); they strive to construct case conceptualizations that will effectively guide interventions, therefore having *treatment* utility (Dobson & Dobson, 2009).

The field of CBT is replete with excellent models for how to organize the data that comprise the case conceptualization (see J. S. Beck, 2011; Dobson & Dobson, 2009; Eells, 2011; Kuyken et al., 2009; Ledley et al., 2010; Needleman, 1999; Nezu, Nezu, & Lombardo, 2004; Persons, 2008; Sturmey, 2009; Tarrier, 2006; Wright et al., 2006; and others). While each of the volumes noted above presents variations that slightly differ from the others, the similarities are most salient. Each model offers the practitioner a comprehensive yet concise way to arrange key facts and hypotheses about the client in such a way that a "picture" emerges that will inform treatment, including the best ways to manage the therapeutic relationship and possible difficulties that may emerge. Key categories of data include:

1. Historical events and/or conditions (e.g., details of the client's upbringing; chronic stressors; traumas, medical problems, and other "diathesis" factors) that played a role in the development of the client's psychological symptoms, complaints, and concerns.
2. The client's hypothesized patterns in thinking (e.g., automatic thoughts, intermediate beliefs, maladaptive schemas) and related cognitive vulnerabilities (e.g., hopelessness, catastrophizing, overgeneralized autobiographical memories, tendency to think in all-or-none terms) that were formed in the context of the factors above, and maintained over the years.
3. Patterns of behavior (including deficits thereof), emotion, and physiological reactivity that also developed as a consequence of the factors above, and that were reinforced over time.
4. Environmental (including social and cultural) context in which the client's patterns of functioning and dysfunction occur and are maintained.
5. The client's coping strategies, including those that compensate ineffectively for his or her difficulties, as well as those that represent significant personal strengths.
6. A range of current situations in which the client's problems manifest themselves, including the precipitants (i.e., stressors) that have brought the client into therapy.

7. Hypotheses and predictions about the clients' responses to intended interventions (which serve as a link to the treatment plan), including potential obstacles.

The manner in which Joey's therapist used the above factors to organize key data is illustrated in Box 6.1, which includes a summary narrative that serves to link Joey's case conceptualization to a treatment plan. This case conceptualization is comprised of information that the therapist has obtained collectively from the initial evaluation as well as at least several sessions of CBT with Joey.

Box 6.1.
Historical Events and/or Conditions:

Joey grew up in a household with parents who suffered from chemical dependencies, and who subsequently neglected him (and at times abused him). He looked up to his older brothers, especially Bob, but they stayed away from the house and Joey has subsequently lost touch with them. Joey was often left alone, and developed fears about "break-ins" and about the "worst thing happening." He felt different from his neighborhood peers in that he did not go to Catholic school.

Hypothesized Patterns of Thinking:

Joey learned that he could not depend on his situation to be stable, and he could not depend on being taken care of. He was often fearful, and learned to "expect the worst." He learned to adapt to being alone. Nonetheless, he developed a "vulnerability to harm" schema, manifested in high anxiety, and possible bouts of depression at times of particular uncertainty. He often thinks in terms of "What if?" He is prone to catastrophize (magnifying the sense of risk), and to under-estimate his resources. He also thinks in "all-or-none," either ruminating and dwelling on his worries, or trying not to think about them at all. Joey does not think highly of himself or his coping skills, even though his history shows examples of his great resiliency. This pattern is representative of an "incompetency" schema. Joey also learned that drinking was a convenient way of "coping," which reinforced his positive view of alcohol.

Patterns of Behavior, Emotions, and Physiological Reactivity

Joey experiences heart palpitations, gastro-intestinal distress, and muscle tension at times of high anxiety. He also becomes depressed when his life situation is in transition. Joey has friends, but seems to lack anyone in his life with whom he is truly close, and he tends to withdraw when he is most pre-occupied with his worries. Joey uses alcohol as his main means to modulate his anxiety and mood, but this is likely making his symptoms worse, including his gastro-intestinal distress.

Environmental Context (including social and cultural factors)

Joey lives alone, and supports himself with a job that is currently in a precarious situation. He likes being with his drinking buddies and his neighbors, but he is not in an intimate relationship, and has no contact with his family. His cultural self-identity is mainstream.

The Client's Coping Strategies and Personal Strengths

Joey's strengths are formidable when one considers that he had virtually no support or guidance from his family while growing up. He managed to graduate from high school and college, get a good job, and earn the high regard of his friends and neighbors who see him as a "stand up guy" who always likes to help out. He tries to keep his anxieties to himself, which sometimes involves withdrawing from others. His main social outlet (and "coping" mechanism) is to drink with some of his friends. He tries "not to think about" his concerns, but then lapses into ruminative worries, which leads him to feel depressed as well.

Current Precipitants and Situations in Which the Client's Symptoms are Manifest:

1. The main precipitant to the exacerbation of Joey's symptoms is the news that his company will be undergoing a restructuring. He fears the worst, and is having images of having no way to support himself, having to leave his apartment and his friends, and having nowhere to turn. He is anxious, depressed, agitated, and tries to cope by withdrawing, "not thinking about things," or drinking.

2. Joey learned (through the internet) where his long-lost brother Bob is living. He wants to contact him, but anticipates being rebuffed, and being alone and disappointed by his family again. He is torn about this (having an "approach-avoidance" conflict), and chastises himself for not having the courage to reach out to Bob. This situation is very meaningful to him, and very much unresolved, though he sometimes says to himself, "I have a job crisis on my hands. I can't be thinking about Bob right now." However, he dwells on both situations anyway, and is taking few problem-solving steps with regard to either situation.

3. Joey has begun CBT on the advice of a neighbor, but he is ambivalent about "needing to see a shrink." He has been very responsible in terms of showing up, being on time, and paying for sessions, but he often jokes in session, changes the subject, tries to engage the therapist in pleasant conversation (e.g. about how the Eagles played on Sunday), and has difficulty going beyond superficial self-reporting on his homework assignments.

4. Joey admits that he rarely (if ever) goes for dental or medical check-ups. He downplays this, but it is significant in that it may represent another manifestation of his anxiety and "vulnerability to harm," he may be ashamed of his fears of doctors and dentists, he made actually need medical and dental care (which he is not getting), and his avoidance of getting the proper care may be a current carry-over of the neglect he suffered growing up.

Hypotheses and Predictions About the Client's Functioning, and Response to Treatment

It is important for Joey to reduce his catastrophizing and ruminating and to increase his active problem-solving, as well as to reduce his drinking as a mood moderator. He under-estimates his coping resources, and may be under-estimating the degree to which people in his life care about him, respect him, and would be happy to help him. Joey will have some difficulty in focusing effectively on his automatic thoughts and "vulnerability to harm" and "incompetency" schemas, as he tends to try not to think about things, and he has still not made peace with the idea of seeing a therapist (there is still some shame involved). With a supportive "mentoring" relationship in therapy (a concept with which he has a positive connotation), Joey's anxiety may be reduced in session, and he may become more disclosing about his views of himself, others, and his future. The issue of contacting his long-lost brother will be important to address actively, as his avoidance of the issue only serves to prolong his sense of alone-ness and irresolution. If progress can be made on his anxiety, and if he can do some problem-solving so as to deal with the high-priority issue of his job, it may be possible to broach the subject of his lack of an intimate relationship, and whether there are fears (or secrets) related to this area as well. Joey's drinking needs to be reduced, but he may be concerned about how he will cope if he does not drink, and who he will socialize with if he does not drink with his buddies. Joey's history of resiliency is a positive predictor, and the therapist will make it a point to give Joey positive feedback on a frequent basis.

Summary of Joey's Case Conceptualization and Treatment Plan

Joey grew up in an unstable household in which major life consequences that were out of the client's control occurred regularly and unexpectedly. Conse-quently, Joey may have a belief that "life is unpredictable and you're only one step away from disaster at any moment." The fact that he was beaten by his father only worsened this effect. In terms of *schema* conceptualization (Layden et al., 1993; Beck, et al., 2004; Young et al., 2003), we might say that this cli-ent has a *vulnerability to harm* schema that serves as a diathesis for any stressor that signifies an unwelcome change in his life. Additionally, he appears under-confident in spite of a history of demonstrated coping, thus his current sense of helplessness may be reflective of an *incompetency* schema as well.

Joey's personal resources or strengths are significant, such as having put himself through college, having expertise in his area of employment, and hav-ing a number of friends and neighbors who apparently like him owing to his genuineness, helpfulness, and pleasant interpersonal manner. However, Joey seems to be unimpressed with his own positive qualities, and is more prone to feeling ashamed. In the past, this shame may have been about having a dys-functional family and not having enough money to attend a parochial school (which contributed to his sense of being alone among family and even peers), not to mention the shame of feeling afraid when he was left alone many nights. Today, Joey seems to be prone to shame in terms of not seeing doctors, dentists, and (until now) therapists, and in generally not confiding in or getting close to others, even though he is a "friendly and helpful" guy.

In terms of socio-environmental context, Joey did not have much affec-tion for his father (owing to the beatings and neglect), but he noted that an unspoken rule in the household was that drinking was an acceptable way of dealing with stress. This lesson from the past, along with presently having a group of drinking buddies who serve as his main source of social support, may support and maintain Joey's use of alcohol as his chief means of "coping."

Obstacles that may impair a successful treatment include Joey's sense of shame in seeing a "shrink," a history of "trying not to think about problems" as his primary non-chemical way to cope, and high anxiety about the cost of treatment in light of his catastrophic expectations about his job security.

The above set of factors suggests some useful directions and considerations for a course of CBT to treat Joey's problems of anxiety, depression, and perhaps alcohol abuse. For starters, the therapist would highlight the collaborative and time-effective aspects of treatment so as to appeal to the client's sense of autonomy (a positive way to reframe his history of being alone), to counteract his sense of shame by emphasizing his active role in helping himself and learning durable skills, and to assuage some of his concerns about a long-term treatment that would be too costly. The therapist may explain to Joey that his alcohol use is a maintaining factor for the anxiety, and perhaps the depression and gastro-intestinal distress as well, invite him to consider the benefits of working to reduce his reliance on alcohol as a "self-medication" device, and yet empathize with his positive associations with alcohol—camaraderie with friends, and immediate relief from anxious suffering. The therapist would be very respectful of Joey's personal strengths and coping skills, noting that the client had overcome early obstacles to get a college education and a good job in his field (the unsettling corporate restructuring notwithstanding), and commenting on the loyalty he had inspired in his friends, which reflected well on his character. This latter strength could be underlined in response to Joey's negative assumptions that his friends would judge him if they got too close to him and knew the "real" him, or would shun him if he didn't go drinking with them. The therapist would base the treatment on a CBT protocol for anxiety disorders (see Clark & Beck, 2010), taking into account the need to deal with Joey's mild depression and possible alcohol abuse as well. The therapist would positively reinforce all efforts that Joey would make to do active problem-solving, to expose himself to negative experiences for the purpose of problem-solving (e.g., actively consulting about his job situation, trying to communicate with his brother Bob, making appointments to see a dentist and a family doctor) and rational responding, and would keep an open ear to any comments the client would make that might indicate misgivings about specific interventions, and/

or remaining in treatment in general. Additionally, Joey keeps most of the details of his interpersonal life to himself, leading one to question whether there are some important secrets in this area (e.g., about his sexual history, sexual orientation). The therapist will be very careful and respectful of Joey's privacy, while still listening intently for client comments that may open doors to the discussion of this important area of his life—important, but not one of his stated reasons for seeking treatment.

1. Historical Events and/or Conditions

The learning histories of clients are very important to ascertain, and an exploration of some of the "high-profile" incidents and scenarios from a client's past can shed light on how he or she has come to have the characteristics he or she posseses today. In keeping with the empirical tradition of CBT, therapists are careful not to engage in undue speculation about the client's history. The client's self-report and/or corroborating facts from other sources are minimum requirements in order to place credence in such diathesis factors as childhood maltreatment, sexual victimization, and traumatic losses, among other distal factors that may greatly influence the course of someone's life. Not all historically salient events need be "traumatic" per se to be relevant to the case conceptualization. All that is necessary is that the historical factors played an important role in the client's psychological development, such as his or her self-image.

In Joey's case, his parents' chemical dependencies, his experiences with abuse and neglect, his being set apart from neighborhood peers by being in a different school, and his separation from his brothers are hypothesized to have played major roles in Joey's feelings of insecurity and vulnerability. An effective treatment plan would involve the therapist acknowledging Joey's past difficulties while helping him to focus on the current evidence of his success in taking care of himself, and the largely benevolent treatment he receives from others at work and where he lives.

2. The Client's Hypothesized Patterns of Thinking

Cognitive-behavioral case conceptualization places strong emphasis on ascertaining the ways in which clients think. Key questions are *"How* do they think?" (e.g., With a tendency to disqualify positive events? With a habit of catastrophizing via "What if?" questions?), and "*What* do they think?" (i.e., the content of their automatic thoughts, intermediate beliefs, and maladaptive schemas). Therapists who are competent at case conceptualization try to understand how the clients' thinking interacts in causal ways with their emotions and actions. By striving to understand clients' thought processes and contents, cognitive-behavioral therapists can make better sense of the clients' difficulties, and can position themselves to generate interventions that have the most promise for effecting positive change. Whether it is during the initial intake process, or during the course of treatment, cognitive-behavioral therapists assess their clients' thinking via direct questioning, via surveying the clients' comments for patterns, and/or by administering questionnaires that specifically tap into the clients' hypothesized beliefs. Key self-report measures include the DAS (Weissman & Beck, 1978), the PBQ (Beck et al., 2001), and the YSQ (Schmidt et al., 1995), as noted in Chapter 2. The clients' developmental history is typically reviewed in order to hypothesize how they came to develop and maintain their ways of thinking, and how these are manifested across a range of current life situations.

Joey showed a propensity for catastrophic "What if?" thinking, as he typically expected the worst and did not have confidence in his own problem-solving or coping skills. These thought patterns were most consistent with a *vulnerability to harm* schema, and to some degree with an *incompetency* schema. Later in treatment, after additional information would come to light, the therapist would hypothesize further that Joey also believed he was *unlovable.* Interventions would focus on counteracting Joey's negative schemas via a mixture of examining evidence against his sense of vulnerability and incompetency, practicing and improving his skills in problem-solving as well as socializing, and engaging in activities that would give him a sense of accomplishment.

3. The Client's Patterns of Behavior, Emotion, and Physiological Reactivity

Joey's initial intake report (from Chapter 5) reveals that he often experiences high anxiety, along with dysphoria. Physiologically, Joey frequently feels tense, and suffers from gastro-intestinal distress that is worsened by stress. Unfortunately, Joey's customary behavioral responses to these problems is to become less interactive with others, with the exception of times that he drinks alcohol, which he views as a way of coping with stress, but which makes him less apt to engage in problem-solving, more dysphoric, and possibly exacerbates his abdominal malaise. A good treatment plan would involve trying to motivate Joey to reduce his alcohol use, and to observe resultant improvements in his work-related and social behaviors, and in how he feels physically (which would become natural reinforcers of his therapeutic changes). Joey would need assistance in improving his social skills without using alcohol to lower his anxiety.

4. Environmental Context (including social and cultural factors)

This may refer to the client's sociocultural milieu, current life situation, physical surroundings, or other factors that provide context within which to better understand the client's attitudes and behaviors. Joey's current environment actually seems unremarkable, in that he gets along well with others at work and in his neighborhood. Unfortunately, Joey has perpetually lived alone, and while he does not complain about this, it emphasizes his lack of a close personal relationship. The treatment plan would follow by helping Joey become more socially involved, both at work and in his personal life. Again, the therapist would collaborate with Joey in reducing the latter's environmental exposure to drinking cues and situations. Also, in light of the uncertainty of Joey's job situation, the therapist would help him to engage in problem-solving so as to maximize the chances that he would remain in a favorable position, even if big changes were to occur in his employment situation.

The client's cultural factors also play an important role in the case conceptualization, especially if he or she is not of the mainstream population in terms of ethnicity, sexual orientation or identity, physical limitations, and other factors (see Chapter 10). Joey, a Caucasian, nonreligious Christian male who (along with recent generations of his ancestors) was born and raised in the United States, presented himself as a client for whom cultural factors were of minimal significance. However, Joey's answers to assessment questions about his relationship history were vague and sparse, leading the therapist to hypothesize that Joey was uncomfortable with this area of his life. Thus, the therapist posited that Joey's sexual orientation might be a cultural factor to incorporate in his case conceptualization and treatment plan.

5. The Client's Coping Strategies and Personal Strengths

In addition to assessing the clients' difficulties and symptoms, CBT clinicians also inquire about their clients' personal strengths (Kuyken et al., 2009). Examining the "supply side" of the clients' functioning has many benefits, in that therapists can:

- Demonstrate that they are interested in learning about the clients as complete individuals, and not just as manifestations of a diagnosis or other dysfunction.
- Offer frank, positive feedback to the clients about their positive characteristics that the clients otherwise take for granted, or believe are unappreciated by others.
- Suggest that the clients already have some skills that can be put to good use in therapy, and that serve as head starts in helping the clients to learn durable self-help skills.
- Note that the clients' personal strengths in one area of their lives may be generalizable or transferrable to other areas, thus leading to new ideas for behavioral experiments.
- Bolster the clients' sense of hope and self-efficacy, leading to improved morale and higher motivation to engage in the worthwhile but sometimes difficult process of CBT.

Joey possessed many strengths, including resilience, intelligence, and a capacity to care about and help others. Unfortunately, Joey largely ignored and discounted these positive aspects of himself, leaving him to focus heavily on his perceptions of being helpless, vulnerable, and different from others. An appropriate therapeutic response would be for the therapist to call Joey's attention to the coping skills that enabled him to survive his upbringing, legitimately praising him for his current successes, and working with Joey to modify his self-critical cognitions in light of his personal assets.

6. Current Precipitants and Situations in which the Client's Symptoms are Manifest

One of the most important uses of the case conceptualization occurs when therapists share their cognitive-behavioral case conceptualizations with their clients, sometimes conveniently in the form of a flow-sheet (see J. S. Beck, 2011). Together, therapist and client examine some of the current situations from the client's life, and spell out how the client's history, environment, patterns of thinking, coping styles, strengths, and symptoms manifest themselves. This review can be especially enlightening when seemingly disparate, problematic scenarios in the client's life can be tied together on the basis of his or her patterns of thinking, which themselves may be tied to salient learning experiences from many years ago.

For example, although Joey described himself as being "a bit of a pessimist," he did not appreciate the ways in which his sense of vulnerability and helplessness impeded his coping and worsened his mood. Prior to starting CBT, Joey simply believed that his negativity was a "natural reaction to the way things are." However, with the help of his cognitive-behavioral therapist, Joey was able to improve his self-monitoring and self-awareness skills. Joey came to see the connections between such aspects of his functioning as his hesitancy to talk about himself when people would sincerely take an interest in learning more about him; his tendency to drink so as "not to think about things"; his declining to follow through on reaching out to his brother Bob; his avoidance of doctors and dentists; his decision not to attend work-related meetings and his procrastination in looking for a new job as a back-up plan in case he lost his current job; and other problems that Joey did not see as being interrelated until he started CBT.

The factors that "connected the dots" were his negative schemas pertaining to vulnerability, incompetence, and (as would be hypothesized soon) unlovability. For example, Joey believed that he did not have much to offer anyone, thus he did not want to "bore" people by talking about himself, even though it prevented others from getting close to him, leaving him alone and anxious, a condition which he would then try to "solve" by engaging in social drinking. Joey dearly wanted to talk to his brother Bob again, whom he once looked up to and had not seen in so many years, but he believed that Bob would want nothing to do with him. To avoid the anticipated rejection, Joey took no action, though he ruminated and engaged in self-reproachful, internal dialogue about "not having the guts" to contact Bob. Joey also did not wish to share much of himself in therapy, at least at first. He opened up more as the therapist pointed out Joey's strengths, and expressed confidence in and respect for him. Joey felt helpless and paralyzed about getting a new job, believing that he was functioning at such a low level due to his anxiety and dysphoria that he would be unable to make a good impression on a prospective new employer anyway. Therefore, he took no steps to look for new employment as a back-up plan. Joey also never went to see medical doctors or dentists, reasoning with himself that he did not need to, but very likely being a result of a history of parental neglect (in which Joey never had regular check-ups and therefore never developed a medical or dental routine), compounded by expectations of pain and harm should he go for an appointment. At almost every turn in his life, Joey experienced anxiety, feared the worse, believed he was powerless in spite of his best efforts to cope and survive, did not have much sense of self-worth, and believed he was better off steering clear of thinking about problems rather than trying to solve them actively.

A significant therapeutic step may occur when the CBT therapist sensitively shares this conceptualization with a client such as Joey. Armed with this sort of conceptual understanding of himself in cognitive-behavioral terms, Joey would already begin to feel more empowered and hopeful, as he would transition from a bewildered sense of not knowing what was wrong with him (other than a precarious job situation) to comprehending the way his problematic functioning fit together, and therefore could be systematically modified. Joey would now be better positioned to collaborate with the therapist in commencing the sort of interventions that are illustrated more specifically in Chapter 7.

In the following dialogue, Joey and his therapist discuss part of the case conceptualization and its implications for gaining a more constructive understanding of Joey's problems.

Joey: There is so much I need to be doing, but I'm really in no shape for any of it.

Therapist: Are you referring to meeting with your immediate boss about the restructuring, attending meetings, looking for a new job, and things like that?

Joey: And trying to get in touch with my brother, and making that appointment with the dentist that I said I would do weeks ago, and helping out with the block party that my neighbors are throwing this Saturday. All of it. My anxiety just causes me to freeze. It's pathetic.

Therapist: Well, I know you're disappointed in yourself right now, and I can understand your concerns about all of these things that you would like to be doing, but I wonder if you could try to

109

summarize how your *thinking* is playing a role in these problems, rather than just condemning yourself. We talked about trying to understand some of your beliefs that are playing such an important role in your difficulties. Do you remember?

Joey: It goes back to that "helplessness" thing, where I just assume that there's nothing I can do anyway, so it seems futile to try. Then I expect the worst to happen, and it preys on my mind, and then I just feel more anxious until I can't even stand to think about my life anymore and I just want to be unconscious.

Therapist: Is that when you get the urge to drink?

Joey: Either that or just go to bed. It's all so stupid. What's the big deal about a block party? Why can't I just get my act together?

Therapist: Wow, you're hard on yourself. Listen to the way you talk to yourself. Believe me, I agree with you that it would be better if you could do all of the things you mentioned, including doing some advance trouble-shooting about your work situation, but I think we'll make more progress if we start by being understanding of your difficulties, rather than being critical of you. For example, this feeling of helplessness that you experience didn't just come out of thin air. Where and when did you learn that?

Joey: Well, I know I had zero control over my family when I was growing up. The only thing that was predictable was that nothing was ever predictable. And now my company is being restructured and I have no control over that either.

Therapist: I know you felt powerless and vulnerable when you were growing up, but you somehow survived, finished school, and made a career for yourself. That doesn't sound like "giving up" to me. It sounds like you *thought* there was nothing you could do, and that bad things would always happen, but somehow you *were* able to manage, and to make some good things happen. I think that's happening again now. You *believe* that you're unable to help yourself, but actually there is evidence that you have the skills and experience to cope with and solve your problems, especially if we can work together to reduce your alcohol use. We need to help you find a better way to deal with the anxiety. What do you think about this conceptualization?

Joey: I hear you. It all makes sense. When I start doubting myself everything seems like a disaster, but the truth is that all these situations are just pushing my buttons, and I could probably handle things reasonably well if I just take one step at a time, like you said.

Therapist: I agree. I think you are more capable than you usually think you are. What did you think about what I said about the alcohol?

Joey: (Laughs.) Yeah, I heard that; I was just ignoring it (laughs again). Oh, man I know you're right, because my family always said that drinking was no big deal, and that it was just a way of dealing with the stress of life, but they were full of [expletive]. So how will I deal with stress and people if I can't drink? What's the miracle cure (laughs)?

Therapist: No miracle. A good plan will do just fine. That's what you and I are going to start working on right now if you would like. But first, I wonder what you think about the way we're trying to make sense of your psychological concerns, and how they all fit together. Which parts seem on target for you, and which parts don't seem to be accurate from your vantage point, and which parts seem somewhat accurate if we could just talk about them more and make things clear? I would greatly value your feedback on this, Joey.

7. Hypotheses and Predictions about the Client's Functioning, and Response to Treatment

A good case conceptualization provides a roadmap for treatment that also alerts the therapist to the possible speed bumps and detours along the way (Sperry, 2010). Regarding Joey, the case conceptualization helps the therapist to recognize some of the major problems that will need to be addressed, including Joey's sense of vulnerability (e.g., anticipation of impending disaster) and incompetence (e.g., sense of helplessness to deal with challenging life situations), which is reflected in the client's high anxiety, propensity for catastrophizing, and tendency to self-medicate rather than manage his problems directly. Given that Joey does not like to talk about himself (believing that he is boring and has nothing to offer), and in light of his avoidance of doctors and dentists, it is remarkable that Joey has commenced CBT at all. The therapist will need to be aware of the very real possibility that Joey may leave therapy abruptly and prematurely. Thus, the therapist needs to create an action plan as soon as possible, all the while giving Joey as much legitimate positive feedback as possible to bolster his confidence.

111

Although a reduction in Joey's use of alcohol is a very high priority in therapy, the therapist will need to be mindful of and empathic about Joey's concerns about the consequences of drinking less. For example, Joey may believe that his anxiety will worsen, and that he will no longer be able to engage in the limited socializing that he currently does. Therefore, these concerns need to be addressed, as Joey will need to be taught nonchemical alternatives to feeling better (e.g., being more physically active), and he will need to gain practice (via in-session role-playing and graded, in-vivo homework between sessions) in conversing more with others at work and in his neighborhood. The topic of dating is conspicuous by its absence, and may represent some important "missing data" from the assessment. Being alone has been a theme in Joey's life (being neglected by his parents, living alone as an adult, not letting people get to know him, expecting that his brother Bob would not want to connect with him again), but so is his belief that he has little to offer others. The therapist should look for the first opportunity to engage Joey in a discussion about the related issues of loneliness and intimacy. It is possible that this will be an important area of assessment and intervention for Joey, but its discussion may also heighten Joey's anxiety to the point where he may wish to discontinue therapy. The therapist will need to handle this topic carefully, respectfully giving Joey the autonomy to discuss it or not. As sensitive an area as Joey's brother Bob is, this may actually be a *less* loaded topic to bring up than the dating/ intimacy issue, and perhaps should be addressed first.

In the dialogue below, the therapist introduces a discussion with Joey about the obstacles to treatment that they have faced together thus far. Note the therapist's respectful tone, as he tries to minimize the risk of activating Joey's schemas of vulnerability to harm, and/or incompetence.

Therapist: I was thinking about what you said last session, about wanting to contact Bob, but then talking yourself out of it owing to all the stress you're under at work. If I remember correctly, I think your reasoning was that you wouldn't be able to keep your mind on the higher priority problem of talking to your boss and looking for a new job if you became pre-occupied with trying to reunite with your brother.

Joey: That's putting it nicely. I think what I said was that if I dealt with both things at the same time I would have so much anxiety I would become a basket case (big laugh).

Therapist: Well I agree that we should address your concerns as much as possible, as soon as possible, up to a point, but not try to be overly ambitious all at once. We want you to get the maximum benefit out of CBT, with a minimum of "side-effects."

Joey: Right, so I think I can put Bob out of my mind until I know how my job situation is going to turn out.

Therapist: Well, if you want to focus on managing your work situation, such as preparing to talk to your boss, attending meetings, and looking for a new job, that sounds good to me. It's just that I wonder if it's really necessary to wait until the entire job situation is settled *before* we can go to the next challenging topic. I would hate to see you lose valuable time because you underestimated how much productive work we could do together.

Joey: I'm not sure what you're getting at.

Therapist: What I mean is that I want to help you get the most out of therapy, and I'm committed to doing everything I can to help you reach your therapy goals. What I've noticed is that you tend not to believe in yourself—it's that *incompetency schema* we talked about—and you jump to conclusions about being helpless, or about "being a basket case," as you just mentioned a few minutes ago. That's the way you tend to think about yourself, and you accept it without question, whereas I think it's possible that you may be able to exceed your own expectations for yourself and improve your self-image.

Joey: Such as by dealing with the Bob situation right now, too? Yikes.

Therapist: Well, let's talk about it first. It doesn't have to be a do or die situation. I'm just suggesting that the way you see yourself is itself an issue we need to work on in therapy. One of the ways to improve your opinion of yourself is to try to do some of the things you don't think you can do, step by step, such as contacting Bob, and such as reducing your drinking, and other things too. But let's talk about it as a team. I want to know your thoughts on this matter. Let's see if we can find some common ground and advance.

Joey's history of psychological survival provides hope that he may be able to overcome his current difficulties. Joey can make significant progress in reducing his anxiety, dysphoria, loneliness, and alcohol use

113

via improving his problem-solving, activity level, communication skills, and by modifying the negative self-talk that stems from his maladaptive schemas.

The Competent Therapist's Active Pursuit of Additional Data

When therapists utilize good questioning and listening skills, they will continually learn more about their clients as therapy progresses, and this added information will add richness to the case formulation. Such information may be about important facts about the clients' history (e.g., having gone through a heretofore undisclosed trauma), or his or her current life situation (e.g., battling an addiction), and/or even about the client's ambivalent, negative, or otherwise complicated reactions to therapy and the therapeutic relationship. When therapists begin to ascertain such information they must handle it with great sensitivity, so that it becomes a potentially useful part of understanding and helping the clients, rather than increasing the clients' sense of shame or exacerbating their fears of being punished.

Competent therapists realize that it requires great courage and trust for clients to disclose painful aspects of their experience to a relative stranger, even if that stranger seems nice and has professional credentials. Thus, competent therapists are cognizant of the phenomenon of "missing data," whereby clients do not offer all the relevant information about their clinical problems, either due to shame, fear, unawareness, ulterior motives (such as when they misuse therapy for undisclosed personal gains, see Newman & Strauss, 2003) or combinations thereof.

The following transcript material illustrates the efforts that Joey's therapist makes to flesh out missing data regarding Joey's personal life. Notice how the therapist gives a rationale, shows respect for Joey's autonomous decision-making as a client, and tries to ask questions in a sensitive manner, using the case conceptualization to craft the dialogue in the most accurately empathic and constructive way.

Joey: The idea of having to move to another city just won't fly with me. That's why I'm so worried about being told that the only way to stay with the company is to transfer.
Therapist: I know that you're very comfortable in your current residence, and with your current neighbors, and that you don't want to

leave. (Perceiving a potential opening to ask about Joey's love life, which he has not discussed to this point.) Is there also someone in your life that you're particularly close to, such as somebody that you're dating or would like to date, who you don't want to leave?

Joey: (Laughs heartily.)

Therapist: Really, Joey, I'm not trying to be funny. I just want to understand the reasons why moving would be difficult for you, and a relationship might be one of those reasons. But I'm curious to know why you laughed at my question. What went through your mind?

Joey: Nothing, don't worry about it. I didn't mean to laugh at you.

Therapist: I know. I didn't take it personally. I just figured my question struck a nerve. What is the nerve?

Joey: Really, it's no big deal. There's no nerve. I just don't want to move.

Therapist: I get your point. I do. (pauses) I have to admit, however, that I wonder why we never talk about the subject of love. I have no idea who you've ever loved in a romantic way, and what experiences you've had in your life in terms of closeness and intimacy, and what effects those experiences have had on your emotions, your self-image, your hopes for the future, and things like that. That's why I asked you whether you were dating anyone.

Joey: (Remains silent, and looks away.) That topic is not easy for me.

Therapist: (Quietly, sympathetically.) Do you want to talk about it?

Joey: I don't know. I never talk about it. It's just a big area of nothing.

Therapist: A big area of nothing. Wow. I'm sorry to hear that. Are you saying that you're alone now, and that you're typically alone? I know that being alone is a big theme in your life. Are you telling me that you've never been fortunate enough to be in a love relationship?

Joey: Bingo (looks away).

Therapist: (Pauses.) What are you thinking and feeling right now, Joey?

Joey: I feel pathetic, and weird, and that you must think that too.

Therapist: I can't begin to tell you how much that is *not* what I think. I'm just trying to put myself in your shoes so I can understand how you feel. At first I wondered if you might be gay, and hadn't come out yet.

Joey: Oh geez, no, don't get that idea. Geez.

115

Therapist: Okay, okay, I hear you. It wouldn't be a big deal to me if you were, but now I'm getting the picture that you've never had sex, and that bothers you.

Joey: Now don't get that idea either! I *have* had sex, but nothing meaningful. I've never had a real girlfriend, and sometimes I worry I never will.

At this point the therapist rules out the need to consider the client's sexual orientation as a relevant cultural factor in the case conceptualization. However, it is clear that Joey is ashamed that he has never had a girlfriend, which has potential importance for his diagnosis (Does he also meet criteria for social anxiety disorder?), for his case conceptualization (Does he also have a schema of *unlovability*?), and the still-forming treatment plan (Does Joey wish to enter the world of dating?). Later in the session, the following dialogue ensues.

Joey: I don't know what I have to offer anybody.

Therapist: That's something you've said before. It really represents a poor opinion that you have of yourself. It seems so excessive and unnecessary, but I gather that you believe it strongly. How do you suppose you developed such a powerfully negative view of yourself?

Joey: I don't want to blame my parents for everything. It's lame.

Therapist: Then don't blame. Just explain the situation. What were the causes, and what were the effects? How do you conceptualize your own sense of not being "relationship material."

Joey: I don't think I've thought that through. It's just a feeling I've always had. I had it when I couldn't go to the same school as all my friends, and I never felt like I fit in at the public school I attended, but that was probably my own fault because I just pitied myself all those years and never did anything to make things better. There were girls who liked me, but I always stayed to myself. And now I've missed my chances, and now it's too late.

Therapist: Joey, I can truly understand if you have regrets, but I really think we need to re-visit this idea that it's too late for you. We've talked about your sense of helplessness about making things better for yourself, and it may be happening again, right now, with this topic. I wonder if you would consider putting this on our agenda.

In the following section, we will touch upon the ways in which Joey and his therapist proceeded to approach the goal list, based on the ever-developing case conceptualization.

FROM CASE CONCEPTUALIZATION TO TREATMENT PLAN

As we have seen, the client's current problem list, evaluated in the context of the client's history and current life situation, becomes a full-fledged case conceptualization when the therapist makes hypotheses about how the client's problems, strengths, and coping mechanisms relate to each other, based on a CBT model. This serves as the foundation for a treatment plan, which is fundamentally comprised of goals, and the tasks or methods to achieve those goals. As agreement on "goals" and "tasks" is a key component to a positive, constructive therapeutic relationship (Bordin, 1979), competent therapists make it a point to invite the client to weigh-in on questions such as, "In what ways do I want to improve myself and my life?" "What are the psychological skills I need to learn and utilize in order to achieve those goals?" and "How will I know when I am making progress?"

Goals

Setting goals is perhaps the first major intervention in itself, as it requires the client and therapist to begin the process of collaborating on determining and aiming toward the most important indicators of client improvement. Therapist and client may not necessarily see eye to eye on these matters, such as Joey's therapist believing that it would be useful to put the topic of entering the dating world onto the agenda, while Joey himself believed that it was "too late" for him, and that he had "nothing to offer anybody." However, it is important that the therapist works with the client as much as possible to find common ground right from the start, as there are studies indicating a positive relationship between perceived goal consensus early in treatment and clinical improvement at outcome (see Dobson & Dobson, 2009). This may be accomplished by empathizing with the client's stated goals, yet trying to make a case for endorsing others too.

Given that there is evidence that early success in treatment is both a predictor of an improved therapeutic relationship (DeRubeis, Brotman, &

Gibbons, 2005) and of a positive outcome (see Wilson, 2007), it is extremely beneficial if therapists can identify a goal or goals right away that are manageable, likely to lead to a reduction in the client's distress, and facilitative of hope and client self-efficacy. This is often achieved by choosing goals that are discrete and concrete, and which have some significance for the client.

In the case of Joey, for example, he and his therapist strongly agreed that it would be beneficial for him to learn some basic anxiety-reduction techniques, such as controlled breathing (that he could practice both in session and every day at home), to increase his level of healthy, enjoyable, constructive activities (e.g., taking part in the neighborhood block party), and to do some systematic problem-solving regarding his job situation (e.g., consulting with his immediate boss and with the human resources department, exploring new job opportunities as a back-up plan, generating options, and weighing pros and cons). The therapist's choice of interventions would target these areas first, though the therapist would also look for the first opportunity to engage Joey in a plan to reduce his alcohol use, as this problem was hypothesized to be a maintaining factor in the client's negative moods and avoidance. The therapist would continue this process by talking to Joey about other possible goals, such as Joey's contacting his long lost brother Bob, making and keeping long-overdue appointments with a doctor and a dentist, and entering the world of dating. The therapist was aware that Joey's anxiety and related schemas of vulnerability to harm, incompetence, and perhaps unlovability were particularly heightened by these prospective goals, and Joey believed that there was little to gain by facing these areas of his life. Therefore, a competent CBT therapist would decide not to force the issue, opting instead to work in a spirit of collaboration with Joey, to strive for some early success experiences in their work on the agreed-upon goals, and to utilize the expected improvements in Joey's mood and self-confidence as leverage to pursue the more tentative (and in some ways more challenging) goals. Note that the above goals are not simply about reducing Joey's symptoms; they are also about increasing his meaningful activities and helping him to acquire improved coping skills with which he could solve important problems in his life.

Supervisors play an important role in making this point to their earnest trainees who may otherwise fall into the trap of agreeing with clients on a list of goals that is comprised solely of symptom-reduction items. Note the following dialogue between a CBT supervisor and trainee, as they pay special attention to how the case conceptualization plays an important role in treatment planning.

Trainee: My client seems to have a very empty life. When I asked her to do an Activity Schedule, I was concerned by how much time she was spending on solitary activities that gave her very little mastery or pleasure.

Supervisor: What is your conceptual hypothesis about how her life has arrived at this state?

Trainee: Well, as we talked about before, she seems to operate on the belief that "If I have a problem, I should cut out the source of the problem in my life." She said as much, directly.

Supervisor: What are the unintended consequences of such a strategy?

Trainee: It's like we saw before. If she has any sort of perceived difficulty with a friend, she just cuts that friend out of her life. When she wasn't doing as well as she wanted to in Community College, she dropped out. When her exercise program wasn't helping her to lose weight the way she wanted, she quit the program. She just keeps eliminating things from her life, one by one.

Supervisor: And now, when you talk to your client about her goals, what do you notice?

Trainee: It's all about eliminating discomfort! Any way you look at it, her main goal seems to be to cut things out of her life that she doesn't like, but she doesn't replace them with anything. Her life just gets emptier and emptier.

Supervisor: And she gets more depressed, more lethargic, and less confident about facing challenges. And the less confident she is, the less likely it is that she will want to try new things to enrich her life. So what can you do about that in terms of her treatment goals?

Trainee: For starters, I could explain this conceptualization and see how much she agrees with it. If she seems to understand, maybe she will be receptive, at least in theory, to talking about *adding* things to her life, and trying to re-build her confidence.

Supervisor: I agree. That would be the way to go. Nevertheless, we already know that she quit going to the gym when she felt sore and tired but didn't lose the weight fast enough. Now we're going to be asking her to "work out" psychologically, which will probably be hard work, and the rewards may be gradual. What do you think might happen?

119

Trainee: She might quit trying. She might quit any of the homework assignments that she finds difficult.

Supervisor: She might even quit therapy altogether.

Trainee: So what should I do? I feel somewhat stuck. If she keeps the status quo, she won't improve, but if I try to help her create new and improved goals, she might quit therapy.

Supervisor: You're right. You're in a tough spot with her, but at least you have a good conceptual grasp of what you're up against. How can you use that understanding to present your ideas for new goals to your client in a particularly empathic way?

Trainee: I guess I could start by telling her that I understand that she feels depleted, alone, and hopeless, and that these feelings reinforce her belief that if she has a problem she should just get rid of it because she believes there is nothing else she can do. But then I could tell her that I believe that has the ability to *solve* problems, rather than just eliminate the sources. I could tell her that I want to help her to try for some new goals in her life, because I feel so badly for her that her days seem so empty and she has so few plans for her future.

Supervisor: And what if she just says that she can't do it?

Trainee: I could stay empathic and tell that I know it's going to be hard, but I could say that it's worth it because it's all about improving her life. I could tell her that I am very committed to helping her do that, and to giving her encouragement to keep trying at those times when she wants to give up on herself. Then I could invite her to work with me to put together a list of proactive goals. We might start with a relatively easier one, if possible.

Supervisor: I think you're right on target. Try to work on that goal list with your client as one of the agenda items next session. Let's see how that goes.

Tasks or Methods

This refers largely to the specific techniques that will be used in the service of pursuing the client's goals. By describing and using CBT techniques in session *and* as homework assignments (see Chapter 7), a clear message is sent to the clients that they will be collaborative partners in learning the methods that will allow them to feel better and to pursue their goals.

In explaining the various CBT techniques that clients may use to help themselves, it is important for therapists to offer a *rationale*, so that the interventions make sense, and so that the constructive purpose is apparent. The following is a sample rationale that the therapist offers Joey regarding methods to prepare him for an important meeting at work.

Therapist: I'm not saying that it's easy and that you should "just go" to the meeting. I know you have trepidations about it. I'm also not saying that you should go in cold, and try to wing it. What I would like to suggest is that we try techniques called "cognitive and behavioral *rehearsal*." They involve advance preparation, using your imagination and some role-playing, so that you can position yourself more favorably when you face the meeting.

Joey: I'm not sure how to do that.

Therapist: I will be happy to explain it fully, and to walk you through it. Let me give you an overview first, and then we can get into the details. The *cognitive* part of the rehearsal is where you envision what you think will happen in the meeting, point by point, as well as the thoughts that would go through your mind. Then we try to help you consider more constructive thoughts you could have to deal with the things you anticipate will come up. The *behavioral* part of the rehearsal is where you and I role-play the interactions you think are going to happen, so that you can practice what you want to say, as many times as you need, so that you will be more ready and confident to actually go through with the meeting, with less anxiety. What are your thoughts on that?

Joey: I can't see how that's going to work. I can't predict exactly what's going to happen in the meeting. I can't prepare for every possibility. There's still going to be uncertainty, and that's what makes me feel nuts with anxiety.

Therapist: I agree with you that we can't prepare you for every eventuality. You're right. However, you're already envisioning worst-case scenarios, so much so that you're already concluding that there's nothing you can do—there's that helplessness and incompetency schema again—and that you're better off not attending. By doing the cognitive and behavioral rehearsal, we can help prepare you to deal effectively with the worst case scenarios that you're already anticipating, so that perhaps there *will be* something constructive you can say to yourself in order to function more effectively, and there *will be* something that you can do to cope and get something useful out of the experience. And

121

then there's always that possibility that you won't even have to deal with a worst-case scenario after all, but it's better to be over-prepared.

Joey: It's easier not to go to the meeting.

Therapist: I know it's easier, but is that *better* for you? You've made a good case that uncertainty preys on your mind, but when you avoid meetings all you're left with is uncertainty. If you attend the meetings, you will have much more knowledge to work with, and if you do the cognitive and behavioral rehearsal, you may even be able to make something positive happen. What do you think about that rationale, Joey?

Joey: I see your point in theory, but it's going to be hard.

Therapist: I will gladly take you through the steps, and work with you until you feel more prepared and less anxious. If you want to start working on this, I'm willing to begin. I know the meeting is coming up soon, and I want to help you gain some good coping tools to give you the best possible chance of attending and doing well.

Benchmarking

Treatment planning involves the use of measuring sticks that will inform the therapist and client if they are making progress on the latter's therapeutic goals. These can be formal, psychometrically sound, self-report inventories such as the various Beck scales that assess the client's symptoms of depression, anxiety, and hopelessness on a regular, periodic basis. In a similar vein, the measurement can be a formal diagnostic interview to assess the client's progress in regard to his or her given diagnosis. Less formally, therapists and clients can agree upon observed, behavioral indicators of how the client is faring in treatment. For example, if a client such as Joey is trying to reduce his alcohol use, he can monitor his alcohol urges and usage on a daily basis, measure how long he waits between experiencing a craving and taking a drink, record his thoughts as he ponders the decision about whether or not to drink, and document the outcome. Indeed, this is an ambitious self-monitoring plan, but it allows the client to collect a great deal of data on himself, which enables him to assess his level of progress across several domains. This provides valuable information about how well the client is responding to treatment, and if and where modifications in the treatment plan should be made. In the next chapter, we will examine more closely the specific interventions competent CBT clinicians use to maximize the client's chances of achieving his or her therapeutic goals.

KEY POINTS TO REMEMBER

- Competent CBT clinicians remember that the initial evaluation (i.e., intake report) is a *starting point* in understanding a client, and that new clinical data will be gathered as treatment commences and progresses, that will lead to a more complete case conceptualization, which itself will be a work in progress.
- Good CBT case conceptualizations include information about the clients' history (and *development* of their problems) and current situation (identifying the factors that *maintain* their problems); the clients' typical behaviors, cognitions, emotions, and physiological responses that represent their symptoms; as well as their personal strengths, presenting a picture of the individual that goes well beyond a general diagnosis.
- Good CBT case conceptualizations have good *explanatory power* (i.e., generating hypotheses about the clients' problems), *treatment utility* (i.e., guiding the clinician to choose well-targeted interventions that have the best chance to succeed), and *predictive capability* (i.e., highlighting how treatment may progress, including potential problem areas in enacting the treatment plan).
- In the collaborative spirit of CBT, competent therapists tactfully share their case conceptualizations with their clients, ask for feedback, and use this information to reinforce the treatment goals.
- Competent CBT clinicians respect their clients' right to privacy (even in therapy!), but are nonetheless constantly on the lookout for additional "missing data" that may make

sense out of problems that have been difficult to comprehend and address thus far.

- A good case conceptualization helps the therapist and client collaborate on setting treatment goals, in agreeing on the methods or tasks they will employ, and in deciding on the measurable benchmarks they will use to assess the client's progress.
- Supervisors play an important role in helping CBT trainees use case conceptualizations to put the treatment on course, such as in focusing on how to build the client's psychological self-help skills, rather than focusing exclusively on symptom alleviation.

7

Implementing Cognitive-Behavioral Therapy Strategies and Interventions

"We can't solve problems by using the same kind of thinking we used when we created them."

Albert Einstein

The competent CBT clinician knows that interventions have maximum effect if they are crafted to the needs of the client. In order to demonstrate this, the current chapter will continue to follow the case of Joey, showing how the therapist's choice of interventions is a natural extension of his case conceptualization and treatment goals, and describing how to manage problems that may interfere with the successful application of CBT methods. The specific core competencies of CBT related to the implementation of interventions are as follows:

1. *Establishing and maintaining a treatment focus.* This area of CBT competency includes successfully structuring and pacing the treatment via the use of well-constructed and conscientiously followed

session agendas, by studiously using the treatment plan as a guide across sessions, and by maximizing clarity of communication with the client.

2. *Applying specific CBT procedures.* The competent CBT practitioner uses a repertoire of "tools" that help clients become more adept and confident in understanding and coping with their behavioral, cognitive, emotional, physiological, and interpersonal problems. As we will see later, these methods include self-monitoring, cognitive restructuring (e.g., rational responding, "downward arrow" technique, modifying intermediate beliefs and schemas), behavioral activation (reducing inertia, increasing a sense of accomplishment and enjoyment, enacting behavioral experiments), arousal-reduction exercises (e.g., relaxation and breathing control), exposures to avoided situations (including imagery work with traumatic memories), anti-impulsivity techniques (e.g., "delay and distract"), problem-solving, graded tasks, cognitive and behavioral rehearsal, and skills training via the use of role-playing (e.g., assertiveness, social skills, communication). A particularly high mark of competency in cognitive-behavioral therapists is their ability to use guided discovery questioning (also known as "the Socratic method") to engage clients in actively participating in CBT, and to teach the clients new, therapeutic ideas collaboratively and effectively. Additionally, therapists' competent design and implementation of CBT homework enables their clients to consolidate their learning of a variety of self-help methods, and to generalize their skills to everyday life.

3. *Recognizing and resolving therapy-interfering factors.* Competent cognitive-behavioral therapists make adjustments in their own methods in order to repair strains in the therapeutic relationship and improve collaboration. They also have compassion for clients whose external problems interfere with treatment, and therefore they do not fall prey to the pat, simplistic belief that "the client really doesn't want to change." Instead, they try to implement problem-solving with the clients. Competent CBT clinicians demonstrate expertise in engaging clients who seem distant and otherwise less than optimally invested in therapy. They also know how to manage crisis situations that interrupt the treatment plan but that require emergency clinical attention in their own right.

On the one hand, cognitive-behavioral strategies and interventions can be targeted specifically to the client's diagnostic areas of concerns, such as by using a CBT manual for a discrete problem such as social anxiety disorder (e.g., Antony & Rowa, 2008). On the other hand, they can also be aimed at the client's psychopathological *processes* (e.g., behavioral avoidance, cognitive catastrophizing, poor problem-solving, impulsivity) that are relevant *across* diagnostic categories (Barlow et al., 2004; Barlow et al., 2011). Given Joey's multiple problem areas and diagnostic ambiguity, this latter approach will be taken, such that Joey's main concerns will be addressed by a range of CBT interventions that are aimed at his chief deficits and dysfunctions.

ESTABLISHING AND MAINTAINING A TREATMENT FOCUS: STRUCTURE, PACING, SPECIFICITY

The Importance of an Agenda

Conducting CBT sessions that include an agenda of relevant topics, tasks, and goals, and that limit passive silences and tangential digressions sends the message to the clients that something useful and beneficial is going to occur. This is not to say that the agenda needs to be rigid, or to communicate the idea that there are no circumstances in which some strategic silence or casual conversation is therapeutic. Some departures from the originally set agenda are fitting and proper, such as occur when a client suddenly brings up a topic that takes priority over the others (e.g., thoughts of suicide). Similarly, although it is generally a good idea to keep the length of a typical session close to its predetermined length (e.g., the "50-minute hour"), there are times when it is most compassionate to allow for some added "injury time," such as when the client is uncharacteristically discussing something with great affect and involvement, at which time an extra 5 or 10 minutes could be especially helpful and enlightening.

The following are examples of comments offered by Joey's therapist, toward the goals of setting an agenda and establishing some structure in a friendly, inviting way. Notice how the therapist creates a "bridge" from the previous session to the current one, incorporates homework into the agenda, and uses current data to inform the priorities of the moment:

- "I was thinking that we could follow-up on some of the excellent work you in did in our previous session. Can you remember some of the main topics we discussed last time, and the points we covered? Maybe those topics can make up the majority of our agenda this time as well, though we can make some changes or additions if you would like?"

- "Let's make sure we talk about your homework as part of today's agenda. I'm curious to hear what it was like for you to try those behavioral experiments we talked about last session. Would that be okay? What else should we put on our list of important topics for today?"
- "What would you like to work on today? Let's make a plan."
- "What are the most important things we should try to cover in this session?"
- "I notice on your Beck Anxiety Inventory that you indicate elevated scores on the items of 'fear the worst happening,' and 'fear of losing control.' Maybe we should pay special attention to these problems in today's session. What do you think?"

The following are some sample comments Joey's therapist made when he noticed that the session had drifted away from the agenda, or otherwise lost therapeutic focus:

- "I'm thinking about our original topic before we got a little bit sidetracked. Can we get back to that discussion again?"
- (Trying to create a natural segue) "What you just said reminds me that we still have to talk about those examples of your 'being more communicative at work' that you mentioned when we originally set our agenda earlier. Let's talk about that."
- "We're getting a little bit late in our session and I want to make sure that we don't overlook some of our agenda items. Let's figure out what we still have time to work on, and maybe make a homework assignment out of whatever remains."

Eliciting Clarity and Specificity

Competency in establishing and maintaining a focus in treatment also involves facility in eliciting relevant *content* from clients, even when they have difficulty expressing themselves. Cognitive-behavioral therapists routinely ask their clients thought-provoking questions; the sort that encourage reflection, introspection, and problem-solving. Needless to say, rigorous questioning—even when presented in a gentle, benevolent fashion—places certain demands on clients who may be feeling depleted of energy and low in self-confidence. Thus, when CBT therapists ask good clinical questions, a common answer from clients is "I don't know." When this answer occurs too frequently, it may bog down the process of therapy, and may reinforce the clients' sense of dependence, helplessness, and frustration. Thus, one of the hallmarks of competent therapeutic questioning in CBT is that the clinician generally *does not take "I don't know" for an answer.* Instead, the therapist empathizes with the client's difficulties, but then encourages the client to venture an educated guess or two, and to get into the habit of generating hypotheses, even when he or she at first feels stymied in coming up with answers.

Similarly, to understand clients well, and to design interventions that will fit their needs, therapists need as clear a picture as possible of their concerns. However, as noted, clients sometimes have great difficulty in articulating their problems, thus placing a roadblock in the way of establishing and maintaining a therapeutic focus. Thus, one of the interventional competencies of CBT is the therapist's ability to guide clients from vague discourse to specific identification of what is on their mind, what is happening in their lives, and what their specific needs are. The therapist's competency in helping the client move from the general and vague to the specific and clear is illustrated in the following, brief dialogue with Joey. Note the therapist's parsimonious comments, keeping the pacing brisk, and implicitly encouraging Joey to try to be more thorough in his self-report.

Therapist: I'm very sorry to hear that you feel so inert and bored. What sorts of activities have you done in the past that gave you a sense of pride or enjoyment?

Joey: Things that got me going.

Therapist: Such as...?

Joey: Anything that didn't involve just lying in bed or staying home alone all the time.

Therapist: An example or two would be...?

Joey: Going to the gym. Being involved in community activities. Things I can't do now.

Therapist: To what do you attribute that?

Joey: I've just lost the energy. I've lost faith in myself. I'm too caught up in my worries.

Therapist: Owing to...?

Joey: Just having a really awful attitude, I guess.

Therapist: Typified by what sorts of things that you say to yourself?

Joey: Things like, "What's the point of trying? It's all meaningless anyway.
I'll just get beaten down by life anyway."

Therapist: No wonder you feel so bored, depressed, and detached from
life. Those thoughts really *are* demoralizing. Maybe we can take
a closer look at those thoughts and evaluate them, now that you
have taken the trouble to identify them so clearly.

In the above example, the therapist's brief questions help propel the
dialogue and shape the client's description of the problem to the point
where targets of intervention become more readily apparent, such as
Joey's avoidance of constructive activities owing to his beliefs that there's
no point in trying and that he will "just get beaten down by life anyway."
Notice how the therapist gives Joey some positive verbal reinforcement
for engaging in the dialogue and producing some promising material for
the session agenda.

APPLYING SPECIFIC CBT PROCEDURES

There are a plethora of "tools" that CBT practitioners can offer their clients
so that they may learn to understand themselves more objectively and
constructively, and to cope more effectively, with an expanded repertoire.
These tools comprise the body of methods most commonly associated
with the term "CBT techniques." Numerous books describe these techniques in great detail, and the competent CBT clinician is familiar with
many of them, using them as central reference volumes (e.g., A. T. Beck
et al., 2004; J. S. Beck, 2011; Bennett-Levy et al., 2004; Dobson & Dobson,
2009; Freeman, Felgoise, Nezu, Nezu, & Reinecke, 2005; Greenberger &
Padesky, 1995; Leahy, 2003; Leahy, Holland, & McGinn, 2011; Ledley et al.,
2010; Martell et al, 2010; Neenan & Dryden, 2004; O'Donohue & Fisher,
2009; Wright et al., 2006; Young et al., 2003). A brief sample of some of the
most commonly used CBT techniques is presented below, in the context of
how they were applied in Joey's case, showing how they fit together into
a comprehensive treatment plan. Following these will be additional sections devoted more extensively to the competent use of guided discovery,
and to CBT homework.

Self-Monitoring

One of the first skills competent CBT therapists often teach their clients is how to "take data" on themselves, thus beginning the process of looking at their own problems through the eyes of an objective, social scientist, and establishing the CBT approach of "collaborative empiricism." Joey was taught to track both his episodes of high anxiety, as well as his drinking. He kept a written log in which he would note the conditions under which he would notice that his anxiety had increased, including the situation, his automatic thoughts, and his behavioral responses to those thoughts (e.g., Did he "shut down" and stop working? Did he take a drink?). In a separate technique, Joey would examine his automatic thoughts and attempt to modify them (see below). Joey also used his log to indicate how much he was drinking, in which situations (e.g., With his buddies; by himself to get to sleep), resulting in what consequences (e.g., Was he late for work the next day?). Joey used subjective rating scales (e.g., 0–100) to gauge the *degrees* to which he experienced certain emotions, or felt the urge to take a drink, or believed in his automatic thoughts (and their subsequent rational responses). By compiling these scaled ratings, Joey was able to note changes in his functioning.

Relaxation and Breathing Control (Anti-Arousal Methods)

In order to obtain some relief from symptoms of elevated sympathetic nervous system activity (i.e., reduce his sweating, tension, and gastro-intestinal symptoms), Joey was taught how to relax via the use of sitting comfortably, closing his eyes, imagining pleasant scenes (e.g., being on the beach), and breathing slowly and diaphragmatically. He practiced this twice (for 10 minutes each) every day, and was asked to use this method at times when he had anxiety-driven thoughts, and when he experienced urges to drink alcohol to self-medicate his anxiety.

Behavioral Activation (Activity Scheduling; Rating Activities on "Mastery" and "Pleasure")

In light of Joey's symptoms of anhedonia and social withdrawal, he was helped to plan activities that would give him a sense of accomplishment (mastery) and pleasure. At first, Joey declined, saying that he did not have the motivation, but the therapist explained that sometimes action *precedes* motivation, and that by doing the things he used to enjoy Joey might be able to jump-start his interest. Joey kept track of his activities on a Daily Activity Schedule (J. S. Beck, 2011), and rated his activity on a 0–10 scale on "M" (mastery; such as helping a neighbor with a repair job) and "P" (pleasure; such as going to a comedy club with two coworkers). As Joey became more activated, he "graduated" to more challenging tasks, such as going back to the gym, and attending lunch meetings at work rather than eating at his cubicle.

Behavioral "Experiments"

Related to the method of behavioral activation, this area of intervention can be summed up by the following instruction: "Think of some things that you *could* be doing that would be potentially helpful, but that you have been *avoiding* owing to negative assumptions and/or low motivation; try to do them, see for yourself what happens, and compare the results with your initial expectations." Joey applied this intervention to a number of areas of his life. For example, Joey believed that his buddies would chastise him for drinking less, but he enacted the behavioral experiment of explaining that he was "cutting back due to doctor's orders," and found that his friends really did not care, as long as Joey was still being sociable. Also, Joey did the behavioral experiment of attending all his company's planning meetings even though he was tempted to avoid them for fear that they would only make him feel worse. Joey discovered that he was *glad* that he showed up, as he had a much better sense of where the company was headed, and what he would have to do to remain employed in his current locale. However, there was one particular behavioral experiment—sending an e-mail to his long lost brother Bob—that Joey at first found too difficult to do, as he expected to be ignored, a prospect he said he could not bear to face. Joey agreed *in theory* that it would be productive to test his hypotheses that Bob would rebuff him, and that he would not be able to cope with the rejection. However, Joey opted to do a "graded task" (another well-known CBT technique), involving writing a mock letter to Bob which he would then read in session as if he were talking to Bob across the room. This task would provide Joey with an exposure exercise (yet another important CBT technique, see below) to his own cognitions and emotions related to his familial trauma and loss, and could potentially pave the way for an actual attempt to communicate with Bob.

Exposure Exercises

Two areas of Joey's life in which he was particularly avoidant were his failure to get a medical or dental check-up for many years, and his lack of willingness to "put [himself] out there" to try to have a dating life. After Joey agreed that it would be beneficial for him to make changes in both of the above areas of his life, the therapist explained that a potentially powerful CBT technique involved "graded exposures" to these avoided situations. For example, Joey was willing first to look at websites for local doctors and dentists, then to make phone calls to ask about their hours and which insurances they accepted, then to make appointments (admittedly, far in advance), followed by driving to each office and entering their respective foyers so as to gain exposures to the sights, sounds, and even the smells of each place, and ultimately to attend his medical and dental appointments, while utilizing cognitive restructuring methods (described below, in the context of other issues). In the area of dating, Joey at first explored dating websites, then joined one of the programs, then wrote a profile about himself, then interacted online with a number of eligible women, managing his anxiety with relaxation techniques and cognitive restructuring along the way.

Cognitive Restructuring (Rational Responding)

Joey was taught to spot his own automatic thoughts, using his increased anxiety or dysphoria as cues that "something upsetting must be going on in my thinking right now." He wrote down his automatic thoughts on an Automatic Thought Record (ATR), utilized a series of key questions to modify his anxiogenic and depressogenic thoughts, and generated rational responses (see Figure 7.1). Some of these questions included, "What evidence supports or refutes what I am thinking?" "What are some other ways I could look at this situation?" and "What constructive action can I take to deal with this situation?" among others. The more Joey practiced using ATRs, the more adept he became in reducing his catastrophic thinking and in increasing his constructive problem-solving (see below).

"Downward Arrow" Technique—Toward Identification of Intermediate Beliefs and Schemas

Joey learned how to probe his own automatic thoughts so as to ascertain the beliefs or schemas that underlie such thoughts. His cue to enact

Figure 7.1 Automatic Thought Record Directions: When you notice your mood getting worse, ask yourself, **"What's going through my mind right now?"** and as soon as possible jot down the thought or mental image in the Automatic Thoughts column.

DATE/ TIME	SITUATION	AUTOMATIC THOUGHT(S)	EMOTION(S)	ALTERNATIVE RESPONSE	OUTCOME
	1. What event, daydream, or recollection led to the unpleasant emotion? 2. What (if any) distressing physical sensations did you have?	1. What thought(s) and/or image(s) went through your mind? 2. How much did you believe each one at the time?	1. What emotion(s) (sad, anxious, angry, etc.) did you feel at the time? 2. How intense (0–100%) was the emotion?	1. (optional) What cognitive distortion did you make? (e.g., all-or-nothing thinking, mind-reading, catastrophizing) 2. Use questions at bottom to compose a response to the automatic thought(s). 3. How much do you believe each response?	1. How much do you now believe each automatic thought? 2. What emotion(s) do you feel now? How intense (0–100%) is the emotion? 3. What will or did you do?
Thurs. late afternoon at the office.	1. I received an e-mail inviting me to a "special meeting." 2. Sweating, shaky.	1. "This is bad. They never have a special meeting unless it's some sort of emergency or major change. My life is about to change in ways I don't want. I don't want to deal with this." (I believe this at a level of 90%) 2. "If I attend this meeting, I am going to be a nervous wreck, and everyone will know it. I will look weak and I will be embarrassed. I will probably be unable to say anything in my own defense or on my own behalf, and I'll just look like a sheep being led to the slaughter." (I believe this at a level of 80%)	1. Anxious (100%) 2. Ashamed (50%)	1. I am jumping to conclusions and catastrophizing. I am labeling myself as "weak" and reading other people's minds. 2. Even if it's bad news, I have been preparing myself for this, so it doesn't have to be the end of the world. (I believe this at a level of 60%). Other people in the meeting will be upset too, so they won't be judging me for being concerned. (I believe this at a level of 95%).	1. Thoughts: 1st thought: 40% 2nd thought: 10% 2. Emotions: Anxious (60%) Ashamed (10%) 3. Actions: I will go to the meeting, and I will prepare something to say if I need to.

Questions to help compose an alternative response:

(1) What is the evidence that the automatic thought is true? Not true?

(2) Is there an alternative explanation?

(3) What's the worst that could happen? Could I live through it? What's the best that could happen? What's the most realistic outcome?

(4) What's the effect of my believing the automatic thought? What could be the effect of changing my thinking?

(5) What should I do about it?

(6) If _____ (friend's name) was in the situation and had this thought, what would I tell him/her?

© J. Beck (1995; 2011). Adapted from *Cognitive Behavior Therapy: Basics and Beyond* (2ⁿᵈ ed.), Guilford Press, and used with permission.

this method was when his emotional reactions seemed disproportionate to the situation (especially when he looked at the situation in retrospect, with less arousal). Joey started by identifying an automatic thought, and then asking himself questions such as, "And what would happen *then?*" or "And what would *that* mean?" in order to explore his implicit concerns lying underneath his surface thoughts. Figure 7.2 illustrates one such "downward arrow" that Joey constructed, highlighting his schema of vulnerability to harm.

Modifying Intermediate Beliefs and Schemas

After using the downward arrow technique, Joey saw that his catastrophic assumptions and related anxious and depressive symptoms were tied to a sense of being extraordinarily vulnerable, just as he was as a child. He then undertook many steps to chip away at his vulnerability-to-harm schema. These included: (1) looking for evidence of his previous successes in dealing with adverse life situations; (2) identifying and writing the lessons he learned from these past coping experiences; (3) replacing catastrophic thinking with the specific steps of problem-solving (see below); (4) engaging in role-play exercises in session (see below) in which he had to counteract his schema through persuasive arguments of the facts; and (5) taking part in the advanced technique of imagery reconstruction (see below) to rationally re-evaluate some of the harsh ideas about himself and his life that he had learned growing up in an abusive, neglectful household.

Imagery Reconstruction (With Rational Responding)

One of the most advanced techniques in the field of CBT is imagery reconstruction combined with rational responding—a method that is often associated with trauma work (see Deblinger & Heflin, 1996; Layden et al., 1993; Resick & Schnicke, 1993; Young et al., 2003). One of the goals of Joey's treatment was to reduce the deleterious impact that Joey's childhood had on his beliefs about himself (e.g., helpless, vulnerable) and the world (e.g., unpredictable, fickle, dangerous). After Joey had settled into treatment and developed a sense of trust and camaraderie with his therapist, the therapist described the option of doing imagery reconstruction techniques. Joey agreed to write successively more detailed narratives of some of his most painful childhood experiences, and then to take part in relaxation exercises (learned earlier), followed by imaginal trips down

135

Figure 7.2 "Joey's" Downward Arrow

AUTOMATIC THOUGHT: "The meeting is going to outline the company restructuring and it's going to be bad news for me." *And what would happen then?*

"I will probably have to take a pay cut, or relocate, or I might even lose my job." *And what would happen then?*

"I won't be able to handle it. I will either fail at my new responsibilities, or be at risk for losing my apartment, or be unwilling to go to a strange new place where I don't know anybody, or I'll be unable to pull myself together to look for a new job." *And what would happen then?*

"I would wind up getting paralyzed, unable to work or to look for work, and I would be without money or a place to live, or a sense of direction, or a purpose in life." *And what would that mean?*

"I will be utterly helpless. It would prove that no matter what I do I am unable to prevent bad things from happening to me. It would mean that my life is going to be one disaster after another, and there is nothing I can do to stop it. It would mean that everything I'm comfortable with would be gone, and I won't have any options."

"memory lane," where the lessons that Joey had learned from his worst memories would be identified and modified. Joey learned to manipulate mentally his imagery so that he could envision being able to defend himself verbally in his memories, and to draw more mature conclusions about his personal worth and strengths—conclusions that Joey then wrote down in detail in his therapy journal.

"Delay and Distract" Technique (to Prevent Impulsive Acting on Alcohol Cravings)

Joey agreed that one of the treatment goals needed to be a reduction in his use of alcohol, especially as a "self-medicating" behavior for his anxiety. In his self-monitoring exercises, Joey concluded that his drinking occurred as often when he was alone and ruminating as when he was socializing with friends. He determined that he would try to "ride out the cravings" and not drink when he was alone. In enacting the "delay and distract" technique, Joey aimed to put as much time as possible between his initial urge to drink and actually taking a drink, starting with 10 minutes and building up to longer periods, at which point his craving often subsided. During his waiting time, Joey would engage in activities that would distract him from his cravings. These activities included such diverse choices as talking outside with his neighbors, exercising, doing some household chores, reading, playing his guitar, or doing audio-visual activities (computer, television, music), perhaps while enjoying a nonalcoholic beverage. Joey's "solo drinking" decreased significantly, though he was still prone to drink when out with his friends, which led to the designing of one of his behavioral experiments in socializing while drinking less (see above).

Replacing Ruminative Thinking With Problem-Solving

Joey and his therapist agreed that Joey would attempt to self-monitor his catastrophic, ruminative thinking and replace it with activities related to problem solving. For example, Joey learned to "catch himself" when he was engaging in repetitive, idle worrying, often by using his muscle tension and stomach pains as cues. At such times, Joey deliberately switched into "problem-solving mode," in which he brainstormed and wrote down some ideas about what he would have to do to safeguard his career (e.g., consult with colleagues; make himself as valuable as possible through being more involved and less withdrawn at work; actively investigate other job options), to manage his money well enough to maintain his apartment until the end of his lease regardless of his job status, and to remain connected to friends without necessarily going out to drink. Joey weighed the pros and cons of various options, created plans of action (e.g., getting to work each day an hour earlier than usual; saving money via less drinking; applying for another job), and then evaluated the outcome. Joey's confidence grew, his energy increased, and his sense of helplessness diminished.

Cognitive and Behavioral Rehearsal

As noted in Chapter 6, this technique involved the therapist helping Joey to imaginally "walk through" an anticipated situation that was producing significant emotional concerns and negative expectations. In visualizing an upcoming meeting, Joey was able to plan how to bring his most constructive behavioral responses to bear on whatever problematic events might occur. Further, Joey could track his "hot" (affect-laden) cognitions associated with the meeting, so as to identify and modify his pessimistic thoughts *in advance* of the actual situation.

Skills Training via Role-Playing

Role-playing is a low-cost, high-benefit intervention that has many potential applications in session with clients, and in supervision with trainees (Milne, 2009). Role-playing can provide clients with repeated, simulated exposures to feared and avoided interpersonal situations; opportunities for building skills (e.g., communication, assertion); creative methods for rationally responding to problematic thinking (e.g., "Devil's Advocacy"); or combinations of the above. Role-playing may also be used effectively in supervision, as supervisors and their supervisees practice would-be interactions with clients, thus preparing the trainees to have a broader, more readily available repertoire of responses to possible client reactions in session.

The following is just a sample of the ways in which role-playing may be used appropriately and effectively in session:

1. When clients have been avoiding a much-needed conversation with someone in their life (e.g., family member, friend, neighbor, roommate, love partner, colleague, employer, employee),

role-playing provides a safe forum for the clients to prepare and practice what they would like to say. It is *safe* inasmuch as the therapists encourage and assist the clients, free of unconstructive criticism, in building the skill to face a potentially challenging interpersonal situation, and to practice communication skills. Further, role-playing potentially provides a great deal of trial-and-error repetition that may be difficult to obtain in real life, with none of the naturalistic consequences. Role-playing may seem to be *subjectively unsafe* to the clients if they harshly judge themselves for their assumed inadequate role-playing performances. This brings up the next use of role-playing, as described in point 2.

2. Role-playing helps flesh out some of the clients' negative expectations regarding their self-efficacy, the response(s) of the other person (including the therapist in the here-and-now of the session), the outcome of the situation being simulated, or combinations of the above. For example, Joey was reluctant to engage in a role-play exercise in which he would try to strike up a conversation with a particular female neighbor named "Miranda" that he liked and whom he expected to see at the next "Neighborhood Watch" meeting. When the therapist tried to initiate the role-play, Joey simply shrugged and laughed nervously. Rather than abandoning the exercise, the therapist said, "You seem to be a little uncomfortable with this role-playing exercise; what are your thoughts about doing this that are making you hesitant?" Joey replied with comments that included, "I'm no good at this," and "I don't know what I would say." The dialogue below provides a look at what followed:

Therapist: Your negative thoughts about *yourself* really get in the way of your trying to express yourself. That's too bad. I think you have some interesting things going on in your life that you can talk about quite appropriately and even engagingly, but we'll never know if you convince yourself that you can't say anything.

Joey: I just get very nervous when I talk about myself. I assume I'll freeze up, or maybe I'll just go on and on like a blithering idiot while I bore everybody. I guess that's all-or-none thinking, isn't it? I guess what I'm saying is that I already feel badly about myself, and I think that if I try to talk to Miranda I'll just make things worse.

Therapist: I understand that you don't want to make things worse, and I definitely agree that the goal is to make things better, and that's what I want to help you do. It's just that you have a *habit* of assuming the worst, such as expecting that you'll either freeze up or obnoxiously go on and on about yourself in that all-or-none way of thinking that you so astutely pointed out! But Joey, can you see how doing a role-play exercise would not have to involve *any* consequences? It's just a way of practicing a very important skill, and even if you have a hard time we can learn from what went wrong and try again. Doing this exercise can really be a "no-lose" situation.

Joey: But I might walk out of here feeling like a total loser.

Therapist: From my vantage point, anything you do to extend yourself beyond your comfort zone—such as doing a therapeutic role-play—is a sign of courage and high motivation, and I for one would be impressed. I feel badly for you that you are so quick to view yourself as a "loser," but that's not something that I would ever think about you.

Joey: So how does this role-playing work? How should we do this?

3. In the "Devil's Advocacy" technique, therapists explain that they will be taking on the role of the client's negative thoughts, while the clients are charged with the task of responding rationally. In this method, it is important for therapists to portray the clients' thinking in an accurately empathic way—in which the substantive and emotional contents of the clients' thinking are displayed frankly, but with sensitivity. When done correctly, the Devil's Advocacy method helps the clients to practice responding rationally to some of their most salient maladaptive thoughts, and it signals that the therapist has been paying close attention to what the clients typically think. In the following sample dialogue, Joey is asked to play the role of the part of his thinking that sees the benefit in trying to talk to Miranda, while the therapist takes the role of Joey's typical "nay-saying" automatic thoughts and beliefs that discourage him from talking to women he likes.

Therapist (as Devil's Advocate): There's really no point in trying to talk to Miranda. She's not going to be interested in me.

Joey (practicing rational responses): I have no idea whether she would be interested in me or not. I've never tried to talk to her or spend time with her on Neighborhood Watch. I'm just *assuming* that there's no point. I need to try, and then judge for myself.

Therapist (as Devil's Advocate): Yes, but if I stay away from her, I can spare myself the humiliation of getting tongue-tied and making a fool of myself in front of her.

*Joey (practicing rational responses):*That's a worst-case scenario. It's not a likely-case scenario. You can't go through your whole life expecting the worst. Sometimes you have to have a little hope.

Therapist (as Devil's Advocate): That may be true, but I just feel too vulnerable to put myself out there like that. I just don't think I can do it, and the last thing I need in my life is another failure experience that will make me lose even *more* confidence in myself.

Joey (coming out of the role-play): That's exactly how I feel.

Therapist (also coming out of the role, but encouraging the two of them to get back into the role-play again): Good catch! This is one of your major themes in therapy—doubting your-self and feeling incapable. This is an opportunity to try a new way of thinking that supports yourself more, and that does not fall prey to assuming that you are too weak to cope. Let's get back into the role-play and keep trying. Take as much time as you need.

Joey: So what did you just say?

Therapist: I'll say it again. No problem. Let's resume the role-play from this point onward.

(Getting back into the role) I'm afraid that I will fail and that will just make me feel even worse about myself.

Joey (getting back into the role): If you try to talk to Miranda, that is already a success, because you are bravely doing some-thing you usually avoid. You could feel proud of your-self just for trying.

Therapist (as Devils' Advocate): But what about all the stress I will feel while I'm trying to do it?

Joey (practicing rational responses): You could look at it as good practice. You're "getting in shape." What's the phrase again?—"You're building psychological muscles." It might hurt, but you're getting stronger.

Therapist (as Devil's Advocate): Are you sure you won't think I'm stupid if I try to talk to Miranda and it winds up going nowhere?

Joey (practicing rational responses): Of course not! But the most important thing is how you will feel about *yourself.* That's where you can practice rational responses that are fair and kind to yourself, so that you can support yourself as you face your insecurities.

Therapist (coming out of the role): That was *great* work! What are your thoughts right now?

Joey (coming out of the role): I didn't think I could do the role-play the right way, but I guess I did. By the way—the way you just role-played me—do I really sound that pathetic?

Therapist: Oh my! I'm very, very sorry if I came across that way. I wasn't trying to make fun of you in any way. I just wanted to emphasize the big fears that you've talked about.

Joey: No, you didn't do anything wrong. I just didn't like the way I sounded...I mean, the way you sounded being me. I guess I just want to change that.

Therapist: You're well on your way, because the rational responses you gave in the Devil's Advocate role-play were very constructive and hopeful. Now you've positioned yourself to write down some of those ideas and to try to think of them or read them when you're getting ready to attend a Neighborhood Watch meeting with Miranda. What do you think?

Joey: It's still scary, but I'm getting closer to being able to try.

4. Therapists and their clients can role-play situations that will test the clients' actual skills in the areas of coping and communication. In the following example, the therapist plays the role of Miranda, while Joey tries to practice what he might say to her at the meeting.

Joey (as if he has just chosen to sit next to Miranda): Hi. Do you know if they posted next month's schedule yet?

Therapist (playing the role of Miranda): I think that's one of the topics of discussion at tonight's meeting. I've been out there walking the block three times this month myself. I think some people are becoming unreliable.

Joey: Oh, sorry to hear about that. (Pauses.) So you're doing extra work? That doesn't seem right. (Pauses.) You know, if that happens again, just let me know, and I will try to cover for you so you'll get a break.

Therapist (playing the role of Miranda): That's very nice of you, but you don't have to.

Joey: That's nice of *you* to say that, but consider it an open offer. (Pauses.) You know, it could all be moot if they put us on the schedule together anyway! Then we'll have to do our block supervision together and nobody will be able to cover for *either* of us.

Therapist (playing the role of Miranda): That could happen!

Joey: Yeah, all the slackers would drop out and then they would be down to their two most conscientious people, you and me! Well, if that happens, I can't say I would mind that.

Therapist (playing the role of Miranda): Thanks for saying that. Let's see how it works out.

[Then the therapist comes out of the role, and does a short debriefing with Joey, as follows]:

Therapist: Joey, that was excellent! You had me thinking that you were going to struggle, but that was really a nice conversation you had with Miranda. You didn't freeze up and you weren't boring or obnoxious like you feared you would be.

Joey: I did brag that I was conscientious.

Therapist: Actually, you complimented yourself *and* Miranda together, in the same breath. That was appropriate and very nice! I don't think your problem is a lack of conversational skills, Joey. I think the problem is that you're massively *inhibited* due to your negative beliefs about yourself. If we make some changes in that area of your life, you may have a lot more success in your social life than you think.

Joey: But what if Miranda already has a boyfriend?

Therapist: That would be a bummer, but that's a separate issue. Right now we're just talking about your ability to create a connection with a woman you like by being a nice conversationalist. I really think there's hope here. How about you?

5. Role-playing can also be used in order for clients to re-enact important moments from their lives, either with realism (i.e., trying to re-create what actually happened) in order to interpret the event and its effects in light of current knowledge and therapeutic goals, or with imagery reconstruction (see above), in which the clients deliberately change the course of events in such a way as to gain a greater sense of empowerment, cognitive-affective resolution, or both (see Layden et al., 1993).

A review of all the sample techniques above illustrates how they tend to fit together if the case conceptualization and treatment plan are well-formed. The techniques are not disparate activities—they are important pieces of the same puzzle, and they tend to create a clear picture when enacted as a package, in the context of a solid therapeutic relationship.

GUIDED DISCOVERY (SOCRATIC METHOD)

One of the most difficult methods for CBT therapists to master is the technique known as "guided discovery," also known as the Socratic method (see Overholser, 2010). The hallmark of guided discovery is helping clients entertain thought-provoking questions about themselves and their lives, such that they learn to think more constructively, flexibly, and independently. Guided discovery is a technique that stands apart from the CBT methods described above, in that it is not discrete and circumscribed, but rather represents a more general style of communicating with the client. The following is a sample list of clinical situations in which guided discovery may be used.

1. *The clients profess to have an absence of thoughts, or otherwise to have difficulty in ascertaining or describing important aspects of their experience.* Here, it is useful if therapists have a broad repertoire of questions that make cognitive assessment sound more like casual conversation. Such questions may include:
   - What did you make of that?
   - What crossed your mind then?

- Did something occur to you at that moment? What was it?
- What was the take-home lesson you got from that situation?
- Now that you've described what happened, what's the "moral of the story" here?
- What does this signify to you?
- What are the implications?
- What did that experience remind you of?

The competent CBT practitioner uses a wide range of questions to flesh out the clients' thoughts in a manner that maximizes conversational comfort. Another mark of competency in helping guide clients to discover their automatic thoughts is in being sensitive to signs of clients' shifts in affect. When clients make physical or verbal gestures that indicate a significant cognitive-affective moment (e.g., a sigh, an uncomfortable shift in posture, a nervous laugh, becoming misty-eyed), therapists can begin a process of guided discovery by caringly noting the clients' responses, and gently asking what they are thinking at that moment. An example might be, "Your eyes brightened just now, as if you had a moment of recognition about something important. What just crossed your mind?"

2. *The clients draw pat, negative conclusions, as if to prematurely shut off all further therapeutic considerations or dialogue.* In this instance, it is useful for therapists to empathically summarize what the client is saying, so as to confirm that the client has been heard. For example, when Joey said that there was "no point in trying" to improve his life situation because "life would just beat [him] up" anyway, the therapist said, "I know you've been through a great deal of hardship in your life, and that you're probably fed up with dealing with problems that seem to be out of your control. I'm truly sorry that your job may be at risk, and that you have to go through all of this in the first place. At the same time, I would hate to just let it go at that, and assume that you don't have the wherewithal to do something useful to help yourself in this sort of predicament." Then, in order to open up the discussion for further inquiry (and perhaps therapeutic discovery), the therapist then added comments and questions such as, "I know you have coped with nearly impossible situations in the past. If you could take a page out of your own coping book from years ago and use it now, what would the instructions be?"

3. *The therapist spots a client's clinically relevant (perhaps counterproductive) belief, but does not want to bluntly contradict the client or otherwise risk getting into a power struggle over whose ideas are "right."* The therapist may ask, "Would you be willing to tell me how you arrived at your conclusion? I know you feel strongly about this, and I gather that it all seems very self-explanatory from where you're sitting, but I hope you'll humor me and spell out your thought process for me. I don't want to just say that 'I understand' until I really do. Can we go through this step by step? Thanks." Such a process may bring the client's reasoning into the light of day for further discussion, exploration, and hopefully modification.

4. *The therapist has a clear message to deliver, but does not want to "give away the answer." Rather, the therapist wants to shape the therapeutic dialogue so that the client "comes around" to a new understanding.* For example, in the following dialogue, the therapist has ascertained that Joey often criticizes himself harshly, while at the same time expressing benevolent admiration for his peers, though they have human flaws and failings as well. The therapist is tempted to state flatly that Joey is engaging in the double standard of being forgiving of others while punishing himself, but instead tries to craft questions in such a way that the client will see this phenomenon himself, as highlighted below:

Therapist: I've noticed that when you talk about the people in your life—your friends, your peers, your favorite colleagues—you are very accepting of them. You never have an unkind word to say about any of them. I'm sure they have their issues and problems, like anybody else, but you don't seem to hold it against them.

Joey: I know some really great people. I wish I could be more like them.

Therapist: Well, what are some things you have in common with the peers you admire most?

Joey: In common? I don't usually think about that.

Therapist: Would you be willing to think about it now? Friends tend to have things in common. It could be an interesting thought exercise to consider how you and some of your most admired friends are similar to each other.

Joey: Hmmm. Well, one of the reasons why I like my neighbors so much is that everyone is willing to help everyone else. Everybody pitches in, whether it's shoveling snow, or helping someone with car trouble, or pet-sitting, or running errands for someone who's sick. We all do things like that for each other.

Therapist: That includes you, right? You're one of those people who helps others, right?

Joey: Well, yeah, I'm more than happy to do my fair share.

Therapist: So you also believe in fairness, and holding up your end of things.

Joey: I also genuinely like my neighbors, and they're very nice to me.

Therapist: So they find you likeable.

Joey: Yeah, I'm lucky that I know such great people.

Therapist: Do you think they consider you to be one of them?

Joey: What do you mean?

Therapist: It sounds like you have at lot in common with the people you appreciate the most, and yet the way you talk about yourself—it's as if you feel you don't belong in the same category as them. So it leads me to wonder, do you think that *they* think you are in the same category as *them*?

Joey: They probably think I'm one of them, because that's the kind of people they are.

Therapist: So they accept you as being one of them? Even though they are so admirable, while you think so little of yourself?

Joey: Well, if they knew the *real* me, maybe they wouldn't like me as much as they do.

Therapist: The *real* you? Wow, so you're discounting all the positive things you do publicly and implying that only your privately held worst thoughts and feelings are real?

Joey: Are you saying that my private misery *isn't* real?

Therapist: Not at all. I'm implying that *both* the positive, outer, public "you" and the inner, private, negative "you" are real. Just like the positive things you see publicly expressed by your esteemed peers are real, and their private difficulties that you probably know less about are real as well. Again, my point is that you probably have a lot in common with people you value, and yet you don't value yourself very much.

Joey: Actually, my neighbors Bruce and Wynn tell me a lot about their personal struggles. Bruce is going through a divorce and Wynn has his own demons. They confide in me.

Therapist: What do you think that says about how they feel about you?

Joey: That they trust me.

Therapist: That's a pretty valuable character trait—to be trustworthy and to earn the confidences of your closest friends. Do you take that into account when you evaluate yourself? Is that part of the *real* you?

Joey: I don't usually think that way. (Long, thoughtful silence.)

Therapist: What are the main points you're taking away from this discussion? I've been grilling you with questions, and you've been a good sport about it, but most of all I'm wondering what lessons you're deriving from our conversation.

Joey: That I'm more like my friends than I think?

Therapist: And the implications of that are...?

Joey: I still like them even though they have issues, because I look at the good in them, but I don't do that for myself.

Therapist: Go on (chuckles).

Joey: Uh...I could be nicer to myself?

Therapist: Is that a question or an assertion?

Joey: Well, truthfully, it's a question, because I'm not sure I want to ignore my shortcomings.

Therapist: I totally agree. We don't want to ignore *anything.* It's *all* data. Let's not have any biases here, good or bad. Let's take stock of your life, both the assets that are worthy of admiration—just like how you feel about your friends and colleagues—and the shortcomings that require your attention and your problem-solving skills.

Joey: I guess we're saying that I could be a little more *constructive* in my criticisms of myself, just like I try to be with Bruce and Wynn. I try to offer sound advice to them that is reasonable, and I try not to make them feel put down.

Therapist: I propose that we make it a point to apply that approach to your evaluations of yourself. Let's stay reasonable and constructive, and offer sound advice that you can use to make your life better. Let's also watch out for times when you are gratuitously condemning yourself, and then let's turn it into something constructive, as you just suggested.

In the example above, the therapist's method of using questioning to help Joey "come around" to some therapeutic points of view produces a richer dialogue than would have occurred if the therapist had simply pointed out that the client needed to be as benevolent toward himself as he was being to others. Further, by engaging in a collaborative discussion, additional information came to light that the therapist had not known (e.g., Joey's serving as confidant to his friends Bruce and Wynn), information which then could be used as positive evidence to support the intervention. Additionally, the give-and-take nature of the exchange was such that the client was able to consider modifying his point of view, in his own words, rather than just saying "yea" or "nay" to the therapist's assertions.

HOMEWORK: TAKING INTERVENTIONS FROM THE "LAB" TO THE "FIELD"

Those who practice CBT competently provide their clients with an *education* in how to help themselves with their psychological concerns. Among other things, this entails instructing clients about the general CBT model and its relevance to their problems, showing them how to self-monitor in a constructive manner, and teaching them to modify their thoughts and behaviors in such a way as to improve their mood, their outlook, and their sense of self-efficacy. There is a growing body of empirical evidence suggesting that the regular use of appropriate homework has a significantly positive impact on client outcomes and maintenance (Burns & Spangler, 2000; Kazantzis, Whittington, & Dattilio, 2010; Rees, McEvoy, & Nathan, 2005). Homework is the means by which clients take the skills they have learned in the confines of the therapist's office (the "lab"), and apply them in their everyday life (the "field"), where it matters most.

The list of possible homework assignments is potentially very long, limited only by the collective imaginations of the therapist and client. Some examples, adapted from Newman (2011a), are presented in Box 7.1.

Techniques that are learned in therapy sessions can often double as homework assignments (e.g., ATRs). Whenever possible, homework assignments are designed by the therapist and client in a collaborative fashion, with a clear goal in mind. When presented correctly, homework assignments present the client with a "no-lose" situation in that their enactment leads either to a positive change or to the highlighting of additional information that will inform further conceptualization and intervention.

Box 7.1.
Sample (Nonexhaustive) List of Homework
Assignments for Clients

1. Read selected material (handouts, publications) about cognitive-behavioral therapy.
2. Listen to your audio-recording of your therapy session. Take notes.
3. Keep a journal of daily experiences (situations, moods, outcomes, etc.).
4. Keep a daily log of your moods, with ratings on a scale of 0–100.
5. Use Automatic Thought Records to respond rationally to negative thoughts.
6. Keep a daily log of your behavioral activities (Daily Activity Schedule).
7. Rate your behavioral activities in terms of *mastery* and *pleasure* from 0–10.
8. Plan new activities designed to improve your mood and outlook.
9. Plan new activities for the purpose of dealing constructively with problems.
10. Brainstorm and make a list of ways to solve a difficult problem.
11. Weigh the pros and cons of each choice in dealing with a difficult decision.
12. Design and enact behavioral experiments to test hypotheses and effect change.
13. Practice "delaying and distracting" to postpone or prevent acting on impulse (e.g., binge eating, smoking).
14. Communicate positively with someone you have been avoiding or neglecting.
15. Assert yourself in an appropriate situation (after practicing).
16. Practice breathing control and relaxation techniques to reduce excessive physical arousal.
17. Alter sleep-wake cycle gradually in a functional direction.
18. If you cannot fall asleep, get up and write down your thoughts.

The following are some of the "do's and don'ts" of assigning CBT homework:

Do

1. Link the homework to subject matter that was discussed in the session, or that had been mentioned previously as being relevant to the client's problems and related coping skills.
2. Prepare yourself to explain the homework in some detail, to offer a rationale, and perhaps to do a brief demonstration (e.g., on paper, or on a whiteboard).
3. Express empathy for the client's concerns about homework, including fatigue in starting it, low self-confidence in completing it, and doubt about its utility.
4. Encourage the client to be an active participant in formulating the homework assignment.
5. Mention that homework is a "win–win" situation, because it either helps the client take a step toward a goal of self-assessment and/or intervention, or it will provide useful information about the client's difficulties in enacting self-help procedures.
6. Explain to the clients that they will not be reprimanded for failing to do their homework! Rather, tell them that research suggests that doing therapy homework improves outcome and maintenance, and gives them extra opportunities to gain the maximum benefit from therapy.
7. Make the point that it is best if the homework is actually done during the week, as opposed to the 5–10 minutes in the waiting room prior to the next session. While it is fine if the client "hands in the homework prior to the deadline," the overriding purpose of the homework is for the client to learn something new and useful in everyday life.
8. Find useful synonyms for the term "homework," if clients respond more favorably to alternative descriptors. Terms that have been used in the literature in place of the moniker "homework" include: "take-home therapy," "experiments," "weekly mission," "practicing being your own therapist," and "show I can do it" tasks, to name a few.

Don't

1. Make the homework look as though it is a hastily assigned, random task. The purpose of homework is not to give the client busy-work, but rather to promote a skill and/or gather useful clinical information from the client's everyday life.
2. Give the client an assignment without checking to see if he or she understands the purpose, as well as the method(s) involved.
3. Abandon the enterprise of homework-giving altogether simply because of the client's poor track record in completing assignments.
4. Fail to make the assignments individualized in some way. Although there are some standard homework assignments (e.g., reading well-known CBT self-help books as companion guides to the therapy sessions) that may be given to most or all clients across the board, it is a sub-optimal use of homework to routinely miss opportunities to tailor-make the assignments to the specific needs and situations of individual clients.

Therapists can assess the probability that the clients will follow through with the homework assignment by asking, "On a scale of 0–100, how likely do you think it is that you will try to do the therapy homework we've designed today?"

If the client says "0," it reflects a sense of helplessness and hopelessness, as the client is already saying that there is no chance that the homework will be done, even before trying it. This issue of assumed incapability and failure can then become a topic of discussion.

If the client says "100," the therapist can give the client positive feedback for being so committed to the homework. At the same time, the therapist may also say, "Sometimes unexpected problems crop up that can get in the way of the best plans and best intentions. Can we spend a few minutes doing some advance troubleshooting, so that we can anticipate the sort of unintended problems that might interfere with your being able to do the homework?"

If the client says any number between 0 and 100, the therapist can invite the client to explain both sides of the issue. For example, if the client says "80," the therapist can reply with the comment, "That's great! Can we talk briefly about your thoughts that comprise the 80% confidence you have in doing the homework as well as the 20% of your thinking that has some doubts?"

RECOGNIZING AND RESOLVING
THERAPY-INTERFERING FACTORS

Sperry (2010) notes that several factors may get in the way of the successful implementation of interventions, including external environmental problems, therapist mistakes, and clients' "therapy-interfering behaviors" (see Linehan, 1993). A thorough review of these problems goes beyond the scope of this chapter, but some examples may be instructive, as described below.

External, Environmental Problems

These factors may or may not be readily apparent to the therapists unless they inquire directly. An example might be a punishing home environment in which the client's therapeutically endorsed attempts to be more assertive and independent are met with hostile responses from family members. Another example is a young student who is in treatment to improve his academic functioning related to attention-deficit problems, but whose progress is held back by the underappreciated hindering effects of a physical environment at home that includes poor lighting and ventilation, loud noises and other distractors, little privacy, and no effective "workstation." A further example is a client who cancels many appointments owing to flare-ups of medical problems, and a lack of a support system to help her get to therapy sessions when she is in too much pain to transport herself. In these cases, the competent CBT therapist does not simply assume that the client is "not really ready" for treatment, or "doesn't really want to change." Instead, the therapist tries to investigate nicely the nature of the obstacles, shows compassion for the client's predicament, and tries to engage the client in some problem-solving to deal with the environmental obstacles more effectively. In the last case (the woman who often cancels due to medical problems), the competent therapist would give the client more latitude to miss appointments without closing the file (see Chapter 9, on termination).

Therapist Mistakes

The process of an otherwise promising course of CBT can be hampered by the therapist's poor technique, inaccurate case conceptualization, insufficient empathy, unintended errors, or combinations of the above (see Sperry, 2010). One very common error warrants mention—the novice

CBT practitioner's overzealousness in challenging the clients' automatic thoughts rather than giving the clients more of a chance to air their concerns without undue interruption. The unfortunate effect is that of micromanaging the clients' thinking, and this can cause a strain in the therapeutic relationship (Newman, 2011a). By contrast, competent CBT clinicians take note of some of the key comments their clients are making, respond empathically, and then wait for a natural pause in the discussion to summarize the sorts of negative cognitive content that the clients are revealing. Competent CBT practitioners know that they have to pick their spots judiciously, so that they give their clients sufficient opportunity to explain how they feel before interjecting their own comments and questions pertinent to effecting cognitive change.

Good CBT does not require the therapist to address each and every dysfunctional cognition the client reveals. Nor does it require that the clients change their cognitions for the better, on the spot. Cognitive-behavioral therapists-in-training sometimes express concern that they are failing to conduct a competent session if their clients do not make substantial changes in their thinking prior to the end of the session (as if the professional mandate is that "Nobody leaves my office until their cognitions are changed!"). In reality, cognitive change—indeed, therapeutic change in general—is a *process*, and many clients need time to ponder what has been discussed in session and to do their homework assignments (perhaps over the course of weeks and months), before they begin to modify their longstanding problematic cognitions. The competent CBT clinician understands this, and tries to nurture this process with caring and patience, all the while remaining active and directive.

Clients' Therapy-Interfering Behaviors

Two important types of therapy-interfering behaviors are the clients' low engagement in therapy, such as when they contribute very little to the therapeutic dialogue, and clients' precipitating frequent crises. Let us take a brief look at how competent cognitive-behavioral therapists approach each of these problems.

The disengaged, silent client

Competent CBT therapists try to ask compelling questions that will stimulate the curiosity of clients who otherwise appear uninterested in having a therapeutic dialogue. Unfortunately, some clients are steadfast in being quiet. In such cases, the client's silence itself becomes a potential area to address (though, by definition, the therapist may be the only one who is speaking, at least at first). In such instances, therapists may choose to offer hypotheses, and to see if the clients offer any nonverbal signs of response. Examples of therapist comments, along with their corresponding conceptualizations, are shown below:

1. (The therapist believes that the client's silence indicates anger.) "I think I may have just said something that struck a nerve for you. If that's what happened, I'm truly sorry to have upset you. I'm open to hearing your feedback about this, if you're willing to talk to me right now."

2. (The therapist believes that the client's silence represents a sense of helplessness and hopelessness.) "When you become so quiet like that, I don't know whether to wait until you speak, or whether I should try to reach out to you with words of encouragement. I hope we can talk about whatever is making you feel so down."

3. (The therapist believes that the client's silence represents apathy, and/or general disengagement.) "I could do all the talking today, but I think I would bore myself to tears. I'm much more interested to hear what you have to say. (Long pause without a response from the client.). Well, it's true that 'you have the right to remain silent,' so to speak, even in therapy, and I have to respect that right. So, I'm going to do my best to say some things that might be useful, but I promise I'll stop and listen if you have something to say."

The examples remind us that the client's active collaboration cannot be taken for granted. When clients are suboptimally engaged in treatment, it is an opportunity for therapists to demonstrate professionalism and optimism under duress, which serves as good role-modeling.

Clients' acute crises

Competency in delivering high-quality CBT interventions is not limited to the routine application of techniques, their related homework assignments, and even their implementation when clients are lacking motivation. Competency also involves being able to intervene in crisis situations with composure, clear-headedness, a strong desire to help, and a repertoire of responses that are well-rehearsed enough that they can be utilized under pressure. The most common, high-profile crisis in working with clients is an exacerbation of suicidal ideation and/or intent. At such times, the competent CBT clinician implements general safeguards that are pertinent to any modality of psychotherapy, such as assessing the client's level of *intent* to try suicide as well as the degree of *lethality* of his or her chosen method for self-harm, increasing the frequency of sessions and/or level of care (e.g., assessing for the need for inpatient supervision), making use of the client's resources (e.g., his or her coping skills; the attention and help of loved ones), and collaborating with the client in generating an agreement for safety, among other steps.

While a complete description of the clinical management of the suicidal client goes well beyond the scope of this handbook on core competencies (see Bongar, Berman, Maris, Silverman, Harris, & Packman, 1998; Wenzel, Brown, & Beck, 2009), a few important points may be noted here. First, when clients are suicidal, time is especially important. Ascertaining the client's state of mind early in the session is much better than discovering at the end that the client is harboring suicidal thoughts. Thus, doing a mood check at the start of the session (e.g., looking at the client's responses on the BDI-II and BHS) is the preferred course of action. If the therapist sees that the scores are significantly elevated in general, and that the specific items about suicidal ideation and hopelessness are endorsed, the therapist is advised to inquire about the client's thoughts and intentions to self-harm, and to make this topic the highest priority item on the agenda. By having the entire session to deal with this problem, there is a greater likelihood that therapist and client can come to an agreement on a plan for coping and safety that will avert the need for hospitalization, while at the same time calling attention to the need for more intensive outpatient care.

Second, a client's expressions of suicidality also provide the CBT clinician with an important opportunity to conceptualize the factors pertinent to the client's vulnerability to such a crisis. Questions to address include:

- Under what conditions does the client experience suicidal ideation and intent?
- Are these conditions the sort of stressors to which most people would adversely respond (i.e., a "real-life" crisis such as losing a job), or are these conditions more idiosyncratically stressful to the client (i.e., a schema-activation crisis, such as feeling abandoned)?
- What are the client's thoughts, beliefs, and schemas pertinent to the experience?

- Is the client actively considering more adaptive alternatives to suicidal thinking? How can these be promoted and reinforced?
- What are the client's resources (including what he or she has learned thus far in CBT)? Is the client making use of them?

The issue of the role of the client's idiosyncratic schema reactions is an important one. While there is an objective difference between having suicidal thoughts in response to suddenly losing your job and your marriage in the same week (a normative, real-life crisis) and wanting to die owing to a bad haircut (a subjective crisis owing to the activation of schemas of unlovability and abandonment, highlighted by the belief, "I'm hideous and nobody could ever love me, so I should just kill myself now rather than be insufferably alone the rest of my life"), it *feels the same* to the schema-activated client. The sensitive, conceptually astute therapist understands this, and does not minimize the client's suffering, even as he or she engages the client in an attempt to modify the thought processes that produced such acute, severe emotional suffering.

Third, competent CBT clinicians try to help clients gain valuable learning experiences as a result of their unfortunate crisis circumstances, such as a better understanding of their own schemas, and increased motivation to use CBT self-help skills to prevent such occurrences later. In doing so, the therapist sends the message to the clients that the goal of successfully dealing with clinical crisis situations is not only about surviving, it is about *thriving*, which requires learning, growing, being willing and eager to get back on track with the treatment plan again, and respecting themselves enough to want to have a brighter future, with less vulnerability.

SUPERVISORY FEEDBACK ON THE TRAINEE'S USE OF INTERVENTIONS

Supervisors help their trainees to develop a healthy repertoire of CBT techniques, and to fine tune each one as needed. The supportive tone of the supervisor must predominate, even as the trainees are being given feedback about how they could have performed a technique "better" in some way. The following are three, brief examples of such supervisory feedback:

Supervisor #1: (Reviewing the Automatic Thought Record completed by one of the supervisee's clients.) You've taught your client well. He made excellent use of his ATR for homework. Here's one little extra bit of advice. Do you notice how several of your client's items under the "automatic thoughts" columns are in the form of a question? Next time, show him how to answer his own question, because *that's the real automatic thought*. For example, when he writes, "What's going to happen to me if I get a panic attack?" he is probably already thinking about a worst case scenario. So, instead of just letting him write a rhetorical question as his automatic thought, instruct him to literally answer his own question, and then he may come up with even more salient automatic thoughts that are lurking in the background anyway, such as, "If I get a panic attack, everyone will think I'm crazy." Try it and see. What do you think about that?

Supervisor #2: I was very impressed, and even moved by your imagery reconstruction technique, especially the part where the client surmised that her dying mother would probably have told her that she loved her, if she had been conscious to do so. I could tell that the client really got the message about her mother's love, and those tears of relief almost made me cry too. That was beautifully done. May I offer one little, additional suggestion? Although this particular client understood the intervention well, not all clients will process this sort of evocative intervention in the way you expect. That's why it's typically a good idea to leave at least 10 minutes at the end of the session for time to debrief, and to get feedback. In this case what you did was fine. In future cases, I would play it safe and leave some extra time for processing. Does that make sense?

Supervisor #3: (Looking at the Daily Activity Schedule that had been completed by the trainee's client.) These are very useful data! There is almost nothing on this form that would indicate that she is doing anything for a sense of mastery. Next time, ask your client to add her *ratings* of "mastery" and "pleasure," because that will put her in a better position to see for herself that she is not trying to accomplish anything that might improve her self-image or life situation. If you ask her to add the ratings, there will be more of a basis on which she can draw her own conclusions, and that may make her more receptive to some of the behavioral activation techniques you've been suggesting. Do you see my rationale?

The phrase that best fits the supervisors' comments above is, "Nice technique! Now here is how you can improve even more!"

Now that we have discussed the core competencies pertinent to the therapeutic relationship, case conceptualization, and interventions, let us turn our attention (in Chapter 8) to the means by which CBT clinicians assess their clients' progress competently, including updating the goal list and diagnosis, if warranted.

KEY POINTS TO REMEMBER

- Establishing and maintaining a focus in CBT requires careful attention and adherence to an agenda, eliciting the client's active participation in the process of hypothesis generation and testing, and modeling a communication style that maximizes clarity and specificity.
- Utilizing CBT techniques competently requires knowing a broad repertoire of "tools" to use both in session, and between sessions in the form of homework assignments. It also necessitates targeting the techniques to the needs of the individual client, based on his or her case conceptualization and treatment goals.
- Using the method known as guided discovery (or "the Socratic method") requires a high level of competency, in that CBT therapists have to craft questions that will help clients explore their own problems with positive, hopeful curiosity, and to come to realizations that are more powerful than if they had simply been given the information by the therapist.
- The competent application of homework is a very important part of the efficacy of CBT. Therapists have to design homework assignments that make sense to the client and have a collaborative feel, that are well-explained, that have a good chance of success, and that teach clients skills of self-reflection and self-help that will endure.
- Competent CBT clinicians recognize and respond constructively to therapy-interfering factors. They modify their own procedures if they are in error, show compassion for clients whose environmental factors work against the process of

---

therapy and try to engage them in problem-solving, and bring a high level of professionalism to those situations in which the clients' acute crises (e.g., heightened suicidality) require immediate, top-priority attention. All the while, competent cognitive-behavioral therapists try to conceptualize the crisis situations, and attempt to help the clients gain valuable learning experiences that they can use to prevent future crises, and to resume working toward planned treatment goals when the crisis has subsided.

- Supervisors in CBT help their trainees to become more competent in their application of interventions through positive feedback and constructive criticism, so that the trainees can gain confidence in their methods while still being motivated to make further improvements.

8

Monitoring and Evaluating Clinical Outcomes

"Success isn't measured by money or power or social rank..., [but]
by your discipline and inner peace."

Mike Ditka

Competent CBT therapists do not judge the status of their cases via subjective impression alone. They utilize an array of methods to assess their clients' progress objectively, indicative of the competent attitude that puts verifiable client wellness ahead of the therapists' desire to assume that treatment is helpful. Ideally, monitoring the client's progress will involve both the therapist's and the client's input (and perhaps feedback from third parties such as the client's family), and will involve observations both in-session and between-sessions, across varying scenarios of stress, and repeatedly over time. Methods will include clients' verbal self-report and self-monitoring, behavioral observations (including those made by interested third parties and interdisciplinary practitioners on the case), empirically-based client self-report inventories, and periodic treatment update plans (see Form 8.1, later) that indicate how closely the clients' goals are being approximated. As there is evidence that clients who learn the important self-help methods of CBT make significant therapeutic gains thereafter (e.g., Jarrett, Vittengl, Clark, & Thase, 2011; Strunk, DeRubeis, Chiu, & Alvarez, 2007; Tang et al., 2005), therapists also assess how well clients are able to utilize cognitive-behavioral self-help skills, including homework.

This chapter will describe the following competencies: (1) monitoring progress and modifying treatment accordingly, and (2) utilizing supervision to monitor and evaluate treatment progress. The former competency will be explicated in the context of the ongoing treatment of Joey, as the therapist keeps tabs on the client's progress across a number of indicators. The latter competency will involve a brief vignette in which the CBT supervisor guides the therapist-in-training to collect data on a client, to assess the client's condition, and to collaborate with the client on making alterations to the treatment plan in light of difficulties.

MONITORING PROGRESS AND MODIFYING TREATMENT ACCORDINGLY

Sperry (2010) has noted the sobering findings that too many therapists make informal, inaccurate judgments about their clients' progress, leading to such problems as early dropout, failure to achieve therapeutic goals, and even (potentially dangerous) unawareness of client deterioration. He therefore makes the compelling point that systematically measuring clients' progress in treatment is a vital, core competency.

The Most Fundamental "Reliability Check": The Therapist's and Client's Respective Views

Competent cognitive-behavioral therapists assess the degree to which clients still meet (or no longer meet) criteria for the diagnostic problem area(s) assessed at intake, and dialogue with clients about the latter's subjective views of their own improvement in treatment. When there is a good sense of shared responsibility and collaboration in the therapeutic relationship, client and therapist often will be in agreement about the client's status, as seen in cases where they are both encouraged by the client's progress, or they are both looking for ways to produce positive changes that have thus far been elusive. Occasionally, the therapist and client will share a sense of alarm that the client's condition is worsening, at which point they may agree that significant changes to the treatment plan are warranted. At times, the therapist and client will have a difference of opinion about how the latter is doing in treatment. For example, a client may profess to be doing well, but the therapist ascertains that the client has not been utilizing the skills of CBT, has not been doing homework, and still maintains schemas that keep him or her vulnerable to symptom episodes. Conversely, a client may complain that he or she is not getting better "at all," a statement that the therapist may view as a manifestation of "all-or-none thinking," and "disqualifying the positive," in light of some evidence that the client's behavioral functioning has significantly improved. In both instances, the competent clinician forthrightly, promptly discusses these differences of opinion with the client to achieve better consensus on the client's actual condition, as illustrated briefly below with Joey:

Joey Reports That He is "Fine," but the Therapist is Concerned

Joey: I'm doing fine. There's not much to talk about today. It's the "same old, same old." Work is bad, but I'm just not thinking about it, and I'm trying my best not to care. That always helps get me through.

Therapist: Aside from not thinking about your work troubles, and trying not to care, are there other signs of "improvement?" For example, are you more active with your neighbors, are you going to the gym, are you finding that you don't need to drink as much, and so on?

Joey: All that stuff is pretty much the same. I'm just not letting everything get to me as much.

Therapist: Is that because you're using the rational responding techniques we practiced? Do you have any ATRs for homework that you want to show me?

Joey: I really haven't had time to do any ATRs this week.

Therapist: I really don't mean to doubt you, Joey, but I want to make sure that the reasons you're feeling better are based on something solid, such as your dealing with your problems more actively and confidently without feeling the need to drink, thinking things through constructively, being active and social again, using your CBT skills regularly as a way of life, things like that. If we can work on these goals, there is every reason to believe that you will not only *feel* better, but you'll *be* better. What are your thoughts about that, Joey?

Joey Later Complains of Being "Back to Square One," but the Therapist Notes Otherwise

Joey: It's been a bad week. I'm as stressed out as ever. I feel like I'm back to square one.

Therapist: Wow, I'm so sorry to hear that. I can tell just by looking at you that you're feeling anxious, worn out, and discouraged. But I'm also wondering why you feel like you've regressed. Your *situation* is one thing, but I wonder if we can take a close look at *you* to see what you're doing *right* to help yourself through a bad week.

Joey: At times like this I just want to collapse. I'm really not doing well.

Therapist: I believe you. I want to hear all about what's going on in your life this week. I also want to focus on everything you have been learning in our sessions together, because in the past few weeks I've been impressed with some of the changes you've been making. Maybe now would be a great time to use some of those tools, like trying to notice when you're expecting the worst and instead trying to think of what is *likely* to happen, and then rehearsing in your mind's eye how you will coach yourself through it, and what positive actions you'll take. I think you can do all that. I've seen you do it already.

Joey: When I feel this bad I sometimes forget.

Therapist: Let's both go over our notes right now and refresh our memories. I understand that you feel very stressed right now, but I'm confident that you have the tools to help yourself, so that you don't *remain* in this negative state of mind for too long, and so you get right back on track in solving problems, as you've been doing so well lately.

In the above examples, there is initially a mismatch between the therapist's and client's impressions about the latter's progress. In order to determine in a reliable, valid way that the client is making measurable progress, both parties will need to agree on the benchmarks.

Client Self-Report Inventories

Using empirically based self-report measures is a convenient, effective way to collect data about the client's functioning on an ongoing basis. For example, clients who attend sessions at the Center for Cognitive Therapy at the University of Pennsylvania routinely take 5–10 minutes prior to each session to complete the Beck Depression Inventory-II (BDI-II; Beck et al., 1996), the Beck Anxiety Inventory (BAI; Beck et al., 1988), and the Beck Hopelessness Scale (BHS; Beck et al., 1985), measures with good psychometric properties that are applicable with a wide range of clients. Clients get into the habit of filling out these inventories, actions that are positively reinforced when their therapists make it a point to review their clients' responses on these questionnaires as a standard part of setting the session agenda. For example, when therapists eyeball the clients' responses, they may find that the clients' symptoms have held steady, in which case it may not be necessary to discuss the issue of "changes in mood" as a major part of the session. On the other hand, the therapist may discover that the client is reporting feeling significantly better. While this may not be *statistically significant* in the sense that it represents only one data point (i.e., competent CBT practitioners realize that consistent and steady improvements in the client's mood are required in order to draw more firm conclusions about the client's progress), it may nonetheless be *clinically significant* as a point of discussion in session. A standard therapist comment could be, "I see that you have been feeling much less depressed and much more hopeful since we last met. To what do you attribute this positive change? Can we talk about this as part of today's session?" In making this sort of statement, therapists show that they are paying attention to the client's responses, adding the point that it is important to talk about what is going *well* in the client's life.

A more urgent agenda item emanates from client self-report responses that indicate a decline in functioning. Again, a worsening of the client's mood may only be temporary, and/or may indicate a response style in which the client magnifies the significance of how he or she feels at this moment (not taking sufficient account of how he or she has been feeling in general over time), but the potential hazards of a worsening in the client's mood warrant giving this problem concerted attention. The therapist must put the client's acute decline in functioning high on the agenda, even while realizing that multiple measures over time are more robust indicators of the client's response to treatment.

In addition to the Beck inventories, there are a plethora of self-report inventories that CBT clinicians can use at multiple times across the course of treatment. Therapists can choose measures that are of particular relevance for their individual clients, such as the Y–BOCS (Goodman et al., 1989) for clients who suffer from obsessive-compulsive disorder, the

STAXI-2 (Spielberger, 1999) for clients who are experiencing anger management issues, and the Young Mania Rating Scale for clients with bipolar disorder (Young et al., 1978), among many others. More standard self-report measures (i.e., applicable to clients across clinical concerns and diagnoses) include the Session Rating Scale (SRS; Duncan et al., 2003), the Outcome Rating Scale (ORS; Miller & Duncan, 2000), and the Outcome Questionnaire-45 (OQ-45; Lambert et al., 2004). The SRS is a brief form using four visual scales via which clients give their therapists end-of-session feedback about how they felt about the session and their treatment. The ORS, by contrast, is administered at the start of each session, though it uses the same, easy-to-use visual scaling method of self-report. Here, clients describe how they have been doing over the past week in the areas of personal well-being, relating with family and others who are close, social interactions (with friends, at school, at work), and global functioning. The OQ-45 measures client functioning in terms of symptom distress, interpersonal functioning, and social role. It includes risk assessment items, and—like the aforementioned self-report measures—is designed to measure client progress over the course of therapy, as well as follow-up periods.

Client Skill Acquisition

To maximize the chances that the clients will maintain their gains and will feel an increased sense of self-efficacy in coping with life's stressors, it is necessary to assess how well they have learned the self-help principles of CBT. There are several ways in which therapists can make this assessment, including observing how often and how well clients make note of their own cognitive biases and/or problematic beliefs, devise more functional alternatives, and instruct themselves on how to put these changes into action. In the following example, Joey makes a skillful self-assessment and self-intervention that demonstrates a good grasp of the principles of CBT, whereupon the therapist responds enthusiastically, praising the client and asking for even more demonstrations of CBT self-help knowledge:

Joey: When I got the bad news, my first reflex was to tell myself that everything was hopeless, and that I was stupid to have gotten my hopes up in the first place, and that there was no point in trying anymore. I was even considering canceling my appointment with you, because I thought, "Why bother?" That's when it occurred to me that this is exactly the sort of situation when

I need to use what I've learned in working with you. I can't let myself feel hopeless. I have to take the bad news in stride and stay constructive.

Therapist: That is super work! You faced an adverse situation, you caught yourself telling yourself a lot of hopeless thoughts that would only serve to make you feel worse, you prevented yourself from quitting, and you reminded yourself of the advantages of trying to cope, especially when you feel most down. That was a great "catch," and I'm impressed.

Joey: Well, I'm trying, but the situation is still not so good.

Therapist: That's true, and I'm sorry to hear about that. While you're showing such good self-awareness and coping, let's build on that right now. For example, aside from telling yourself that you have to work against feeling hopeless, what are some things you can tell yourself in order to take the next step? What can you do to start the process of doing problem-solving, right now? You've got momentum on your side. Let's keep it going!

Joey: There are about three or four important calls I have to make, because I really need to talk to the people involved directly. I don't think e-mails are good enough. And I have to be at my best when I make those calls, because I have to sound confident and composed.

Therapist: That's great that you're willing to face this situation so constructively. Can we do some role-playing right now? We could enact some of those calls, and see how it goes.

Joey: I think I have to clarify what my goals are, and what I want to say.

Therapist: That's excellent. Let's do that first, and then we can do a role-play or two, if you think that would help. What *are* your specific goals here?

In the example above, Joey is dealing well with a difficult situation, and the therapist is being supportive as well as encouraging the client to utilize more skills, right then and there.

Beyond the therapist's observation of the client's behavior, some measures have been developed to assess the client's skill level in understanding and utilizing CBT self-help principles. The Ways of Responding (WOR; Barber & DeRubeis, 1992) questionnaire asks clients to write what they would do and think in order to cope with specific, vividly imagined hypothetical stressors. The Performance of Cognitive Therapy Skills Scale (PCTS; Strunk, et al., 2007) is a research instrument used by trained raters who observe videos of clients' sessions in order to rate the clients' self-help skills in the areas of behavioral self-activation, spotting and modifying automatic thoughts (such as by working on Automatic Thought Records), and working on their beliefs or schemas. The Cognitive Therapy Awareness Scale (CTAS; Wright et al., 2002) is comprised of 40 true–false questions covering key concepts in CBT such as identifying cognitive errors, thought recording, and activity scheduling. It has been used to quickly and conveniently measure clients' understanding of the basic terms of CBT, though the authors acknowledge that the CTAS is not a comprehensive measure of CBT skills per se.

A clinically practical measure of client acquisition and utilization of CBT skills is the recently developed Skills of Cognitive Therapy (SoCT; Jarrett et al., 2011). This questionnaire—of which there is a client version (for self-report) and a therapist version (for observer ratings)—includes eight empirically derived items, rated on a 5-point Likert-type scale (from "never" to "always or when needed"). Aside from the advantages of easy use, the SoCT has generated data suggesting that higher scores (i.e., better comprehension and use of CBT skills) from both clients and therapists both during and at the conclusion of treatment predict the probability of positive response to a standard course of CBT (i.e., significant improvements in depressive symptoms). The items of the SoCT tap into such skills as clients' demonstrating an understanding of how their thoughts and behaviors contribute to their mood disorder, their active weighing of evidence pertinent to their depressive thoughts, the degree to which they participate in activities to improve their mood, and how customarily they use methods such as Automatic Thought Records to generate alternative ways to think, among others.

A central component of skill acquisition in CBT is homework. All other things being held equal, clients who tend to do therapy homework regularly, and with some investment of time and effort, will tend to get more out of treatment for the long run (Burns & Spangler, 2000; Detweiler-Bedell & Whisman, 2005; Kazantzis et al., 2010; Rees et al., 2005). Given this, it is very important for CBT clinicians to work with their clients to generate homework assignments on a regular basis, so that the clients have the chance to avail themselves of the advantages that homework confers. Exceptions can be made at times when clients angrily reject homework and threaten to leave therapy if the therapist insists on assigning homework (see Newman, 2011b, for a lengthy clinical example of how to deal with this sensitive problem).

Third-Party Observations of the Client

Many clinicians are familiar with the following scenario, in which they believe that a client is making progress, only to have a relative (most often the client's parent or spouse) call to express concern about the client, perhaps leaving a message detailing examples of the client's dysfunctionality about which the therapist was unaware. Although the therapist in such instances must respond judiciously in light of the ethical mandate to maintain confidentiality—thus, the therapist will need the client's consent to return the call to speak to the worried third party—the therapist cannot simply ignore this information. Given that outpatient therapists cannot know everything about their clients' between-sessions functioning, some feedback from other close observers of the clients can be helpful in obtaining a more complete assessment of their progress, especially in complex cases.

A more welcome scenario occurs when therapists receive spontaneous messages from third parties that indicate that the client is doing very well, such as when a client's parole officer confirms that the client's urinalyses for illicit substances have been consistently "clean," or a client's mother confirms that her anorexic daughter has been more willing to sit down to meals with the family, or a client's wife happily reports that the depressed client has been getting up in time to go to work every day. Whether the news is worrisome or promising, these additional sources of information can be very instructive in assessing the client's status. As such, it can be advantageous to elicit the client's official permission to be in contact with those individuals who play the most important roles in his or her life, especially when those persons reside with the client. Therapists explain the rationale for such potential outside communications (e.g., they potentially provide extra safety, better communication, confirmation of the client's progress or difficulties), and the therapists affirm that nothing will be kept secret from the client (e.g., "There are many things that you say in treatment that I cannot tell anyone else without your consent, but if anyone *else* tells me something about *you*, I will share that information with you so that nothing is going on behind your back"). If this policy of increased openness of communication is established early, it becomes a potentially important element of evaluating the client's response to treatment.

Another form of "third-party" observation involves the input from other healthcare professionals who are sharing the case. Appropriately making use of interdisciplinary consultation is one of the foundational competencies of psychotherapy (Kaslow, 2004; Rodolfa et al., 2005), and typically will require the clinician to explicitly gain the client's signed consent when the interdisciplinary professionals are not part of the same in-house team. Examples include an outpatient CBT clinician contacting the staff at the facility where the client has temporarily been hospitalized; a nonphysician CBT clinician discussing the coordinated care of a client with the psychiatrist who is prescribing and supervising their shared client's pharmacotherapy; a CBT psychiatrist doing some problem-solving with the client's social worker about additional resources (e.g., a day hospital program) for a client who needs more treatment time than the psychiatrist can offer; a CBT therapist confirming a "therapeutic meal plan" with an anorexic client's nutritionist, and others. These interdisciplinary consultations allow each professional on the case to compare notes on how the client is faring. Consensus is desired, but contrasting views between the different practitioners can shed light on some of the client's problems in collaborating with treatment. For example, an eating disordered client's apparent progress in CBT may be cast into doubt if the therapist discovers that she has been avoiding her appointments with the nutritionist—a problem that will need to be discussed in the CBT session. Similarly, a CBT therapist may learn from a bipolar disorder client's psychiatrist that the client's medication blood levels have been low, perhaps indicating less-than-optimal adherence to his or her pharmacotherapy. This finding may alert the CBT practitioner to assess and perhaps modify the client's negative beliefs about his or her medication (see Newman, Leahy, Beck, Reilly-Harrington, & Gyulai, 2001; Sudak, 2011; Wright et al., 2006).

Treatment Update Planning

A key part of assessing clients' progress in CBT is the Treatment Update Plan (TUP). This is a formal procedure that takes place periodically (e.g., every 3 months), and is especially relevant for longer courses of treatment, in which therapists and their clients need to assess repeatedly the clients' status to determine future directions in treatment. Form 8.1 shows a TUP that was largely completed by the therapist, but shared with Joey for his verbal and written input (as well as his signature) at a designated session. This particular TUP template is based on the form that is used at the home clinic of the author, but it is by no means the only model that a competent cognitive-behavioral therapist may construct.

Form 8.1

"JOEY'S" TREATMENT UPDATE PLAN (TUP)

Name: Joey   DOB: DD/MM/YYYY

Today's Date: "Today"   Diagnostic Code: Axis I   300.02; 296.21

Axis II   None.   Axis III: None.   Axis IV: Employment stress   Axis V: GAF

Current : 80

Intake Date (date) three months ago   BDI: 18   BAI:36   BHS: 6

Last Session (date) today   BDI: 9   BAI: 12   BHS: 5

Total # of Sessions to Date: 11   Total # of Sessions Since Last Update: 11

☐ Base Line   ☐ No Improvement   ☐ Slight Improvement

☑ Moderately Improved   ☐ Greatly Improved

PROBLEM LIST	PATIENT'S STRENGTHS	FACTORS THAT IMPEDE TX
1. High anxiety over job uncertainty.	1. History of independent problem-solving.	1. Sense of stigma about being in therapy.
2. Excessive use of alcohol to "cope."	2. Capable of forming close friendships.	2.
3. Estrangement from siblings.	3. High level of skills in his professional field.	3.
4. Beliefs that encourage him to "fear the worst" as a "necessary" way to think.	4. Sardonic, entertaining sense of humor.	4.
5. Belief that he has "nothing to offer" in a relationship, therefore avoiding trying to initiate one.	5.	5.
Other:	Other:	Other:

OVERALL GOALS FOR TX	MEASURABLE OBJECTIVES TOWARD EACH GOAL	DATE OF NEXT TUP
1. Reduce excessive anxiety.	1. Beck Anxiety Inventory scores consistently Below 10.	3 months later

2. Reduce alcohol consumption.	2. At least 3 days per week of no drinking at all.	3 months later
	Complete cessation of binges.	
	No more than 10 drinks per week.	
3. Reduce patterns of catastrophic think-ing and replace with problem-solving.	3. Initiate meeting with direct supervisor about the implications of the restructuring.	3 months later
	Begin to investigate other job opportunities.	
4. Either make peace with separation from siblings, or try to re-initiate contact with Bob.	4. Write "mock" e-mail to Bob. Process the as-sociated thoughts and feelings in session.	3 months later
5. Increase motivation and hope about being in a romantic relationship at some point.	5. Write a profile for a dating website.	3 months later
Other		

Names of Medications:

1. _____None._____
2. _____
3. _____
4. _____

Prescriber: __Not applicable__
Phone Number: __Not applicable__

Client's Summary and Comments: *I am starting to feel better. Less anxious and tense. Better stomach, which is probably helped by drinking less, which has not been as difficult as I thought it would be. Being in therapy does not seem as strange as it did in the beginning, and Dr. Newman and I have worked on things that make a lot of sense to me, like my habit of expecting the worst. I think I can see the light at the end of the tunnel. I don't know for sure if I will talk to Bob again, or try to have a girlfriend, but at least I'm not sweeping it all under the rug anymore. I have more confidence in myself and my future.*

Therapist's Summary and Comments: *Joey has experienced a significant reduction in his anxiety, even though his job situation is not yet resolved. This change reflects his skill in noticing and modifying his catastrophic thinking about losing his job and becoming destitute. He is also becoming more proactive about his job situation, such as in investigating his options, and not just passively going back and forth between the extremes of ruminating about the restructuring and the potential harm to his salary and career and drinking to forget about his worries. His drinking has reduced significantly, and he reports no binges in the last two months. Joey is now doing cognitive-behavioral rehearsal about contacting Bob, and is taking graded steps towards entering the dating world. Joey notes that he will likely terminate before the next treatment update review in three months. Joey knows that he has the option of having booster sessions, if he wishes.*

_____Joey_____
Client's Signature

_____Cory F. Newman, Ph.D._____
Therapist's Signature

Date
_____Today_____

Date
_____Today_____

☐ Treatment will continue through next treatment period

☐ Boosters through next treatment period

☑ Termination during next treatment period

Not applicable
Supervisor's Signature
(if applicable)

An inspection of the present TUP shows a number of important features, including a five-axis *DSM*-based diagnosis (indicating Joey's coded diagnoses of Generalized Anxiety Disorder, and a single-episode Major Depressive Episode that is mild); scores on his Beck Inventories (showing improvements on the BDI and BAI since intake); a list of the client's problems and strengths (as well as potential obstacles to treatment, such as Joey's sense of stigma); a list of goals for therapy and their specific, measurable benchmarks; a review of the client's adjunctive pharmacotherapy (not applicable in Joey's case); and brief written narratives both by Joey and by his therapist, followed by signatures and a checkbox indicator of whether treatment is expected to come to a conclusion prior to the next 3-month TUP.

Competent therapists know how to present and share their assessment with their clients in a way that is authoritative yet non-*authoritarian;* collaborative in terms of discussing their respective views of the clients' progress toward their goals, and in conjointly discussing how to overcome roadblocks in the way of those goals; and sensitive with regard to disclosing such data as the clients' official diagnoses. In Joey's case, his Major Depressive Episode had been changed from a designation of "moderate" at intake to the level of "mild" at present. Although he still met criteria for Generalized Anxiety Disorder, the reduction in his BAI score (that had been gradual and steady) indicated that he was on his way to a remission of this problem. Significantly, the provisional diagnosis of Alcohol Abuse (at intake) could now be ruled out altogether, as Joey was exceeding his goals in this area. Further, the therapist gave consideration to adding the diagnosis of Social Anxiety Disorder, which he would have included at the initial assessment if he had been aware of Joey's long-term avoidance of dating and corresponding schema of unlovability (as typified by his belief that he had "nothing to offer" a potential girlfriend). However, in light of the fact that Joey was very sociable in nonromantic, nonfamily relationships when he was not depressed, combined with the fact that he was making progress in addressing his fears of dating and in improving his self-image, the therapist chose not to add this diagnosis, opting instead to consider it a "subclinical" problem that warranted further monitoring. The therapist took a similar approach to the consideration of the diagnosis of Avoidant Personality Disorder in terms of recognizing that Joey met several (but not verifiably *four*) of the criteria for this disorder at intake (e.g., avoiding occupational activities for fear of criticism, disapproval, or rejection; fear of being ridiculed or shamed in an intimate relationship; viewing himself as being socially inept and inferior to others), and deciding not to add this diagnosis at a point in time when the client in fact was making improvements in facing uncomfortable and unfamiliar situations, including scenarios in which he might be evaluated by others. Joey was happy to have the chance to write his feedback on the TUP, and befitting Joey's personal strength of a "sardonic, entertaining sense of humor" (see Form 8.1), he commented to his therapist that his TUP showed that he had been "downgraded from a Category 1 hurricane to a tropical depression."

UTILIZING SUPERVISION TO MONITOR
AND EVALUATE TREATMENT PROGRESS

Although CBT supervisors are charged with the important responsibility of helping their supervisees gain the knowledge, skills, and attitudes to practice CBT competently, they know that their top priority is always the well-being of the clients under their supervisory care. Thus, every supervision session routinely involves an update about the clients' condition, a review of how well they are responding to treatment, and a plan for how the clients will benefit from upcoming sessions. For their part, the supervisees put the needs of their clients first by being willing to make accurate, comprehensive disclosures to their supervisors about what is happening in their work with their clients, even if such disclosures risk making the supervisees look as though they are not succeeding in their work. This reflects the competent attitude noted earlier, that the "image" of the therapist as someone who is succeeding takes a distant backseat to a veridical overview of the clinical status of the clients. Supervisors have a central obligation to create a safe, accepting environment that will facilitate the supervisees' willingness to present the facts, and supervisees have a corresponding mandate to work in active collaboration with the senior clinicians who are overseeing their cases, and who are ultimately responsible for their care (see Ladany, Friedlander, & Nelson, 2005). A practical way to facilitate this competent, client-focused, give-and-take between supervisees and supervisors is for the former to make recordings of sessions available for evaluation, and for the latter to invest the time to listen to them or watch them. This is an effective way to stay close to the data in supervision (Newman, in press).

In the following vignette of a supervision session, the trainee therapist actively seeks the help of the supervisor in dealing with a challenging client whose condition is unstable. The supervisor responds by assisting the therapist trainee in evaluating the client's progress (or lack thereof), in suggesting well-conceptualized interventions, and in using best practices in CBT.

Supervisor: (Reading the trainee's session note.) The client's Beck scores have gone way up.

Trainee: I'm really struggling with "Miss Q." This is the third time I thought she was doing much better, only to have her come to the following session in full-crisis mode. I don't know whether to mistrust what she tells me, or mistrust my own judgment, or both.

Supervisor: Well, I appreciate your candor. Let's follow up on that "trust" issue you just brought up, but first things first—did you assess her risk for suicide?

Trainee: Absolutely, just like the previous two times. She starts the session by saying things such as, "I don't really want to die, but I don't want to live if I'm going to keep screwing up my life." Then I ask about what triggered her suicidality, and it's usually something in her personal life where she lashes out at someone she loves, and then they withdraw, and then she feels unloved and abandoned, and then she wants to die. Then I try to offer her support and we talk about how she can learn skills to control her anger and her related behaviors, and we put together a safety plan, and by the end of the session she convinces me that she is not going to hurt herself and that she doesn't need to be in the hospital.

Supervisor: That was a good summary. It really fits with what I saw on the video from your session with her three weeks ago. Did you record this current session we're reviewing now?

Trainee: Yes.

Supervisor: I think this is one I should see as well. Do you want to spend part of this supervision session watching it together?

Trainee: It won't be easy to watch, but if you can guide me in helping Miss Q and getting her more stable, that would be great.

Supervisor: Okay, let's do that in about 10 minutes, but I have some questions for you first. Without having to assume that you can't trust her and you can't trust yourself, how can you *conceptualize* this pattern of hers, based on everything you know about her?

Trainee: Well, it starts with the fact that her diagnosis is borderline personality disorder, but I don't like labeling her like that.

Supervisor: Well, let's not label her. Let's just look at the facts of her functioning and try to make sense of it. What could account for her quick decline from doing well to feeling suicidal, and how can you use that knowledge to inform your treatment plan?

Trainee: Well, speaking of mistrust, Miss Q has a strong mistrust schema, and it usually results in her making accusations, such as to her sister, and to her boyfriend, and then they get fed up with her and either lash out or withdraw, and then Miss Q's anger turns into despair because her schemas of abandonment and unlovability get activated. That turns into what looks like hair-trigger hopelessness and suicidality, but then she faithfully lets me know how she's feeling, and she always cooperates with the safety plan. Fortunately, she's never actually made a suicide attempt. Unfortunately, she looks back at all the havoc and she feels like a loser who keeps screwing up her life, and round and round we go. I don't know how to make solid progress with her.

Supervisor: Again, that sounds very well conceptualized, and it doesn't require mistrusting her self-report or your clinical judgment. However, now that this is the third time Miss Q has had a sudden decline in functioning, we have to find a way to change the pattern, maybe starting with a strategic change in the treatment plan.

Trainee: What would you suggest?

Supervisor: Well, I'll state a couple of ideas right now, but I'll resist telling you too much until we have a look at the video, at which point we can both weigh in. The good thing is that the evidence suggests that Miss Q is well-connected to you, and is repeatedly willing to enact a safety plan. That's positive in its own right, but it also suggests that she may have some skills in cooperating with additional self-help suggestions, and maybe that can be a big part of the next session. I also think we have to approach her problems from multiple angles.

Trainee: I was thinking that too. I was thinking that I need to educate her more about schemas, how they get triggered, how they lead to under-controlled emotions and behaviors, and how that leads to consequences that reinforce the schemas.

Supervisor: Right! And what's another therapeutic angle you have to take?

Trainee: Skill-building. Such as anticipating certain situations and practicing how she wants to respond in advance. Maybe we can use some role-playing exercises.

Supervisor: Excellent. What else?

Trainee: Hmmm. Self-soothing? Maybe some sort of plan for taking care of herself when her negative affect is high. We haven't talked about that yet.

Supervisor: You're definitely on the right track. That would be a good way to update her treatment plan in light of what's been happening. In the meantime, continue to monitor her condition vigilantly, have her keep filling out the Beck inventories, continue with the safety plans as needed, and maybe try to see her twice per week instead of once. Also, feel free to contact me between sessions if you need an emergency supervision session.

Trainee: Thanks. That's good to know. Can we talk more about the details of the new plan?

Supervisor: Yes, let's watch the video right now and use it as a springboard for some ideas.

In the above vignette, the client's needs get the lion's share of the attention, but the supervisor also tries to nurture, support, and teach the trainee. The supervisory collaboration is excellent, with both parties being respectful of each other, and toward the client. Supervisor and trainee conceptualize and hypothesize, and they do this in the context of objective measures of the client's moods and ideation, her past behavior, and the raw data of the session video.

EVALUATING OUTCOMES

The term "outcome" is not uniform, and therefore warrants some defining. Perhaps the most common definition is the client's psychological status (e.g., remitted diagnosis; increased level of global adaptive functioning; improved status of cognitive and behavioral changes; enhanced stability and wellness of mood state) at the time that regular therapy sessions end, commonly known as "termination" (see the following chapter for greater focus and depth on this subject). Within the scope of this definition, a client who shows improvements of the sort noted above at the time of the final, regularly scheduled therapy session would be considered to have had a positive outcome. At the same time, the concept of outcome has to take into account the *durability* and *maintenance* of treatment benefits beyond the completion of a formal course of therapy. Some clinical disorders such as bipolar spectrum illnesses, schizophrenia, substance dependence, and others that have a more longitudinal course and a propensity for phasic relapses require an even more long-term definition of outcome. In these latter cases, the best outcome (of course) involves permanent remission of the mental illness, but reasonably good outcomes may be signaled by increases in the latency between symptom episodes, shorter durations, and lessened intensity of symptoms (see Lam, Hayward, Watkins, Wright, & Sham, 2005; Scott et al., 2006).

Ideally, if and when clients experience a recurrence of their symptoms following a period of improvement, they will have already been coached in advance by their therapists to self-monitor the symptoms, to apply what they have learned in CBT, and to assess whether they can recoup from this temporary setback in such a manner that reinforces their sense of self-efficacy and hope. Clients in CBT are taught not to view lapses in their psychological condition in an all-or-none fashion—such as in feeling demoralized, self-reproachful, and believing they are dependent on therapy (or worse, that therapy can't really help them) at the one extreme, and being stoic and self-denying (thinking that they must never go back to therapy again because it would be an admission of failure) at the other extreme. The middle ground approach involves:

- Knowing that symptoms generally do not "go to zero," and that some recurrences are to be expected, but not dreaded.
- Recognizing that re-emergent symptoms do not necessarily signal a full-blown relapse, and that a prompt, proactive response to these symptoms may effectively prevent a relapse.
- Knowing that recurrences are not signs of failure in treatment, or signs of dependency on treatment, but rather serve as opportunities for the clients to enact their CBT skills to help themselves through the situation in more effective ways than they have in the past.
- Feeling free to decide to return to treatment for booster sessions, or for another round of treatment, if necessary, especially if life circumstances have become particularly harsh.

In sum, clinicians look for objective signs that their clients are improving *during* the course of treatment, that they are significantly better at the *end* of a regular course of sessions, and that these gains are largely *maintained* (if not built upon) long after therapy has been completed.

KEY POINTS TO REMEMBER

- The competent monitoring of clients' progress in CBT requires the regular, repeated use of multiple, objective methods of tracking their response to treatment.

- Therapists need to actively involve the clients in evaluating the latter's progress.
- Several, convenient, client self-report measures can be used to monitor the client's symptoms, to assess their views about their treatment, and to gauge their proficiency in utilizing CBT self-help skills. Competent therapists pay special attention to indicators that the client's condition is declining and use this information to take corrective action.
- The quantity and quality of clients' use of CBT homework is an important measure of their skills in practically applying the lessons of therapy, and therefore is a predictor of their likelihood of achieving and maintaining gains as a result of a trial of CBT.
- Gaining signed permission from clients to communicate with family members and other professionals in charge of their care assists therapists in obtaining a more comprehensive, global view of the clients' functioning and response to CBT.
- Treatment Update Plans (TUP) are formal, written, periodic assessments of the client's condition that are shared with the client, and that shape ongoing goals and interventions.
- Competent CBT supervisors provide a safe environment in which supervisees can disclose the problems they are having in making progress with clients. Supervisors invest time in listening to or watching their supervisees' session recordings, so as to stay close to the data.
- The competent evaluation of client "outcome" emphasizes maintenance, long-term tracking, and the constructive management of clients' episodes of symptom recurrence.

9

Maintaining Treatment Gains and Planning for Termination

"Give us the tools and we will finish the job."

Winston Churchill

In the same way that therapy sessions are enhanced by having strong, well-structured openings and closings, the course of therapy as a whole also benefits from a positive, well-planned beginning and ending. The merits of firmly orienting clients to CBT at the start of treatment was discussed in Chapter 2, and the current chapter will focus on the therapist competencies that are necessary to help clients attain a sense of mastery and hope as they approach and come to an agreeable conclusion of therapy—a conclusion in which the clients will feel a positive sense of resolution, and will be in a favorable position to maintain the gains they have achieved in therapy.

HELPING CLIENTS MAINTAIN TREATMENT GAINS

One of the most significant findings in the empirical literature is that good CBT has staying power (Hollon, Stewart, & Strunk, 2006). Clients who benefit from a course of CBT tend to learn skills that maximize the chances that their therapeutic gains will be durable. Aside from the benefits accrued from learning skills while in therapy—perhaps bolstered and reinforced through regular homework assignments—long-term maintenance of gains is assisted by having a plan of action. In other words, rather than just ending therapy when the client has shown consistent, stable progress, as if to say, "You are ready to go, so good luck to you," competent CBT therapists help their clients prepare for termination by thinking ahead. "Thinking ahead" entails a number of things, including,

- *Anticipating future stressors* (e.g., predicting high-risk situations). For example, Joey came to recognize that drinking in response to stress worsened his situation in a number of ways, therefore he worked with his therapist to design a plan to prevent relapse. While this plan did not necessarily entail absolute abstinence, it did suggest several courses of action Joey could take in response to his tell-tale signs of high anxiety (e.g., catastrophic thinking, gastro-intestinal distress, avoidance of solving problems) *before* he would act on an urge to have a drink. Joey agreed to utilize many of the methods described in the previous chapter, such as rational responding, relaxation and breathing control, and taking part in activities that would give him a sense of accomplishment, rather than simply becoming inebriated. In doing so, Joey was investing in his newly learned coping skills, while systematically increasing the period of time between his urge to drink and actually drinking, which is an effective anti-impulsivity plan. Further, Joey and his therapist identified a number of situations that might occur that would likely require him to put the above plan into action, such as if he were to experience a change in his employment, or meet with his brother. For Joey, relapse prevention was about being aware of these (and other) upcoming situations, and being ready to implement well-practiced, constructive coping skills.
- *Cognitive rehearsal of how the clients might coach themselves through difficult moments.* Late in treatment, Joey showed great skill in spotting his "worst-case scenario" thinking, to the point where he no longer allowed himself to utter comments such as, "I'm going to fall apart," or "I can't do this." Instead, he would mentally walk himself through the anticipated situation, and instruct himself on what he would have to say to himself to produce optimal

confidence, and to put his energies into problem-solving, rather than catastrophizing. Joey became adept at generating and compiling a running list of constructive self-statements to use in anticipated, difficult situations, including, "I'm going to meet this problem promptly and head-on, therefore at the very least I'm going to be proud of myself," and "The sooner I know what I'm up against, the sooner I can start doing what I need to do."

- *Keeping a handy compendium of items generated as part of treatment for regular review* (e.g., coping cards, completed Automatic Thought Records, recordings of some of their therapy sessions, a list of support people with whom to connect during difficult circumstances). Joey kept a folder with his best ATRs, which he found extraordinarily helpful to review when he noticed that this anxiety was up and his confidence was low. By reading exemplars of his most helpful rational responses, Joey reminded himself that he had the cognitive wherewithal to keep situations in perspective, so that he would *not* collapse. Further, Joey recorded many of his therapy sessions, enabling him to listen to previous sessions as reminders of his work in CBT. Joey made sure these digital recordings were password-protected, and gave each session a distinct file name so that he could identify its main focal points. Again, Joey showed his sense of humor by saying that he named his sessions as if they were episodes of "Friends," as in, "The one where Joey..."

- *Creating a "to-do" list for future psychological accomplishment,* using the skills the clients have acquired in CBT to succeed even further. Joey was very pleased that he was now openly discussing his goal of re-connecting with his brother Bob, and he felt proud that he had written a letter to him. Joey took the successive steps of reading the letter aloud in session, and later sending it to Bob. Even more so, Joey's goal was to re-establish a relationship with his brother, or to accept with equanimity the possibility that Bob might never respond. Similarly, Joey was now active on two internet dating sites, and he was exchanging messages with a number of women. His next goal was to meet one or more of them for casual dates, such as coffee. However, in the long run, Joey wanted to establish a serious, committed relationship, and he was now more determined than ever that this was going to happen. Again, it was not possible to know *when* this would occur, and Joey did not necessarily have to remain in therapy until he had a girlfriend, but this goal represented a natural product and extension of his work in CBT.

- *Asking for the client to "Have a CBT session with yourself"* (see J. S. Beck, 1995). This can occur when the frequency of the clients' sessions has been tapered down, and clients can fill in the gaps in the schedule by conducting a full-scale self-help session for themselves at home, perhaps during the same day and time slot in which they would have met with their therapist. When Joey no longer attended sessions every Tuesday, he occasionally put himself through a simulated CBT process at home, in which he filled out a self-report mood inventory; reviewed the stressors of the past week and assessed how he coped; took stock of his personal strengths and positive events so as not to forget or otherwise discount them; did at least one ATR regarding a current, ruminative worry; planned some activities for mastery and pleasure for the coming week; and did some systematic problem-solving (with a written plan) about a current concern (e.g., how to be polite but assertive toward a woman he met on-line who he felt was crossing his boundaries against his wishes).

In helping clients such as Joey with tasks such as those above, competent therapists succeed in emphasizing the importance of clients "working their program" of CBT as a way of life, so as to maximize wellness and coping into the future. In the real world, relapses happen, and absolute cures of emotional disorders are rare indeed. However, if therapists and their clients explicitly talk about relapse prevention as a key agenda item, clients will have the best chance of being prepared for the sorts of stressors that might otherwise set them back later on.

THE COMPETENT TERMINATION OF TREATMENT

"Termination" of treatment is a general concept that can take on many forms (Davis, 2008). The most favorable form of termination occurs when both the therapist and client agree that the latter has achieved his or her goals and has progressed to the point where regular, planned sessions are no longer necessary. The client leaves treatment feeling confident and hopeful, with his or her presenting problems largely resolved and with symptoms significantly reduced. The therapist and the client feel very positively about what they have accomplished as a collaborative team, and the client has learned the conceptual and technical self-help skills that will help him or her maintain the gains acquired in therapy (Sperry, 2010).

Although not all terminations can occur this ideally, there are important steps that therapists can take, perhaps starting very early in treatment, in order to maximize the chances that the conclusion of treatment will be a positive experience. For example, some clients may wish to cease attending sessions before they have had sufficient time to learn the self-help methods of CBT. As noted earlier, competent CBT therapists routinely ask their clients for feedback so as to better understand the latter's thoughts and feelings about how therapy is going for them thus far. When there are signs that the client is dissatisfied or otherwise unsure about staying in treatment, the competent therapist will try to do some collaborative problem-solving in the hope of continuing the work of therapy in a more mutually agreeable vein. On the other hand, competent CBT clinicians effectively and diplomatically manage situations in which termination and a referral seem called for *because* the client has not made sufficient progress to date. Additionally, competent practitioners know how to navigate clinical situations that may appropriately involve several distinct trials of treatment with the same long-term client at times over the years. This chapter will shed light on some of the parameters involved in the scenarios above.

Termination: An Overtly Discussed Agenda Item in CBT

Termination is an issue that is easy to avoid, but imperative to discuss. Preparation for the ending of treatment should be started well in advance, perhaps even from the very outset of treatment (see J. S. Beck, 1995). For example, the therapist's consent forms may indicate that treatment will be time-limited, perhaps even specifying a typical range of number of sessions. Similarly, when the therapist and client establish an initial treatment plan, this may involve an overt statement that the status of treatment will be evaluated on a periodic basis (e.g., every 3 months), often in the form of a written "Treatment Update Plan" (the TUP, see Chapter 8). This process, aside from being good practice in monitoring the quality of the treatment and the client's progress, allows the topic of termination to be discussed with appropriate notice. Therapists can address the subject of termination as part of their routine dialogue in which they allude to the goals of therapy, and how these will manifest themselves in the lives of the clients long after treatment is complete. Consider the following comments and questions put forth by CBT therapists early in treatment:

- "What do you think some of the signs will be that you're getting well and that you can see the 'finish line' of our work together?"
- "As we go through this treatment, we will measure how well you're doing. At some point, we will probably decrease the frequency of our sessions as you improve, and if you continue to do well we will talk about coming to a conclusion of our sessions."
- "In CBT, we pass the baton to our clients. In other words, I will teach you some coping skills that you will practice in your everyday life, to the point where they will be like second nature to you, and you will benefit from using them well into the future."
- "Thinking ahead, when the day comes that you walk out of this office for the final time, having benefitted from treatment and feeling confident and hopeful, what changes do you expect you will have made in your life?"

Such comments and questions make the points that the client's ultimate independence from therapy is a goal in itself, that the therapist has confidence in the client's ability to learn, grow, and be autonomous, and that therapy has a direction. Good CBT is neither mysterious nor amorphous. As such, competent practitioners of CBT keep their clients informed about what they are trying to accomplish, how they will try to do this, and approximately how long it may take.

Clients sometimes bring up the topic of termination themselves, and therapists with good listening skills will hear "hints" from the clients that they have questions or concerns about the issue of ending treatment. The following is a small set of examples of such client comments. Some are direct and transparent; others, less so.

- (Exasperated tone) "How long do I have to come here?"
- "What's going to happen to me when you finish your internship here?"
- "What if I'm not better by the time I'm supposed to be?"
- "You know, you're the only person I could ever talk to about these things."
- "If I don't do the homework, are you going to kick me out?"

- "My last therapist stopped seeing me because I had a hard time getting to a lot of sessions. Do you have a 'use it or lose it' policy too?"
- "Hey, if I start to have a hard time again, is it okay if I call you again and come back?"
- "Can you be my personal coach forever (laughs)?"

One can probably vividly imagine the range of affect expressed in the client comments above, from a sense of exasperation at being mandated to attend therapy in spite of having no interest to do so, to a sense of anticipatory anxiety and loss at the thought that the therapist will not always be there, and everything in between. In the spirit of CBT, therapists will want to flesh out these comments a bit more before responding in ways that may miss the nuances of the clients' thinking. For example, early in Joey's treatment he asked his therapist the question above, "What if I'm not better by the time I'm supposed to be?" The following dialogue highlights the discussion that ensued. Note that the therapist does not simply give a pat answer; he tries to gain a better understanding of Joey's concerns first.

Therapist: That's a fair question and I'm more than happy to get into that with you. What are some of your concerns about not improving in a timely way?

Joey: You know I'm worried about my career, and that includes worrying about my money situation. I chose CBT because I heard it didn't go on and on and I wanted to make sure I had some cost certainty about my therapy. The last thing I need is another worry.

Therapist: I completely understand your financial concerns. I want to make sure that we are both very active in this treatment so that you can make improvements as soon as reasonably possible. That's why we do things such as having an agenda to stay organized, and homework assignments so that you learn self-help skills that you can use on your own.

Joey: Okay, that's fine. I know you're doing your best for me, and I know we're going at a good pace here—sometimes a little *too* fast, but that's okay because that's better than going nowhere and dragging— but I'm still worried that I'm not going to make progress, and then we're going to have to stop, and then where will I be?

TherapistT: So it's not just the cost factor. You're also worried that you're not going to improve even if we both work hard, and then you're going to be left out in the cold if we have to stop therapy. Am I on track about that? What goes through your mind?

Joey: I picture one day coming in and you saying to me, "Well, Joey, I've done all I can do for you, so I think our work is done. Sorry."

Therapist: First of all, that's not going to happen. I would never just dismiss you from therapy like that. We're partners in this process so I'm fully committed to discussing every important issue with you openly and in advance, such as how and when to end therapy.

Joey: Alright, that's fine, but I worry that I won't be able to get over my anxiety, and that my job situation will get worse, and time will run out for me, and I'll be in worse shape than ever. Then you might just tell me I need medication and tell me to go see someone else, and then I'll be back at square one.

Therapist: Joey, I appreciate your trusting me enough to be so open with me about your worries. It gives me a chance to set the record straight, and it's also an opportunity for us to do some problem-solving, rather than catastrophizing, which is one of the major goals on the treatment plan. Even if we both decide—*together*—that you could benefit from having a medication consultation, that doesn't mean our work ends. Many clients benefit from a combination of CBT and medication. So we don't have to end CBT if you go on meds. But that's getting way ahead of ourselves. Right now, I think we have to continue working hard at our treatment plan, and *seeing for ourselves* how you're doing, rather than looking ahead at worst-case scenarios. Just to make sure I'm communicating well, what are the main messages that you're getting from me right now?

Joey: That you won't just pull the plug on me, and we're going to continue to be very active with the CBT and see what happens, and that needing meds might happen but we're not there yet and even if we were, I could still continue with CBT.

Therapist: What else?

Joey: Uh, that worrying about money is legitimate but this therapy goes at a good pace, and I'm learning skills, so there's a good chance I'll do okay, and I won't go broke in the process, and that I don't have to catastrophize so much.

Therapist: (Laughs.) Well, something like that. I hope I sounded sympathetic too!

Joey: Yeah, you did. (Pauses.) It's weird. I'm worried about being in therapy too long and spending too much money, but on the other hand I'm worried about therapy ending too soon and not getting better in time. I'm putting myself in a "Catch-22."

Therapist: We could turn this into a homework assignment if you're okay with that. Would you be willing to use ATRs to address your worries, and to try to come up with some rational responses that will modify some of your worries about "not getting well in time?" Also, could you specifically address your anticipatory thoughts about "being back at square one" and being in a "Catch-22?" If you could work on those, that would be excellent!

In sum, the competent CBT clinician does not shy away from a discussion of termination, and makes it a point to handle the client's concerns empathically, with good assessment skills, and with an eye toward problem-solving.

Termination and the "Longitudinal" Case

Although CBT is considered a time-limited treatment (with its emphasis on using time effectively, and teaching clients to have better psychological self-sufficiency), there are some clinical problems (e.g., bipolar disorder) that tend to recur naturally, and thus may be best suited to a therapeutic approach that involves periods of CBT sessions separated by periods of inactive treatment. In other words, rather than there being one discrete period of treatment ending with one definitive termination, some cases are best handled more longitudinally. For example, a client with bipolar disorder underwent a course of CBT when she was a freshman in college, involving approximately 20 outpatient sessions, some of which were spaced out over time in the form of "booster" sessions. She came back for two "check-up" sessions over the next 2 years, and then she returned for another "module" of ten sessions during her senior year when she was under stress owing to applying to and interviewing for medical schools. Five years later, when the client returned to the area as a medical intern, she came back for another round of CBT sessions when she noticed that sleep deprivation was putting her at risk for mania. She terminated when her internship was over, as planned. Then, almost 10 years later, the same client returned yet again for CBT sessions when she was experiencing an increase in stress owing to work–family conflicts, and the sessions were

189

held whenever the client could find the time (sporadically over the course of 2 years), finally culminating in yet another "termination." Overall, this client spent the vast majority of an almost 20-year stretch in taking her medication, functioning well, and not needing to see her CBT clinician. However, it was very helpful for her to be able to return for periods of CBT sessions when most needed.

When the Client Unilaterally Stops Attending Sessions

Sometimes clients suddenly stop attending therapy, without discussing the matter, and without achieving their therapeutic goals sufficiently. This is typified by the scenario where the client fails to show up for a scheduled appointment, and then does not return the therapist's follow-up calls. Similarly, the client may cancel an appointment, but never reschedule. As there is evidence that premature termination of this sort is associated with poorer long-term outcome (see Dahlsgaard, Beck, & Brown, 1998), it is important for CBT therapists not to let their absentee clients simply disappear without a good faith effort to communicate and perhaps re-engage. Tact and professionalism are called for here, as CBT therapists do not wish to give the message that they alone know what is in the clients' best interest. The message that therapists need to send is one of congenial concern. This can take the form of an official postal letter—with a nondescript return address that does not signal to the world that the client is receiving mail from a mental health professional—or a voicemail message. The following monologue represents the therapist's attempt to communicate with a client in such a manner, complete with rationales and suggestions for how to proceed:

Therapist: (leaving a secure voicemail message to a client who has missed recent sessions and who has not answered the therapist's previous calls): "Hi, it's Dr. Newman. I'm following up because it's been a long time since I've heard from you, and I'm wondering how you are. I hope that your being out of touch means that you're doing well and that you don't think you need to come back. If that's true, I want to wish you all the best, and I also want you to know that my door is always open if you wish to schedule a booster session or two in the future. In any event, I hope you'll call me back just to let me know how things are going for you. Additionally, if you're interested, I would also like to invite you to have a wrap-up session, where we could review the work we've done and establish a long-range game plan for maintenance. Just call me and I'll be happy to see you as soon as the two of us can coordinate our schedules. On the other hand, if you're not feeling well, or something went wrong in one of our previous sessions that you're unhappy about, I would be very open to hearing what's on your mind, and I would be very motivated to help in any way I can. If you would prefer to see another therapist, and you would like my input on who that could be, I would be glad to offer you referrals. So, I guess what I'm saying is that I hope you're well, and I hope to hear from you, and I would be happy to see you, even if it is just for a session that pulls all our work together and creates a relapse prevention plan for you. Take care."

If the client does not respond to a voicemail message, it is wise to follow up with a letter—using the same friendly tone as the voicemail exemplar above—stating that the file is now closed, but that the client is welcome to get back in touch in the future. The letter may also add the names of one or more other therapists and their contact information, in case the client may wish to be referred elsewhere.

In cases where a client is clearly having significant psychological difficulties yet has been missing from treatment, the therapist's message can be a little more urgent about the client's absence from therapy, yet still communicate respect for the client's autonomy. The following represents an excerpt from a formal letter sent by a therapist to address this more serious situation:

"If you would prefer not to have any further sessions with me, I will assume that you have good reasons and of course I will respect your decision. I hope that you are seeking help with someone else, because it is very important that you be in active treatment at this critical time when you are experiencing so many personal difficulties and symptoms. I also hope that you are continuing with your medication, or at least that you are meeting with your psychiatrist to discuss your options. It is very important that you not be left without care. If I can be of help, I would be happy to meet with you. The most important thing is that you are in regular treatment with a qualified professional who can help you."

In the message above, the therapist makes it clear that the concern is all about the client, and not about the therapist's caseload or ego. The therapist's letter also serves as a clear message that a sudden, unplanned termination without further disposition is disadvantageous to a client, especially one who is still quite symptomatic and perhaps at some risk.

The Timing of Termination with Challenging Cases

Achieving the proper timing for a termination of therapy is somewhat of a balancing act. On the one hand, there is an ethical mandate not to abruptly abandon clients in need. On the other hand, there is a countervailing ethical consideration to avoid unduly prolonging a course of therapy beyond noticeable utility. In actual clinical practice, the middle ground between these two unfavorable extremes often is wide, leaving therapists and clients with ample leeway to collaboratively determine the best course of action in winding down and ending a course of treatment.

With certain types of clients who pose ongoing management challenges (e.g., chronic, significant risk of self-harm; low collaboration with the treatment plan; frequent crises; repeated gestures to cross the therapist's boundaries), there is a temptation for the therapist to end therapy, citing the fact that "the client is not improving." However, in such cases, it may be true that therapy is providing the most important sense of stability and anchoring in the client's life (and therefore has value), and even though measureable positive change has been elusive, an abrupt cessation of treatment might be patently deleterious to the client's health. So what is a therapist to do? The following assertion serves as a useful heuristic: *"Be quick to set standards and limits in therapy, but do not be so quick to terminate therapy itself."* In other words, if a client seems to be greatly in need of professional supervision, but is not necessarily showing signs of making gains in therapy, it is better to set high standards for the client and therapist to meet (e.g., keep focusing on goal-attainment; keep assigning challenging homework assignments; keep seeking professional consultations on the case), rather than to summarily end treatment.

It should also be noted that even if there is compelling evidence that a client is not improving as a result of treatment, it is inadvisable to end that treatment while the client is in a heightened state of risk (e.g., suffering from a current, tragic life event; experiencing an exacerbation of suicidal ideation; presently going through a manic episode; experiencing problems and complications on concurrent pharmacotherapy). In such instances, a competent therapist can provide such clients with much-needed supervision and support until the crisis has passed, at which point it may be appropriate to consider termination with an appropriate referral.

To reiterate, when a client is not making progress in therapy over a significant period of time, it does not necessarily signal the need to end treatment, but it certainly indicates that the therapist and client need to openly assess the roadblocks to progress, revisit and perhaps alter the treatment plan, and address the function—both adaptive and not so adaptive—that therapy is serving in the client's life. This strategy serves as the happy medium between letting therapy go on and on without paying attention to the costs and benefits (on the one hand), and impulsively ending treatment (on the other hand). Finding the "happy medium" is an example of competent CBT therapists demonstrating a thoughtful, measured approach to handling problems.

In order to facilitate communication with a challenging client on the potentially sensitive and loaded topic of termination, the therapist may choose to bring up the matter of the client's inadequate progress and their possible consideration of termination as part of a formal, periodic Treatment Update Plan (TUP, see Chapter 8). This can be done every 3 months as a routine part of therapy, with the therapist and client both having the "homework" of preparing for this review session in the week leading up to it. Thus, the question of, "Should treatment continue through the next 3-month period, or should we aim to conclude therapy during this time?" is brought up in a formal context, rather than at the spur of the moment when the therapist and/or client are feeling discouraged. Competent therapists should also be ready and responsive in addressing the topic of termination if and when the client brings it up spontaneously. Ideally, the therapist should start by listening to the client rather than immediately responding in a manner which could be construed as being defensive. This situation can serve as a positive opportunity to take stock of what is missing in the treatment plan, and to increase a sense of collaborative problem-solving.

Dealing Sensitively With a Sense of Loss at Termination

The end of therapy can be an emotional time for some clients, and the competent therapist is quite attuned to and aware of this happenstance. Many therapists themselves experience a sense of wistful sadness at saying goodbye to clients with whom they have worked so closely, and with whom they have developed a genuine bond. In some respects, the positive termination of therapy is like a high school graduation, in that it is a time when both therapist (teacher) and client (student) can feel enormously proud, reflecting back on what the client has accomplished, with the client looking to the future both with excitement and with some understandable trepidation. Therapy termination can be different from a high school graduation in that there are times you *can* go back if you wish. Booster sessions can be an important part of a longer-term termination *process,* in which the client weans off therapy with less and less frequent sessions, and/or has the safety net of knowing that he or she can return for periodic "check-ups" if desired.

It is important for therapists not to underestimate the emotional impact of termination for some clients, some of whom entered therapy feeling alone and/or misunderstood, and who found a rare sense of acceptance and bonding with their therapist. While it is true that one of the goals of treatment often is to help such clients build a support system of their own outside the therapist's office, it may still be the case that the end of treatment represents a significant loss. Empathic therapists truly understand this. Though therapists generally cannot convey the message that, "I will always be there to help you again in the future, just when you need me," they may be able to say, "My door is open for you to return for booster sessions in the future, provided that I am available." Similarly, though therapists with good boundaries cannot state that termination now signals a change to a more personal relationship (even if the clients would welcome such a stance), they can make it clear that they have valued the time they have spent working together, and that they will think about the clients in the future, perhaps welcoming communications from them about how they're doing.

Joey's Termination from CBT

After 4 months of CBT (totaling 17 sessions), Joey believed he was doing better across all the leading indicators of his functioning, and the therapist largely agreed. Joey's symptoms of anxiety had decreased markedly and consistently, his diagnosis of depression was now in partial remission, his use of alcohol had been dramatically reduced, and he was doing much more problem-solving at work instead of catastrophizing and avoiding. Further, Joey had gone to see a doctor and a dentist (and he had already gone back to the dentist for two of the four fillings he needed!), he had sent an e-mail to Bob (and was coping well with the lack of a response), and he had had some casual dates that aroused more anxiety than attraction but he was "learning the ropes" and willing to continue trying. Joey opted to have three more sessions on an every-other-week basis, and then wanted to leave the door open for future booster sessions if he were to encounter particularly challenging situations. The therapist said that he would be happy to do this, but added that since therapy should not just be about crisis management, he wanted Joey to be prepared to bring in written examples of his CBT self-help (e.g., ATRs) if he were to return. The therapist explained that this would maximize the chances that Joey would stay "fresh and sharp" with his cognitive-behavioral skills, that he would make the most of any follow-up session, and that he would be using the follow-up session from a position of strength as an active collaborator, rather than feeling weakened and "back to square one," as he was so prone to thinking.

Joey's third every-other-week appointment, his 20th session overall, was his final CBT session. He explained that his job situation was not entirely resolved, but it was looking more and more that his position would not be eliminated or transferred. Joey stated that he was reaching a point of acceptance that he would probably not hear back from Bob, and that he was experiencing disappointment rather than a sense of personal rejection. Joey's schemas of vulnerability to harm, incompetence, and unlovability were not entirely gone, as certain situations could still trigger his anxiety (along with his urge to drink), but they were dramatically less prominent and pervasive in his life, and his confidence was higher than ever. Of great significance was Joey's proud assertion that he was now dating his neighbor Miranda (of role-playing fame from Chapter 7). Joey said that he probably did not need this session, but that he "couldn't resist coming in to brag about Miranda," and to say "thank you for everything." At the end of the session, Joey humorously, wistfully said, "I'm going to miss my 'Tuesdays with Cory'." The therapist and Joey shared a heartfelt, back-slapping hug, and therapy ended.

TERMINATION OF SUPERVISION

Appropriate supervisory termination can be managed by using similar parameters as therapy termination, even though the relationship is different, and the types of termination are fewer (Davis, 2008). Supervision is a mandatory part of a new clinician's training, and the trainee must meet certain requirements in terms of skills and accumulated supervisory hours, while the supervisor has ultimate responsibility for the care being given to the supervisee's clients. Termination of supervision is often done on an academic calendar, involving formal points of evaluation (e.g., on a quarterly basis). Often, the date of termination is determined by an academic schedule, and is known well in advance (perhaps from the start). Supervisors have to use their authoritative power most benevolently and wisely, because trainees often have less flexibility and power to unilaterally terminate with their supervisors than clients have in ending their work with their therapists (Newman, 1998). When handled properly, the supervisory relationship results in good care for clients, a steep learning curve of CBT methods for the trainee, the positive professional development of the trainee, and ultimately a transformation in the supervisory relationship from one which is hierarchical to one that is more collegial. In the latter sense, supervisory terminations generally do not involve a sense of an *ending* of a relationship, but rather an evolutionary progression.

A "good" termination of a supervisory relationship usually involves the supervisor's positive professional evaluation of the trainee, such that the latter is now endorsed as being qualified to go to the next level of training or professional standing. Supervisors give their supervisees feedback during training, so that any problems can be worked on during the prescribed period of time in which they are working together. As Davis (2008) notes, "Termination evaluation is not the time for surprises" (p. 231), therefore it behooves the supervisor to apprise supervisees of any additional or remedial work they need to do to receive passing marks. In cases where the therapist-in-training is finishing a practicum or rotation in a given setting, termination of the supervisory relationship would not be complete without a timely, thorough, well-considered clinical disposition of all the supervisees' cases. The clients are also going through termination (or a referral to a new therapist) at that time, and their needs must be held paramount by both the supervisor and the therapist-in-training—an example of a mandate for "conjoint competency" in the service of the clients.

KEY POINTS TO REMEMBER

- A comprehensive relapse prevention plan helps clients anticipate future stressors so they can do advance problem-solving

---

and use cognitive rehearsal to prepare effective ways to cope; to utilize notes, session recordings, and simulated therapy sessions with themselves in order to stay "fresh" and "sharp" in using CBT self-help skills; and to formulate new goals for further growth and life enhancement after therapy is completed (i.e., not resting on their laurels).

- In CBT, the topic of ultimate termination is discussed early, openly, and constructively.
- In some cases where clients have long-term needs, "terminations" occur at the end of discrete periods of treatment (or "modules"), separated by significant periods when the clients function successfully and independently. Overall, the therapeutic relationship may exist and continue for the long run, as therapist and client resume their work when necessary.
- Competent CBT clinicians are alert to signs that clients are at risk for premature termination, thus they ask the clients for feedback and try to do collaborative problem-solving so as to keep an appropriate process of therapy moving forward constructively.
- Competent CBT clinicians successfully navigate the middle ground between terminating treatment too abruptly (i.e., risking abandoning the client) and continuing with treatment too far beyond the point of diminishing returns.
- Termination can stir up significant feelings of loss for clients, and competent CBT practitioners handle this with great empathy and sensitivity.
- In CBT supervision, a good and proper termination involves the supervisor giving constructive feedback, the supervisee being endorsed legitimately to advance to the next level of training or professional standing, and (perhaps) the supervisory relationship becoming more of a collegial relationship for the long run.

10

Practicing Cognitive-Behavioral Therapy with Cultural and Ethical Sensitivity

"I am not Athenian or Greek but a citizen of the world."

Socrates

The term "culture" refers to the unique behavior patterns, attitudes, values, worldviews, and lifestyle shared by a group of people that distinguish them from other groups (Tseng & Streltzer, 2004; Whaley & Davis, 2007). Clinicians are increasingly expected to be culturally sensitive and culturally competent. Cultural sensitivity involves the clinician's "awareness of cultural variables in themselves and in their client that may affect the therapeutic relationship and treatment process" (Sperry, 2010, p. 198). Cultural competency involves the clinician's ability to understand and be responsive to clients from the perspective of their particular subgroup, acknowledging the importance of cultural differences in assessing psychopathology and in designing appropriate interventions; being mindful and respectful of cultural strengths; and valuing the expansion of one's knowledge base in order to maximize meeting the needs of clients from a variety of backgrounds (López, 1997; Sue, 1998). This chapter summarizes some of the ways in which competent CBT clinicians strive to make adaptations to improve their therapeutic relationship skills, case

199

formulations, and interventions to be optimally effective with clients from diverse backgrounds. Later, the chapter will address the competent therapist's adherence to codes of professional ethics, and the manner in which expert therapists enact the principles of "positive ethics" to maximize the well-being of clients in complicated clinical situations.

CULTURAL SENSITIVITY AND
THE THERAPEUTIC RELATIONSHIP

The start of therapy is a time of uncertainty and trepidation for many clients, as they wonder how therapy will proceed, and ponder questions such as, "Will I feel comfortable with my therapist?" and "Is therapy going to help me, or will it be useless, or even worse?" These natural concerns of the new client may be amplified if there are cultural differences between him and herself and his or her therapist, particularly if the client is of minority status, and the therapist is not. Minority clients often experience higher levels of uncertainty and fear as they enter therapy, "...and in fact historically have been discriminated against in the mental health system (Moffic & Kinzie, 1996)" (Kinzie & Leung, 2004, p.39). As a result, they may also harbor a significant sense of mistrust, borne of their own past experiences with the health care field, and/or as a result of high-profile cases of malfeasance perpetrated against their compatriots (see Mayo, 2004). Additionally, more than the typical mainstream client, persons from certain cultures are particularly fearful of being labeled as "crazy," and perhaps being judged and/or shunned by their kinfolk (Kinzie & Leung, 2004). Competent CBT clinicians need to be understanding and accepting of the minority clients' wariness, rather than being insistent on their collaboration.

Another aspect of cultural sensitivity is the accurate empathy that therapists need to communicate to clients regarding the inherent stressors the latter face simply by virtue of their experiences as minority clients. Three important questions that culturally sensitive therapists can ask at the start of treatment include:

1. "What hardships have you experienced as a result of your ethnicity, sexual orientation, or physical challenges?" If the client offers a substantive answer, the therapist follows with:
2. "How much do you think these hardships play a role in the problems that are bringing you to therapy at this time?"; and,

3. "What are your thoughts about working with someone like me, who may not be of the same background or may not have shared your experiences?"

Such questions communicate the therapist's high level of motivation to understand the client's negative experiences related to his or her minority status, and to be sensitive to the client's potential misgivings about taking part in therapy with a clinician from the mainstream or a different culture. Therapists of minority clients would do well to be prepared to think carefully about what it must be like to live under the following circumstances (among many others):

- Struggling to speak English as a second language, encountering people who disparage you because of your accent and unusual idioms, and who assume you must be "stupid."
- Having the mixed emotions of being happy to become a resident in a "free" country, while feeling the anguish of being separated from family members who are not free to enter this country as well.
- Looking the part of being well assimilated into the mainstream, while harboring feelings of being "a stranger in a strange land."
- Being secretly gay in a staunchly religious family, in which some of the family members have openly expressed hostility against gay persons.
- Being torn between a sense of reverence for and obligation to one's elders from "the old country," and wanting to live under the rules and mores of the "new country."

These experiences represent levels of vulnerability and trauma that mainstream therapists may never have personally experienced, and it is appropriate for the therapists to acknowledge this.

Competent therapists who wish to maximize their rapport with clients from diverse backgrounds make a special effort to gain familiarity with the customs and life-cycle rituals that are so important to their nonmajority clients. For example, the therapeutic relationship is enhanced when a non-Hispanic therapist can demonstrate an appreciation for a Latina client's pre-occupation with making arrangements for her daughter's *quinceañera* ("Sweet 15 party"), or when a non-Jewish therapist can sensitively inquire about the *shiva* that took place at the home of a Jewish client whose father recently passed away. If therapists show an active interest and make a good-faith effort to learn about the culture of their minority clients, they will not only improve the connections they make with such clients but they will also accumulate a fund of knowledge that will help them better understand and relate to future clients from similar backgrounds.

DEVELOPING EFFECTIVE CULTURAL FORMULATIONS

Sperry (2010) describes the competency of developing effective cultural formulations as involving, "...the capacity to develop a compelling explanation for the client's presenting problem and maladaptive pattern when cultural factors are operative" (p. 196). In order to ascertain the degree to which cultural factors play a role in the client's psychological concerns, Sperry (2010) recommends assessing a comprehensive range of variables, including the client's cultural identity (including race, ethnicity, nationality, and religion), gender and sexual orientation, migration and country of origin, socioeconomic status, level of acculturation, language, explanatory model for their illness, and others. He describes convenient questionnaires that can be used to assist the clinician in assessing these variables, though it is also possible for therapists to ask the clients directly about these matters, or to include general open-ended questions on these topics as part of the clients' customary pre-treatment self-report forms. Sperry (2010) especially emphasizes the factors below, which he notes are often given short shrift in the assessment process:

Cultural Identity

This variable addresses the question, "To which particular cultural group and/or place of origin does the client have a sense of belonging?" At times the client will be very straightforward, saying (for example), "I am a proud Latina who was born in Mexico but the United States is my home, and my Catholic faith is very important to me." Others may be less definitive—in fact, the client's unclear sense of cultural identity may be an important part of his or her distress. As an example, one client stated at the outset of therapy that he "never felt like [he] belonged," no matter where he was. He explained that as an African-American child adopted by well-to-do Caucasian parents, he was often one of the only persons of color in his primary and secondary school. Later, when he went to college and experienced a larger cohort of African-American students, he felt out of place with them as well. In spite of his objective successes in school and sports, as well as having a fairly large group of friends, this young man declared that he had a "huge identity crisis" and therefore felt "lost among others," even when they were treating him well.

Acculturation

Acculturation refers to the process by which immigrants and their descendants adapt to and integrate into the mainstream culture. Three important indicators of a client's level of acculturation are: (1) How much and how well he or she uses the mainstream language versus his or her mother tongue (or the language of his or her elders); (2) his or her generational position (e.g., Was the client born elsewhere? If not, were the parents, grandparents, or great-grandparents foreign-born?); and (3) social activities (e.g., Does the client prefer interacting with mainstream peers, or those from his or her specific cultural background?). A competent assessment of the client's acculturation takes into account the potential conflict that may exist between a client who is well assimilated into mainstream society, and the client's family who is not.

For example, a young woman whose heritage was South Asian was born in the United States, she spoke in a manner that sounded like any of her mostly Anglo-American friends, and never dated men from her own culture (she preferred Caucasian men from European-American backgrounds). Her parents, who came to the United States as adults, were more traditional in their customs and in their expectations for their daughter. This client vaguely mentioned "conflicts of opinion" with her parents, but rarely discussed these matters in any detail in session. Instead, the client offered nondescript statements such as, "My parents can be so old-fashioned and difficult." It was the therapist who ultimately took the initiative to ask about the client's parents' views of their daughter never dating men from their family's cultural background. This question opened up an area of discussion in therapy that the client had never intended to broach. At first, the client took umbrage, tersely asking, "Are you saying that I should 'stay with my own kind'?" The therapist quickly attempted to make repairs to this strain in the therapeutic alliance, saying, "Oh my goodness, I'm so sorry I gave that impression, which would be so offensive if that was what I was implying!" The client relaxed a bit, and the therapist continued, "You and I can agree that you are free to be romantically involved with anyone of your choosing, but we would both be in denial if we ignored the impact such openness has on your relationship with your parents, which I would imagine is important to you." Notably, this exchange not only led to a richer discussion about the client's relationship with her family of origin, but also opened up the topic of the client's negative views about her ethnic heritage, and the impact this had on her self-image.

If it is determined that the client was indeed born in a different land, the culturally sensitive therapist will strive to obtain a rich, thorough history that may include illustrative reminiscences of the client's place of birth and upbringing. Additionally, therapists need to be particularly mindful of assessing for past *trauma*, especially if the clients have relocated to their present locale under adverse, dire circumstances (e.g., escaping from famine, war, persecution).

Explanatory Model for the Illness

Competent therapists assess their clients' attributions regarding their illness by asking such questions as, "How do you explain your symptoms?" and "In your opinion, what are the major causes of your situation and your related distress?" The culturally competent clinician listens carefully for answers such as "stress," "biochemical problems," "genetics," and "trauma," which are part of the "scientific mind-set of mainstream culture" (Sperry, 2010), versus such attributions as, "It's a punishment from God," "A curse was placed on me," and "The injustices of this society." The latter answers lead the therapist to follow up with more questions that will flesh out the client's culture-based beliefs.

Illness Perceptions and Treatment Expectations

Related to the above, the clients' illness perceptions include their beliefs about the proper terms for their symptoms (e.g., *ataque de nervious*, see the glossary from the appendix of the *DSM-IV-TR*), the course and consequences of their illness, and the methods they expect will ameliorate or cure their difficulties. Examples of the ways in which culture may play a role in the above include a client who has been instructed by his religious congregation to seek treatment to "reverse" his homosexuality (an expectation that cannot be validated or accommodated by a competent therapist who delivers evidence-based treatment); a client who believes that "having greater faith" is curative whereas "self-help" is sacrilegious; and a client who believes that only redress from an unjust society can begin the healing process. Not all culturally influenced treatment perceptions pose such difficult problems, but these are the sorts of issues that competent cognitive-behavioral therapists will face across the span of their careers.

A culturally sophisticated case formulation takes into account all of the above variables, allowing the clinician to understand the client's concerns in a way to communicate accurate empathy, and to adapt interventions in a way that will earn them cultural credibility with their clients. In some cases, little or no adaptation is required, as the client's self-identity, level of acculturation, explanations for his or her distress, and his or her expectations for treatment all lie within normative limits of the mainstream population. Here, the standard CBT protocols for the clients' problems can be used with little or no modification. However, when cultural factors play a larger role in the case formulation, the competent therapist will find ways to successfully collaborate with the clients, such that the best practices of CBT may be utilized within a framework that shows respect for the clients' culture-based beliefs. Effective cultural formulations are not typically "all or none." In other words, the clinician is not making a dichotomous choice between a standard, normative CBT case conceptualization *versus* an alternative model that is completely matched to suit the client's minority status. Rather, the question is, "Too what *degree* (on a continuum) does the case formulation need to be modified to be optimally sensitive in order to best understand the context for the client's well-functioning and dysfunction alike?" The clinical examples in this chapter illustrate this point, in which there are particular *areas* of client concern that require the therapist to be culturally sensitive, the scope of which is different for each client.

A related task of the culturally sensitive therapist is to be mindful of two sets of cultural norms—those of the clients and those of the mainstream population—in order to gauge the clients' problems across situations on the respective continua of adaptive functioning. For example, Huppert and Siev (2010) describe the case of an Orthodox Jewish woman who suffered from severe obsessions and compulsions related to violating laws of religious observance, especially the dietary regulations of *kashrut* (keeping kosher). Her case was described as a particular form of obsessive-compulsive disorder known as "scrupulosity," in which a desire for certainty and perfection along with an intense fear of committing and promulgating sins led the client to be markedly dysfunctional *within her own cultural community.* Although the therapist in this instance had to be knowledgeable about the customs of the client's religious group, he also needed to be aware of when the client's beliefs were a function of obsessive-compulsive symptoms, superimposed on the client's cultural rituals. For example, the client's community followed strict rules about separating dairy products from meat products, therefore it would not be unusual for a person from this cultural sphere to believe that she could not accept an invitation to come to dinner at the home of a person who did not adhere to these regulations. In other words, the culturally sensitive therapist would not view this as a manifestation of social anxiety or avoidance. However, in the Huppert and Siev (2010) case, the client feared that she was tracking specks of spattered milk around the house with the soles of her shoes, mixing the milk with meat particles that she feared she had also spread accidentally, thus causing widespread culinary contamination that would be sinful for her, her family, and anyone to whom she might bring a dish. These beliefs and related fears went way beyond cultural matters into the realm of frank psychopathology. The authors describe going to great lengths to treat the "scrupulosity" problem while showing respect for the client's culturally *normative* mandates.

By contrast, the following example highlights a client who is *not* demonstrating marked dysfunction, but rather is suffering from ambivalence and guilt surrounding his trying to balance his life between the norms of his elders (who are not acculturated), and the norms of mainstream society (which he has adopted as his own). The client is a 32 year-old man who is living with his parents and who has no plans to move out, even though he is gainfully employed. If we think only in terms of the norms of white, Anglo-American society at large, we may hypothesize that there may be excessive interdependency between this client and his parents. Thus, we may posit that a goal of treatment would be to help this client gain more confidence, independence, and assertiveness skills so that he may find a residence of his own (or with a peer). However, this client is Asian-American, the only child of immigrant parents. In this case, the culturally competent therapist would *not* assume that an appropriate treatment goal necessarily would be for this client to leave his parents' abode. The norms of this client's ethnic heritage may dictate that it is appropriate and necessary for the client to demonstrate *filial piety* toward his elders, such that the client would believe it is his duty to take care of his aging parents, perhaps irrespective of his own desires to relocate (Chen & Davenport, 2005). Again, the therapist should not *assume* this is the case—for example, the client may be very "Americanized" and thus may be less moved by the demands of filial piety than he is inhibited by social anxiety—however the culturally competent therapist is *aware* that the client's remaining with his parents may fit well within the norms of his heritage. Further, the therapist will be attuned to the possibility that the client feels quite *ambivalent* about which set of standards to use as guidelines for his life, and that this sense of being torn between two worlds may be a significant part of his subjective stress.

The following dialogue is an excerpt from an early session in which the issue above is addressed. The client prefers to be called by his Americanized name of "Ken." This is already a clue to the therapist about the client's challenges in navigating two cultural worlds.

Ken: There is always so much pressure to do the right thing, and to make my parents proud. They have nobody else but me, and I am their whole world. They came here to the States with nothing, and they always told me that they wanted to create a better life for me. How can I let them know that I am unhappy, after all of their sacrifices?

Therapist: It sounds like you are very sensitive to the needs of your parents, and that you wish to honor their sacrifices. That is very considerate of you. It also sounds like you would like to make some changes in your life. What changes are you considering?

Ken: I don't know if I *can* make any changes. I'm doing exactly what I'm supposed to be doing right now. If I make any changes, such as wanting to get married and move into our own place, it will be harmful to my parents. At the same time, if I keep things the way they are, I am just becoming more unhappy, and then they tell me that they are a burden to me, which is partly true, but it just makes me feel guilty, like I am failing them.

Therapist: Is the issue of marriage and moving out of your parents' house hypothetical, looking ahead to what could be true in the future, or is there actually someone in your life right now with whom you would like to create a life together, apart from your parents?

Ken: There isn't anyone special in my life right now, but that's the point. If I continue along this path, I can't imagine how I'm going to find someone. I don't want a situation where I am expected to marry someone who is from my own culture and traditions and who will accept my parents living with us.

Therapist: But clearly you have some strong feelings of loyalty to your parents and their culture and beliefs, and that's partly why you are so torn. There are two different sets of beliefs and goals about which you feel very ambivalent.

Ken: How can I live both lives? How can I respect them, and respect myself at the same time?

Therapist: Maybe we can start by trying to articulate the two sets of beliefs and goals. Maybe we can also look at your belief about what it means to "fail" your parents. Let's try to gain some clarity about this conflict. That could be a good starting point in terms of understanding your situation with the utmost respect for all its aspects.

As the case of "Ken" illustrates, formulating a sensitive, effective case conceptualization of clients who come from minority ethnic backgrounds involves considering the possibility that the clients experience *mixed* feelings and a *range* of thoughts about the mores of their culture, as well as conflict about how much respect they have for the customs and expectations of their own subgroup in comparison to the majority population within which they may reside. These feelings may be even more pronounced in younger clients, whose life experiences have been interconnected with the world at large to a degree their elders could scarcely fathom. Culturally competent therapists must realize that *even if minority clients have doubts about the customs of their culture, this does not give the therapist license to be critical of those customs.* At the same time, therapists need to help such clients to explore their own path toward transcending the ways of their elders, if that is their choice. All the while, therapists must also be very attuned to the clients' feelings of guilt, anticipatory anxiety about being criticized by their families and community, and real-life consequences that may befall them if they opt for a more assimilated lifestyle. Sometimes, when a client says, "I want to make my own decision, but my family will hate me," it is not necessarily a cognitive distortion! On the other hand, sometimes this thought *would* be a cognitive distortion. The point is that by being culturally sensitive therapists *take into account* the impact of the clients' minority status on their life situation, but they do not *assume* the nature and scope of this impact in stereotypic ways.

Culturally Competent CBT Clinicians are Aware of Their Own Faulty Assumptions

To deliver competent CBT, therapists must be adept at self-monitoring the problematic beliefs that may interfere with their effectiveness, and at modifying these beliefs by considering more objective alternatives. From a cultural standpoint, it is not unusual for mainstream therapists to hold faulty or overgeneralized beliefs about their minority clients—beliefs that will hinder the establishment of an effective case formulation, not to mention a sense of connectedness in the therapeutic relationship. The following are some brief examples:

- A therapist has an African-American client who has had great professional and economic success in the field of information technology. In light of the client's high socio-economic standing, the therapist does not think of the client as someone who has been affected by disadvantage and societal prejudice. However, a culturally competent therapist would assess this client's history, asking about his experiences with prejudice and discrimination. In doing so, the therapist might learn that his client still feels embittered toward society over his father's incarceration, thus enabling the therapist to gain a better understanding of the client's difficulties with overgeneralized anger.
- A therapist has a young adult client who is in a wheelchair owing to a spinal injury, and the therapist assumes that this condition is the main reason for the client's dysphoria. The therapist fails to ascertain that the client attributes her depressed mood largely to the disturbing obsessive-compulsive symptoms that have been a problem since well before she suffered her injury. The therapist later is surprised to find that the client is able to drive a specially modified vehicle, and that she has a boyfriend. The therapist earnestly attempts to understand the impact that the client's paralysis has had on her life, but in the process underestimates the wider-ranging consequences of her OCD, including the discord her OCD symptoms are fomenting in her romantic relationship. In this case, a more competent approach would have involved the therapist asking the client directly about her views about the factors most responsible for her choice to come to treatment. In doing so, the therapist would be less focused on the client's physical challenges, and more attentive to the client's obsessive rituals, and their adverse effect on her romantic relationship.
- A therapist has a male client who complains of loneliness. The therapist asks many questions about the client's social behaviors and attitudes, always referring to interactions with the opposite gender (e.g., asking the client, "Do you have many opportunities to meet single women?"). Only after some time has elapsed does

the client at last reveal that he is gay, whereupon the therapist is embarrassed to realize her faulty assumption. Then the therapist overcompensates, animatedly inquiring about opportunities for the client to meet other gay men, overlooking the client's chief concerns that he is unable to tell his friends and family the truth about his sexual orientation, and therefore feels estranged from them. The therapist oversimplifies the client's "loneliness" as being about not having a boyfriend, whereas the client's loneliness is more of a feeling of alienation from others owing to his sense of being an outsider in his family and in society as a whole. A more competent assessment would have taken into account the personal consequences of this client's secrecy, while empathizing with his sense that he was hindered from being more communicative by the very real evidence of the prejudices of others.

In the previous examples, therapists draw erroneous conclusions that are least partly based on assumptions made about the clients' membership in their respective sociological groups. Such errors get in the way of the therapists' ability to look at the data. They may fail to ask the right questions, and/or filter out useful information through inattention. The phenomena depicted above are not necessarily cases of malevolent prejudice, but they represent biases nonetheless—biases that can interfere with an accurate case conceptualization, and that can hinder the development and maintenance of a positive, collaborative therapeutic relationship.

By the same token, in a noble attempt *not* to fall prey to stereotypes, and instead to treat everyone as equals, therapists may try to act as if there are *no* differences between people based on culture and mores, which is the opposite extreme set of assumptions. Here, the therapist is failing to be sufficiently culturally competent because actual differences in the belief systems and societal experiences of the client's subpopulation are not being taken into account as potentially important factors. For example, in an attempt to treat a client from an East Asian country as she would treat any other client, a therapist misinterprets the client's avoidance of discussing her home life as a matter of simple "resistance" or lack of insight. A more culturally competent hypothesis might have taken into account the client's desire not to say anything that might bring shame to her family. By being "color blind," the therapist misses an opportunity to conceptualize her client as nobly bearing her family's burdens on her own. Consequently, the therapist does not ascertain ways to gently address this issue.

210

PLANNING AND IMPLEMENTING CULTURALLY SENSITIVE INTERVENTIONS

A thorough summary regarding the ways in which competent CBT practitioners may modify standard interventions so as to provide a better fit with various cultural groups requires entire volumes. Indeed, as part of the continuing education that therapists must undertake to be maximally competent in meeting the therapeutic needs of cultural sub-groups, texts such as Hays and Iwamasa (2006) are indispensible. The authors educate their readers about the role of culture on such important therapy-related factors as cognitive style and language, values, health beliefs, stigma, the therapeutic relationship, as well as CBT methods such as cognitive restructuring, problem-solving, and "culturally sensitive assertion training." Another valuable resource is Martell, Safran, and Prince (2003), which describes CBT approaches to the treatment of lesbian, gay, and bisexual clients, educating the reader about the stressors of being a sexual minority, and helping the reader to craft more culturally informed case formulations and interventions.

Culturally competent therapists find ways to *adapt* standard interventions in such a manner that they will be respectful of the clients' values and practices (Whaley & Davis, 2007). Therapists are open to receiving feedback about which methods will be acceptable to the clients, and which ones will not. An example is a therapist of a devoutly religious person who is not satisfied with a secular, rationalist argument about why he need not condemn himself for an "unforgivable sin." The therapist in this instance is willing to work with the client to consult a suitable clergyperson in order to address the client's self-punitive thinking from a religiously authoritative perspective. A similar instance is the case of a woman who maintains the belief that "I should not rely on myself, because I should have faith in the Lord." This view would seem to be at odds with one of the basic tenets of CBT, which is to empower clients by teaching them coping skills that will increase their self-efficacy. However, her culturally competent therapist was able to accommodate the client's beliefs by opening a discussion about how it may be possible to improve the client's self-efficacy as a *manifestation* of faith (e.g., "By making choices and solving problems I am showing faith in the qualities that the Lord gave to me as a gift of His wisdom and love"). The result was that the client was able to benefit from CBT, and her functioning came to fit the healthy norms both of the secular society at large, as well as of her own deeply religious community.

211

Another expression of cultural competency involves the CBT clinician's recognition that not every culture values the same methodologies of thinking. Whereas Westerners may be responsive to Socratic arguments in which logical inconsistencies cause cognitive dissonance that must be resolved by modifying at least one viewpoint, those of Eastern heritage may be more inclined to accept two apparently opposing states as being part of the natural paradoxes and balancing of life (see Nisbett, 2003). Here, the culturally astute CBT practitioner might choose not to use the Socratic method as much, but rather to work within the realm of finding "balance" and "acceptance" as a way to diminish emotional distress and hopelessness.

For those clients whose cultures are more apt to stigmatize the concept of mental illness and its treatment, an extra emphasis on the *educational* aspects of CBT may be particularly helpful. Organista and Muñoz (1996) report that the use of therapy manuals and homework assignments helped Latino clients to think of therapy as being more akin to a classroom experience, thus alleviating some of the stigma attached to meeting with a therapist. Expounding on the theme that the methods inherent to CBT make it an advantageous approach for some minority groups, Whaley and Davis (2007) write that, "The emphasis on behavior change through skills training and practical exercises may address the need for personal and group empowerment expressed by many populations of color" (p. 572).

Another appealing adaptation of CBT is the likening of "cognitive bias" with sociocultural bias. For example, in her training courses on CBT, world-renowned lecturer Christine Padesky has used the term "prejudice" to explain the concept of dysfunctional thinking that gratuitously condemns oneself without taking due account of all of the facts. As many minority clients are all too familiar with the harmful results of cultural prejudice, they may be especially motivated to fight against their own cognitive prejudices, and instead work to adopt a more balanced, fair-minded, even-handed, affirmative approach to "talking" to themselves (in the context of their automatic thoughts and rational responses). One might imagine the extra emotional impact of the following therapist comment, made to a client of color who habitually engages in self-punitive comments while simultaneously disqualifying her personal assets and accomplishments:

"Your negative thoughts about yourself keep getting promoted, again and again, without merit, based on 'the good old boys' network, whereas your positive thoughts about yourself, which have truly earned a promotion, keep getting overlooked and kept down because they're not in the 'in group.' It's an unfair system that really needs to change. I think we need a little 'revolution' in your thinking. Let's help your positive thoughts about yourself to 'rise up.' What do you think about that?"

SUPERVISORS: THEIR ROLE IN DISCUSSING CULTURAL ISSUES

Supervisors play an important role in assisting their supervisees to recognize and manage cultural issues that may be relevant to their work with their clients. As novice therapists may not always be assertive or proactive in raising sensitive issues in supervision, it is up to the supervisor to initiate an inquiry about cultural issues as they may pertain to the supervisee, the supervisee's clients, or their interactions (Iwamasa, Pai, & Sorocco, 2006). In doing so, supervisors contribute to a sense of safety that will enable therapists-in-training to feel more free to bring topics related to diversity into the supervision agenda. "Differing cultural worldviews of the client, therapist, and supervisor and the ability to adequately address issues of race and culture can be critical to change in the treatment and lead to development of increased self-esteem for student clinicians" (Anderson, Khowaja, Rosales, Schroth, & Street, 2011, p. 9).

As implied above, supervisors can readily include themselves (e.g., their own experiences and/or knowledge base) in the discussion of diversity, such as when they acknowledge to their supervisees that the latter may have a better understanding of a given client by virtue of their sharing a similar heritage, or when the supervisors offer their own cultural knowledge to assist the supervisee in gaining a better understanding of a client. At the same time, nonminority supervisors should not *assume* that a minority supervisee is able to relate easily to a client from a similar minority group. There may be intra-ethnic differences between client and therapist-in-training (e.g., respective levels of "advantage and privilege") that can cause tension in the therapeutic relationship, the likes of which will need to be addressed openly, and with supervisory oversight. The key is that the supervisor needs to be alert to cultural matters so as not to omit this important area of discussion that is potentially so important to case formulation, treatment, and the professional development of novice therapists. The quest for cultural competence and expertise provides an enriching experience for therapists and supervisors alike, leading to a better understanding of a wider range of clients, a broadening of perspectives and insights, and a greater sense of community with persons from all walks of life.

PRACTICING WITH ETHICAL SENSITIVITY

Competent therapists need to have a healthy respect for and a working knowledge of ethical guidelines and mandates (APA, 2002). The word "guidelines" is used deliberately, as many of the ethical issues that confront therapists on a regular basis are not black and white, instead requiring the careful consideration of a variety of factors, how they interact, and how they translate into promoting the best interests of the client, safeguarding society (as in the "duty to warn"), and representing the field of psychotherapy with professionalism and trustworthiness. These are lofty goals, sometimes requiring that therapists take their time, weigh the issues carefully, and make it a point to consult with peers or mentors in the field.

Respecting the Client's Decision to
Say "No" to an Intervention

CBT presents therapists and their clients with a powerful technology for therapeutic change. One of the most striking examples is the category of interventions known as "exposures," such as when phobic clients are brought into contact with their feared scenario(s); post-traumatic stress disorder clients are coached to re-experience horrific memories in a planned, systematic, re-educational way; and obsessive-compulsive clients are made to confront situations without the "benefit" of their dysfunctional rituals. While there is substantial empirical support for these interventions (see Clark & Beck, 2010), ethically sensitive therapists remember that their clients have the right to refuse interventions they believe will be too difficult or upsetting. These clinicians do not engage in power struggles with their reluctant clients, eschew labeling them pejoratively as "resistant," and refrain from giving clients "take it or leave it" ultimatums. Instead, ethically astute practitioners find ways to collaborate with these clients so that the latter ultimately receive the highest "dose" of CBT they can tolerate, even if it is less than the therapists ideally have to offer.

Although CBT therapists understand that aggressive interventions can lead to significant client improvement and empowerment, they also realize that clients may feel empowered by asserting themselves with their therapists, ostensibly saying, "There is a limit to what I will experience in treatment, and I want those limits to be respected." Ethically sensitive therapists rightly wish to give their clients the opportunity to achieve the maximum benefits from CBT, and therefore will continue to present their clients with the option of taking progressive steps toward more robust interventions. At the same time, competent therapists respect their clients' autonomy, including the right to say "no" to certain CBT procedures, without fear of therapist censure and/or abandonment.

Cultural Responsiveness and Boundaries

Therapists are stewards of their ethical code (e.g., APA, 2002), which addresses (among many other issues) the conditions, parameters, and prohibitions pertinent to the therapeutic relationship. For example, certain types of dual relationships are deemed potentially exploitative of clients, and therefore must be avoided. Secondary to these professional norms, but important in their own right, are the interpersonal norms of the client's culture that suggest what is appropriately polite, proper, and perhaps necessary to establish a working relationship. The culturally and ethically competent therapist is flexible in how he or she will interact with clients—provided that this flexibility still remains within acceptable professional norms—so that optimal comfort and trust can be established between therapist and client.

For example, an example of boundary flexibility can be seen in the sensitive handling of the Hispanic concept of *personalismo* (Organista, 2000), which refers to the sharing of personal information as a means by which to establish familiarity and trust. Therapists who work with Latino clients may need to be a little more willing than usual to answer the clients' personal questions (within reason) to provide the proper climate for clients to make their own disclosures. In other words, therapists who ordinarily disclose only their training background and credentials may suddenly find themselves having to decide whether or not to answer questions about their age, marital status, whether they have kids, and whether they have ever personally experienced the client's difficulties, among other nonprofessional queries. While each therapist must decide for himself or herself what the limits of comfort and professional propriety ought to be in such instances, it may be useful to stretch a little bit when encountering clients for whom *personalismo* is a critical factor in establishing a therapeutic relationship.

Similarly, therapists who typically do not accept gifts or favors from clients may need to consider saying "yes" to Latino clients' token offerings and gestures, lest the clients feel a lack of connectedness with their therapist. Again, expanding the limits of boundaries with certain clients is not the same thing as disregarding boundaries. Professional and ethical rules mandate certain boundaries and limits irrespective of the mores of different ethnic cultures. The point is that there is a *range*, and the astute clinician makes adjustments within this range, based on the cultural preference of the clients. Sometime that means that therapists will be more familiar than usual, and sometimes it means that therapists will be more formal.

Although professionals from the major, industrialized Western societies tend to value individualism and privacy, many people who hail from other heritages may value familial support and collective well-being to a greater degree. As a result, mainstream therapists need to be aware of the possibility that the client will benefit more from inviting the family to be more involved in his or her treatment (with the client's consent), than in assuming that confidentiality in the strictest sense is the client's preferred course (Kinzie & Leung, 2004). Again, competent CBT therapists respect and adhere to ethical guidelines (such as those that govern the principles of confidentiality), but they also realize that the practical applications of these guidelines are not always uniform, and their assumptions about "what is in the best interest of the client" may require some culturally informed filtering.

"Positive Ethics"

As noted, competent therapists know, respect, and comply with ethical regulations. Expert clinicians are additionally familiar with the concept of "positive ethics," which refers to the practicing of therapy in a way that places greater emphasis on doing "the greatest good," rather than in avoiding doing something "wrong" (Knapp & VandeCreek, 2006). Stated another way, positive ethics is about *not practicing so defensively* that self-protection becomes the paramount concern. Another way to construe "positive ethics" is that it is a search for superordinate principles that will guide therapists to manage those clinical circumstances in which different ethical principles seem to conflict with each other, and/or to astutely anticipate, articulate, and prevent ethical dilemmas before they occur (Sperry, 2010).

A most important point is that the concept of positive ethics in no way is in *opposition* to the ethical code as it stands. Rather, it is a realistic and humanistic approach to the mature, thoughtful, sensitive, professional management of situations that cannot be neatly accounted for or predicted by a static document. Consistent with this value, Knapp and VandeCreek (2006) add that in instances where a therapist chooses to adhere to one ethical principle at the expense of another, every effort should be made to limit the degree to which the nondominant principle is overshadowed. Being "ethically sensitive" means that in addition to being as faithful as possible to the written ethical codes, competent therapists remember that their decisions—even those based on sound professional principles and widely accepted policies—have the potential to create unintended consequences for some clients. Thus, there will be times when ethically sensitive clinicians have to consider courses of action that do not necessarily fit neatly into pre-determined boxes, in the service of making a sensible, good faith effort to do what is best for the client (as seen in the two case examples below). The goal is to seek a virtuous solution to a complicated clinical problem, rather than simply meet the minimum standard of proper response (which may protect the therapist, but stop short of finding an optimal solution for the client).

Confidentiality dilemma

A 19-year-old college student, attending CBT for depression and generalized anxiety, reports to his therapist that he is not attending classes, and that he typically drinks alcohol late at night, sleeps most of the day, and is becoming increasingly apathetic about his life. He states that his parents have no idea that this is happening, and that "they don't care anyway." The therapist does all that she can to encourage the client to stop drinking, to attend class, to schedule healthy activities, to take a referral to see a psychiatrist for a medication consultation, and to reveal to his parents the difficulties he has been experiencing, as a "behavioral experiment" to test his theory that "they don't care anyway." The client does not comply with any of these therapeutic suggestions, misses two sessions, and (upon his return to treatment) tells his therapist that now he is getting oxycontin off the streets. The client adds that he is "sleeping all the time and not eating anymore." Although the client is above the age of 18 and denies suicidality, the therapist gives strong consideration to calling the parents (who live on the opposite coast) to disclose their son's condition, to encourage them to travel to be with him, and to work together to brainstorm further treatment options. The therapist shares her thoughts with the client, and offers to hold a family session. She also gives the client the option of calling his parents from her office, so as to be in charge of explaining the situation to them with the therapist's assistance. He curtly says, "Do whatever you want, but I'm not calling them." The client leaves without signing a formal consent to release information to his parents.

In this instance, does the therapist's plan to involve the client's parents represent a breach of confidentiality, given that the client is not actively, imminently suicidal, or—given the client's downward trajectory in functioning and lack of collaboration in treatment—would it be more harmful to the client if the therapist did *not* contact the parents? Further, what sort of protections are the parents entitled to, who have entrusted the care of their beloved son to the perceived stewardship of a University Health Center thousands of miles away? In this instance of gray-zone ethics, the therapist contacts the client's parents, informs the client that she is doing so, documents her clinical rationale copiously in the chart, makes it clear to the client and his parents that she is committed to providing therapy for this young man, and states overtly that her goal is to help the client to function at his best so that he can live independently and safely. The parents fly across the country, attend a therapy session with their son, and the mother remains in the area to "supervise" her son for the remaining weeks of the semester. In light of the mother's presence, the client's addictive behaviors decrease, he meets with his therapist twice per week, and he is able to finish the semester. Later, the client and his parents decide that the client will take a leave of absence the following semester, live at home, and receive treatment locally during that time. The client subsequently contacts the therapist and reports that he was "shocked" that his parents would actually "drop everything" and fly across the country to come help him. In this scenario, the therapist's actions emphasized the principles of beneficence toward both the client and his family, while taking steps to minimize harm to the client's autonomy.

Hospitalization dilemma

A 35-year-old woman who lives alone reports that she is "always suicidal" and has been for years. She describes previous hospitalizations as having been detrimental to her, having "nothing to do" with her long-term despair and serving mainly to produce a traumatic sense of loss of autonomy. One day she calls her therapist, telling him that she does not want to live anymore. The therapist urges her to check herself into a hospital, but the client flatly refuses, adding that "If you try to hospitalize me against my will, you'll *really* be killing me." The therapist—earnestly trying to protect the client's life, but also trying to respect her autonomy—engages the client in a 2-hour phone therapy session, whereupon the client simply hangs up after saying, "I'm tired and I want to go to bed; thank you for caring." The therapist tries to call back, but the client does not pick up. He ponders his choices—call the police and have the client involuntarily hospitalized, which is the customary and professionally safe thing to do, or take the chance that the 2-hour session was sufficient to deal with the crisis, assume that the client will not try suicide, and take no further action at that moment. Remembering that this client has been hospitalized many times—yet her suicidality continues unabated—while hypothesizing that the trusting therapeutic relationship they have formed may be their best safeguard in the long run, and determining that the client had not actually taken any steps to harm herself, the therapist opts *not* to call the police. Instead, he calls the client first thing the next day and strongly suggests that they meet for an impromptu session as soon as possible to solidify their outpatient treatment plan. The client comes to session, still remarks that she hates her life, but thanks the therapist profusely for not having her hospitalized, saying, "I know from experience that being in a hospital only makes things worse." The therapist replies, "We have to do better than 'not making things worse;' we have to help your condition *improve,* and I'm going to need your collaboration more than ever if we're going to make treatment work on an outpatient basis."

In retrospect, the therapist took a significant short-term risk in deciding *not* to call the police, but he was taking a number of factors into account: (1) the client had not yet taken any self-harming actions; (2) he provided a two-hour phone session in the midst of the crisis; (3) the client made it clear that her suicidality was chronic, and not just acute, and that it would be a sign of understanding and respect if the therapist did *not* hospitalize her; (4) their therapeutic relationship—which arguably was a long-term, anti-suicide, safeguarding factor, would be harmed significantly if the therapist called the police; and (5) there is a basis in the psychology literature for eschewing involuntary hospitalization for clients such as this, except in the most extreme, life-threatening emergencies (Paris, 2007). Further, the therapist followed up with a session right away, and made it clear that this crisis situation called for more intensive therapy and an updated treatment plan. In doing so, the therapist was respecting the client's autonomy and acting with beneficence, but minimizing the potential harm to her well-being by intensifying the treatment going forward.

In the examples above, the respective therapists would have been behaving ethically by maintaining strict confidentiality in the first case, and by calling the police in the second case. Many would argue that these actions would have been most prudent, most consistent with practicing "by the book," and representative of competency. The point of this overview of "positive ethics" is not to state otherwise, but rather to emphasize the complexities of real-life clinical dilemmas, and how expert therapists manage them. Such therapists take responsibility for their actions, remain committed to the well-being of the clients, document their clinical decision-making, and (when possible) make use of consultation.

KEY POINTS TO REMEMBER

- In trying to understand a client from a nonmajority population, the competent therapist stays close to the middle ground, neither ignoring the implications of the client's membership in a societal subgroup nor assuming that he or she fits a stereotype.
- Competent therapists are accepting and understanding of the wariness of clients who are from oppressed groups, and work hard to establish a working relationship that is most comfortable for the clients.
- Competent CBT therapists are aware of their own overgeneralized assumptions about their clients, and take steps to learn about their nonmainstream clients as individuals.
- Competent CBT case conceptualization involves assessing such factors as the clients' cultural identity, level of acculturation, explanatory style for their illness, and expectations about the sorts of interventions that are necessary.
- If clients are critical of the customs and mores of their self-identified culture, competent therapists remain respectful of these customs and mores, bearing in mind that the clients may be ambivalent, and may still have respect for their elders and heritage.

- Whenever possible, competent CBT practitioners *adapt* their interventions to fit the cultural sensibilities of their clients. The goal is to increase comprehensibility and empowerment, and to reduce stigma. Emphasizing the *skill-building* and *time-effective aspects* of CBT are helpful in this regard.
- Competent therapists are knowledgeable and respectful of their ethical code. Expert therapists also incorporate the principles of "positive ethics" into their practice, in which finding the best solution for the client and others is the priority, more so than simply making the choice that best reduces therapist liability. Therapists realize that this is a complicated process, often requiring consultation and careful problem-solving.

11

Becoming a Highly Effective and Competent Cognitive-Behavioral Therapist

"It's what you learn after you know it all that counts."

attributed to Harry S Truman

This final chapter summarizes the chief ways in which aspiring CBT practitioners achieve competency, how they maintain their effectiveness, and how their work may ascend to levels of expertise. A central part of this process involves making good use of supervision early in one's career, as well as learning and utilizing best practices as a supervisor throughout one's career.

ATTAINING COMPETENCY THROUGH REPETITIONS AND SIMULATIONS

The seemingly mundane concept of *repetition* is germane to attaining competency in CBT. Therapists who are early in their training and careers may not have had the opportunity to perform large numbers of CBT procedures with many clients in practice. However, these novice therapists may benefit greatly by making it a point to practice *simulations* of a range of CBT techniques (see McCullough, Bhatia, Ulvenes, Berggraf, & Osborn, 2011), such as progressive relaxation, controlled breathing, rational responding (along with the use of ATRs and related guided discovery questions), imagery induction (such as for cognitive rehearsal of upcoming situations, or past trauma exposures), and other methods. Simulations can take place most readily in supervision sessions—thus highlighting the importance of CBT supervisors making use of role-playing when meeting with supervisees—as well as in formal training sessions that involve experiential exercises among the workshop participants (Milne, 2009).

Yet another valuable source of practice is in the therapist's self-application of CBT methods. There is much to be gained, for example, when therapists engage in asking themselves guided discovery questions instead of drawing pat, negative conclusions, or in behaviorally activating themselves when their initial inclination is to abandon their daily plans and cancel engagements owing to lethargy and dysphoria, or in facing an anxiety-arousing situation promptly rather than procrastinating. With each self-application of a CBT technique, therapists gain valuable experience in the basics of these procedures; learn first-hand where the "bugs" in the program may lie (e.g., having automatic thoughts that discount the importance of writing things down); feel a greater sense of congruency and integrity as people who are willing to "walk the walk" in order to help themselves; and improve the accuracy of their empathy in helping clients overcome their difficulties and misgivings in using CBT techniques. For example, in supervision it can be a very helpful homework assignment for clinical trainees to fill out several ATRs of their own. The supervisor typically will instruct the supervisees *not* to write about deeply personal issues (unless they want to share these exclusively with their own therapists), but rather to focus on training-related concerns, such as a fear of upsetting a client. This type of exercise gives the novice therapist an opportunity to gain valuable repetitions in enacting a CBT skill, as well as providing them with first-hand experience in what it is like for clients to learn and perform these self-help skills, including encountering occasional pitfalls.

Of course, whenever possible, it is ideal for CBT therapists-in-training to gain as much actual experience as possible in delivering CBT to as many clients as can be managed safely and responsibly. Some novice therapists train in settings that will afford them intensive experiences with a particular client population, thus helping them to accelerate towards competency in a specialty area. Others obtain training is such a way that they gain valuable experience across a range of client populations. Either scenario is a viable route toward competency, provided that these therapists possess the self-awareness and motivation to know the limits of their knowledge, and to make every effort to fill in the gaps in their training as they move forward.

The process of developing CBT competency described above is significantly assisted by obtaining competent CBT supervision (Newman, in press), by being an ongoing, avid reader of articles and books on CBT (Ledley et al., 2010), and by taking advantage of opportunities to become protocol therapists in research trials involving CBT (Newman & Beck, 2008). Good supervision enables novice CBT therapists to stretch beyond their comfort zones to work with challenging cases, and to learn to use a wide range of interventions, all with the knowledge that their supervisors will provide timely, informed, supportive oversight. Novice CBT therapists who make it a priority to keep up with the literature will succeed in establishing a positive habit that will heighten their learning curves in understanding and performing CBT, and that will help them maintain a high level of competence throughout their careers by valuing keeping up to date on developments in the field. Additionally, as clinical research trials often require intensive supervision for all participants, typically involving the use of video-recordings of each session (along with adherence and competency ratings), novice therapists can readily progress to higher levels of competency by taking part in studies whenever the opportunity is presented. It is not uncommon for pre-doctoral CBT therapists to be chosen to serve in this important role if they have demonstrated a high level of responsibility and related professional attitudes that signal promise as a competent CBT practitioner (Newman & Beck, 2008).

RETAINING COMPETENCY: OVERCOMING FATIGUE AND "SAFETY BEHAVIORS"

Even the best therapists can stray from procedures that have worked so well with so many clients. What factors may best account for even the most experienced therapists' occasionally drifting away from tried-and-true CBT methods? Two factors stand out: (1) fatigue, and (2) therapist "safety behaviors." Regarding the former factor, CBT requires a lot of energy, including preparation in advance of sessions, high levels of attentiveness and communicativeness in session, and a great deal of active, involved, "in the trenches" teaching of psychological skills. The highly competent CBT clinician needs to enter into each therapy session with a constructive mindset, and with the intention of making something positive and memorable happen. Fatigue may detract from this level of commitment. On the hopeful side, a recent summary of the extant research on mindfulness-based stress reduction (MBSR) suggests that therapists—from those in training to seasoned professionals—can benefit significantly from learning the self-application of mindfulness principles to reduce "burn out," and to increase empathy and compassion for both clients and themselves in spite of the high-stress work of conducting therapy (Davis & Hayes, 2011). By extension, we may hypothesize that therapists can counteract the therapy-interfering effects of fatigue by engaging in personal pursuits that enhance a sense of wellness and "being in the moment," such as yoga, recreational activities, creative hobbies, and other pastimes that they may find enjoyably absorbing, engrossing, and in contrast to the work of being a mental health care professional.

A second factor that potentially detracts from the expert delivery of CBT—therapist "safety behaviors"—has to do with the therapist's belief that a given client may be too vulnerable to participate in the rigors of CBT (Waller, 2009). While there are times when CBT therapists may appropriately postpone an intervention in favor of a better-timed moment, "drifting" from CBT may occur when such postponements become the rule, rather than the exception. When therapists often opt to play it safe—intervening in ways that will help the clients feel better in the immediate moment, but perhaps at the expense of helping clients stretch therapeutically beyond their limited comfort zones—they shift the therapy from CBT to a largely supportive therapy. This shift risks watering down the interventions. CBT incorporates everything that is empathic and nurturing about supportive therapy (Gilbert & Leahy, 2007), while adding the important component of skill-building, which may entail some discomfort in the process. Therapists who too often underestimate their clients' ability to manage the stress of learning new psychological skills will become less directive in session, resulting in time being used less efficiently, flattening the clients' learning curves for self-help methods, and leading to their own becoming "out of shape" in conducting highly effective CBT. The remedy for therapists' excessive safety behaviors is a reassessment of their belief that clients have a limited capacity for withstanding stress in session, along with the development of particularly supportive ways of introducing and conducting active CBT methods with clients (as described in earlier chapters).

THE ONGOING DEVELOPMENT OF SELF-REFLECTION

As noted in the first chapter, two of the core values espoused by competent CBT practitioners include a willingness to apply CBT methods to help themselves (for practice, for wellness, and for better empathy with clients), and to embrace being a "student" throughout their entire career and life (thus remaining humble while improving with age and experience). The advanced skill of "self-reflection" embodies these values, and is an essential part of working toward the development of expertise in delivering CBT. As Bennett-Levy (2006) notes, self-reflection represents an advanced level of skill, enabling therapists to strengthen the therapeutic relationship by being optimally aware of their own reactions in and between sessions, and allowing supervisors to model a valuable skill to trainees. The following are examples of therapist self-reflection in action. In each case, the therapist's ability to study himself or herself makes it possible to maintain a high level of competence and professionalism, to conceptualize cases more completely, and to learn from personal experience in a positive way.

1. A therapist has a 1:00 pm appointment with a court-mandated client, someone who has a history of arriving late for sessions. A half-hour before the scheduled session, the therapist finds himself deciding whether or not to run a quick errand after lunch. He assesses the situation, realizes that he will be late for his 1:00 pm client if he takes care of his personal task, and initially opts to go out on the errand anyway. He pauses for a moment, and wonders why he would do this, as he typically values being on time for his clients. *Asking himself what he is thinking at that moment, the therapist tunes into his own thoughts,* which are, "That client often keeps me waiting, so why shouldn't I keep *him* waiting for a change?" Immediately, the therapist realizes that this is a dysfunctional cognition, as he is allowing his own behavior to be shaped inappropriately by the client, rather than continuing to operate under rule-based guidelines that are more professionally driven. Further, the therapist recognizes that he has been more annoyed with his client than he has previously allowed himself to acknowledge. As a result, the therapist becomes more mindful of his own negative responses to this client, and how these may be affecting therapy. Further still, the therapist begins to hypothesize the ways in which this client may be adversely affecting others in his life, perhaps inducing anger in them as well. This line

of thinking then becomes part of the case conceptualization. The therapist decides to forego the errand, and prepares to put the topic of the client's habitual tardiness on the agenda with a calm sense of clinical purpose.

2. A client whose problems are often maintained and exacerbated by her avoidant behaviors reports that she has once again felt "paralyzed" in finishing an important report for her employer. As the therapist attempts to help her client to do some problem-solving in order to begin to write in spite of her assumptions of incompetence and failure, the therapist realizes that she herself has been putting off submitting a manuscript. The therapist realizes that she too has some assumptions about not being able to do her work adequately, and thus she has found the process of writing her paper aversive. Immediately she feels greater empathy for her client, resulting in her communicating with extra warmth and validation as the two of them struggle to manage the client's negative assumptions and related anxiety. As she attempts to give the client a suitable homework assignment, the therapist makes a silent pledge to herself to follow her own assignment so that she can get back to work on her own paper. Meanwhile, the therapist makes sure that the client understands that she will not be criticized for any difficulties she might encounter in the process. As the therapist put it, "However you respond to the assignment will be useful information for us so we can keep doing good problem-solving." The therapist also feels more compassion toward herself, as she determines that, "If I truly believe that it is not helpful when my client 'beats herself up,' I will not do this to myself either." This outlook becomes a boon to the therapist's wellness, which serves to help her in clinical practice.

3. A client tells his therapist that she has not been paying enough attention to him, in that his weekly Beck Depression Inventory scores have recently worsened significantly, though the therapist has not made any mention of this in session and instead has proceeded as usual, as if nothing untoward were occurring. The therapist looks at the chart and realizes that, indeed, she has been insufficiently aware of the exacerbation of the client's symptoms. At first she says to the client, "But you haven't *said* anything about feeling worse, your agenda has been the same as always, and you have looked great." Almost the instant the therapist makes

these comments she realizes that she is focused more on excusing her own oversight than in conceptualizing the situation, in making repairs to the therapeutic alliance, and in determining a clinically appropriate way to proceed. The therapist recognizes that the client's behavior is quite consistent with his habit of presenting a "perfect" image to the world while he silently suffers, feels alone, says nothing of his emotional pain, and maintains the belief that "others should notice if they really care." The therapist therefore gains a valuable glance into the way that the client's modes of operation play themselves out with others, including the therapist herself. However, the therapist acknowledges (both to herself and to the client) that she has a professional responsibility to notice the client's suffering with greater perspicacity than untrained others. She apologizes for not having noticed the client's worsening condition, offers to work on understanding the reasons for his decline in functioning, and suggests that they begin to collaborate on ways to intervene effectively. The therapist decides that she will wait until later (after the alliance has been repaired) to overtly bring up the client's maladaptive habits of disguising his pain while expecting others to read his mind. In the meantime, the therapist does some rational responding silently in her mind, in response to automatic thoughts such as, "I have ruined our good rapport," and "A good therapist would not have been so careless." Her rational responses include, "This is a *strain* in our therapeutic relationship, but all of our previous good work together will be the strong foundation that will help us cope with this situation and go forward positively," and "My oversight is an important matter, but my 'goodness' as a therapist does not hinge on this one event, but rather is reflected in how I learn from this situation." Further, the therapist recalls that she used the words, "You looked great," in explaining to the client how she missed the signs of his decline. She begins a process of asking herself whether she finds herself so attracted to her client that she is at risk for losing clinical objectivity, instead seeing the client as an admired (even desired) peer. With courage, professionalism, and determination to treat the client properly, the therapist consults with a trusted colleague about this situation in order to get frank, helpful feedback. This is an important hallmark of competency.

4. A therapist-in-training hesitates to use role-playing in sessions with clients, even though her supervisor has suggested that this method would be useful. She recognizes that her avoidance of role-playing is linked to her expectation that she will perform the technique poorly and that the client will lose confidence in her. The therapist-in-training reasons to herself that gaining exposure to this feared and avoided intervention could help her habituate to the anxiety of role-playing, could improve her clinical skills, and could help modify her negative thoughts via coping and mastery experiences. Thus, she decides to enact a role-play exercise with the client as a "double intervention" (for herself, as well as for her client who needs assertiveness practice). Both parties benefit, and the therapist-in-training becomes more inclined to use this valuable technique in the future.

Self-reflection is equally important for supervisors, especially as their behaviors have important impact on both the supervisees and their clients. When a supervisee is showing signs of anxiety, it is useful for the supervisor to consider how he or she may be contributing to this state. Supervisors can sometimes underestimate the power they wield over their supervisees, who often are all too aware of the impact of the supervisors' official, summative evaluations on their status in a training program, and (indeed) on their career trajectory. Supervisees also may have very little to say about their options for switching to another supervisor, and any difficulties they have in working with one supervisor may have a ripple effect in how they are perceived by other supervisors who are faculty in the same department (Newman, 1998). Thus, competent supervisors need to be supportive and nonpunitive as they appropriately spell out the parameters of supervision, such as the number of clients the supervisees must see, the number of recordings of sessions and the amount of case-related paperwork they are required to submit, and the skills they will agree to practice and learn (see Box 11.1 for a sample supervisory "contract").

In general, supervisors who model the competency of self-reflection foster this ability in their trainees, who in turn become more adept in helping their clients to self-reflect and thus become more proficient in self-applying CBT. The results are that the clients feel more of a sense of self-efficacy and therefore improve the maintenance of their therapeutic gains, while their therapists develop into expert CBT practitioners and

Box 11.1.
Sample Supervision Contract

Clinical Objectives for Practicum Supervision

1. Treat 3–5 clients in cognitive-behavioral therapy over the course of the academic year. When clients are unavailable in any given week, take part in role-playing exercises in supervision for practice.
2. Write all therapy notes and reports promptly, and maintain them in an organized fashion in the client's chart so they may be co-signed by the supervisor. (I understand that my supervisor must take ultimate professional responsibility for the care of the clients.)
3. Protect my clients' confidential information by keeping the charts in a secure place, using disguised information whenever possible, and refraining from discussing their cases outside of the training settings.
4. Apply the structure of cognitive-behavioral therapy to each session, including setting an agenda, evaluating the client's mood and thought processes, and reviewing and assigning homework.
5. Learn to combine good, general clinical skills (e.g., warmth, empathy, tact, genuineness, listening) with the specifics of cognitive-behavioral therapy interventions (e.g., role-playing, rational re-evaluating, collaborative empiricism).
6. Describe the client's problems in terms of problematic behaviors, affect, thoughts, and underlying beliefs or schemas.
7. Be optimally present and on time for the client's sessions, as well as the supervision sessions.
8. Proactively arrange for appropriate clinical coverage when unavailable to see clients.
9. Proactively seek consultation with the supervisor or another available, suitable, licensed mental health professional when special problems arise with clients that may not be able to wait until the next, formally scheduled supervision session.
10. Submit at least four video-recordings of sessions over the course of the academic year (with the client's signed consent), and achieve a score of at least 40 on the Cognitive Therapy Scale on three of them.
11. Actively read articles, chapters, books on cognitive-behavioral therapy and be prepared to discuss them as part of the supervisory process.

231

12. Actively adhere to ethical principles of the profession, and the legal statutes of [name of geographic jurisdiction], and be prepared to discuss and solve ethical and/or legal dilemmas in supervision.
13. I understand that my supervisor will give me formal, evaluative feedback on a quarterly basis throughout the academic year.
14. I understand that my supervisor will be available for supervision sessions as scheduled, and to assist in matters of clinical crisis.
15. I understand that my supervisor will view and rate at least four complete recordings of cognitive-behavioral sessions that I conduct.

supervisors who "pass down" the capabilities of self-reflection to the next generation of trainees, and the positive cycle continues.

HIGH COMPETENCY: MAKING THE LESSONS OF CBT MORE MEMORABLE AND INSPIRATIONAL

An important manifestation of expertise in delivering CBT is the therapist's ability to teach the clients the conceptual and practical self-help skills of CBT in a manner that will maximize the clients' *retention* of the information, as well as their *motivation* to use it. In the same way that many of us can remember particular teachers who helped us learn to love a particular subject owing to the enthusiasm they displayed, the warm encouragement they offered, and the intellectual appeal they brought to the material, highly competent therapists can have the same positive impact on their clients. The result will be better outcomes, and better maintenance—not in every case, to be sure, but more so and with more clients. While "testimonials from satisfied customers" do not substitute for empirical evidence, they nonetheless shed light on the sorts of processes that clients may find especially helpful, offering us hypotheses that may be tested later. With that in mind, the following are a few comments (from post-treatment "thank you" cards) offered by actual CBT clients over the last 20 years at the Center for Cognitive Therapy at the University of Pennsylvania. None of the material below risks identifying the clients. Rather, these notes bring up themes that were reiterated independently by many clients over time.

232

- "You never let me get away with saying 'I don't know.' It bothered me at times but it made me think, and now I have a better understanding of my myself and my life than I had before. Thank you for making me work so hard to think things through!"
- "Thank you for the way you took the time to explain things to me. You never talked down to me, but you never talked over my head either. You always found a way to give me the information I needed, or told me how to get it for myself. Therapy was never a mystery. You made sure I understood things, and now I have more confidence in myself because I 'get it,' and I know what I have to do to help myself."
- "Your analogies and stories helped me so much, and each image you described really was worth a thousand words, as they say. I'll never forget the way you described all the ways my life was like a baseball game, which suddenly helped me coach myself so much better. Now I manage my life the way I would run my team of high school baseball players, and I'm not even angry when the umpire blows a call!"
- "The turning point in therapy for me was when you were willing to do an Automatic Thought Record of your own and to show it to me. That was really practicing what you preach! After you did that I really felt I could trust what you were telling me, and I saw you as being on my side, and not just telling me what I ought to do."
- "When I stopped believing in myself, you believed in me. When I thought I couldn't cope for another day, you convinced me that I could. When I felt ashamed of myself for my failures, you reminded me what was good in me. When I forgot how to use my CBT skills, you patiently walked me through them again. You never let me quit, and I knew that you were in my corner. When I started to get better, and learned to use my CBT skills, you were my biggest cheerleader to keep me going forward. I'm going to miss you, but your lessons will always be in my mind, and your caring words will always speak to my heart."

These messages emphasize the importance of the therapeutic relationship within the work of CBT. Additionally, they all indicate an expectation that the positive effects of treatment will leave a positive, enduring mark. As one of the comments above suggests, one of the creative ways that therapists can improve their clients' understanding and retention of important therapeutic material is via the use of metaphors, stories, analogies, hypothetical questions, and any similar method that makes a "picture" become worth a thousand words (Blenkiron, 2010; Newman, 2000). One of the best ways to accomplish this goal is by using information that a given client finds particularly meaningful, such as an allusion to his or her profession, personal values, ethnic or cultural mores, hobbies, areas of particular interest (e.g., sports, literature, movies, music, politics), all in the service of making a therapeutic point. In order to accomplish this goal, therapists need at least two areas of strength: (1) to be facile in formulating case conceptualizations that take into account the clients' personal interests, values, and experiences in the shaping and maintaining of their clinically relevant beliefs; and (2) to have their own fund of knowledge about as wide a range of topics as possible outside of mental healthcare per se, so as to have more information on which to draw, increasing the chances that clients will resonate with what the therapist has to say. In other words, *lifelong learning across a range of topics is helpful to the therapist's building of expertise in delivering good CBT.* The following are some examples of a therapist using the case conceptualization (e.g., knowledge of what the client would find most compelling in a discussion) in combination with an external knowledge base to give a concise, meaningful therapeutic message to clients that they would be likely to remember and use.

- The client was a judge by profession, suffering from chronic depression typified by a pessimistic thinking style. She had been loath to work on generating rational responses for homework, saying that they did not truly represent what she believed. The therapist, using a U. S. Supreme Court analogy, asked the client to think of rational responses as "dissenting opinions," and asked her to write her best versions of these dissenting opinions for homework. This re-packaging of rational responses in the language of jurisprudence increased the client's willingness to engage in rational responding, and was reinforced by the therapist's collaborative willingness to validate the merits of the client's "majority opinion" (i.e., her typically negative thoughts).
- The client was a middle-aged man whose main avocation was a passion for ice hockey. He often had differences of opinion with his therapist, insisting that the therapist's feedback was off target, arguing that only he (the client) was in a position to judge

accurately what was happening in his own life. Using a hockey metaphor in order to gain the client's maximum attention, the therapist said,

"In the hockey game of your life, you have a front row seat, right up against the glass. Nobody has a better feel for the power, the speed, and the emotion of the 'game' than you, because you are right where the action is. By contrast, I am sitting 12 rows back, watching the hockey game of your life from a different vantage point. I can't possibly appreciate the sheer impact of the game the way you can, but I can see patterns develop on the ice because I'm higher up, whereas you are *too close to the situation* to see these patterns. I think you and I can work together to understand this game better. You can teach me about the raw power and emotions of the game, and perhaps I can send you messages about the patterns in the play." The client then said, "How can *I* get that seat 12 rows up too?"

Seeing this as an opportunity, the therapist replied, "By learning some distancing techniques—methods that will help you gain perspective and evaluate your life more strategically and less impulsively." The client's interest was piqued, and the tone of argumentation decreased.

- A suicidal, adolescent female client expounded on the meaninglessness of life, and was dismissive of the therapist's efforts to engage in a discussion about what would make her life more worthwhile and hopeful. When the therapist learned that the client's music idol was Kurt Cobain, the leader of the grunge rock group Nirvana who killed himself in 1994, he decided to educate himself about this rock star by obtaining *Rolling Stone Magazine's* tribute issue on "The Life of Kurt Cobain," and reading it thoroughly. He also purchased two of Nirvana's albums and familiarized himself with some of the lyrics. He engaged the client in discussions about Nirvana's music, which made her more talkative in session (including their agreement on the hypothesis that the song "Heart-Shaped Box" was probably a dark tribute to Kurt Cobain's therapist). Then, seizing the moment when the client expressed grief over the musical world's loss of Kurt Cobain, the therapist asked the client to do the homework assignment of listing at least five reasons why Kurt Cobain should *not* have committed suicide. The client gladly brought in a long list of written reasons, leading to a discussion of the reasons why the client herself would similarly be wise not to kill herself.

Effective therapists go out of their way to send therapeutic messages that are "packaged" in such a way that they are acceptable, comprehensible, and memorable for clients. This means understanding what matters to clients, and tailoring the lessons of CBT to make them more personally interesting and/or meaningful for clients.

COMPETENCY IN CBT SUPERVISION

Leaders in the field of CBT have previously spelled out their hypotheses about what constitutes best practices in CBT supervision (e.g., Liese & Beck, 1997; Padesky, 1996), serving as the basis for empirical reviews and studies that are making their mark on the field presently (e.g., Milne et al., 2010). In studying supervision methods and their results, Milne and colleagues define effectiveness, "...as demonstrating that clinical supervision had an impact on the supervisee's learning in terms of changes in attitudes and skills, or...produced a favorable outcome in terms of patient benefits" (p. 281).

Using the best-evidence synthesis (BES) approach to reviewing 24 studies that were representatively rigorous in methodology, Milne et al. (2010) determined that some of the central features of competently delivered CBT supervision involved observing the trainee's work directly (e.g., via video-recordings), providing feedback, and using multimodal methods of teaching (e.g., didactic instruction, role-playing, modeling the application of techniques, readings, video demonstrations). The authors added that there were additional aspects of supervision that were not as consistently used across the 24 studies, but that merited further research both on theoretical and on professional grounds. These methods include such foundational competencies as creating a healthy supervisory alliance within appropriate boundaries, modeling and teaching cross-cultural responsiveness, teaching critical thinking skills, promoting the reliable and valid monitoring of client outcomes, and encouraging supervisee self-reflection; as well the functional competencies of setting supervision goals, training supervisees to structure sessions effectively, to conceptualize cases, and to teach their clients to use a wide range of CBT self-help techniques. This line of research has resulted in the testing of a new instrument to measure supervisor behavior called SAGE (Supervision: Adherence and Guidance Evaluation; Milne & Reiser, 2008). A related summary of CBT supervisory skills and responsibilities—both foundational and functional—as described by Newman (2010), is presented in Box 11.2.

Box 11.2.
Sample (Nonexhaustive) List of CBT Supervisor's Responsibilities

1. Take ultimate professional, ethical, and legal responsibility for the clients under the care of the supervisees. Monitor cases regularly, take confidential notes, and review and sign the supervisees' clinical notes promptly.
2. Be available for regular supervision sessions (e.g., weekly), and provide for supervisory coverage in the event of being unavailable to the supervisees.
3. Establish clear goals and objectives for clinical supervision. Make the process of supervision clear and predictable, rather than mysterious.
4. Give supervisees feedback on a regular basis, including providing formal evaluations on a quarterly basis. Review recordings of the supervisees' sessions with their clients or otherwise directly observe their work. Evaluate the supervisees' progress in constructive ways that will encourage them to advance and grow as beginning professionals, but be prepared to identify supervisees who may require special remediation in order to ensure their ability to provide a reasonable standard of care to their clients.
5. Promote the professional development and autonomy of supervisees, yet balance this goal with being available for consultation (and perhaps direct participation) in complicated, critical, or dangerous clinical situations that the supervisees face with their clients.
6. Be a role-model for ethical behavior, professionalism, and expert clinical problem-solving. Respect the supervisees' boundaries, and use the power imbalance in the supervisory relationship wisely and compassionately.
7. Emphasize the importance of the therapeutic relationship, and behave in a collaborative and benevolent manner with supervisees

---

237

so as to demonstrate good relational skills. Demonstrate the ways in which supervisees can think like empiricists, yet communicate with warmth and caring.

8. Assist supervisees in learning the skills of CBT case conceptualization.

9. Assist supervisees in learning a wide range of CBT interventions. Use methods such as role-playing and video demonstrations in order to facilitate this goal.

10. Guide supervisees toward valuable resources such as the literature, instructional media, interdisciplinary and interfacility contacts, conferences, and opportunities for professional presentations, among others.

Direct Observation

It is best if supervisors periodically listen to (and/or view) recordings of sessions conducted by their supervisees (with the knowledge and consent of the clients). The benefits for the supervisees include receiving feedback on the totality of the way that they conduct CBT sessions, being able to chart their own progress as CBT trainees via their periodic scores on the CTS, and feeling valued by supervisors who invest extra time in their training. The benefits for supervisors are also significant, in that they gain a more holistic view of the CBT that is being conducted under their professional auspices, they can offer feedback that is more well-informed by virtue of their having reviewed more data, and *they can learn from their supervisees.*

Direct observation as a supervision method also pertains to the supervisors providing their trainees with opportunities to watch CBT performed by more experienced therapists. This may involve observing and discussing professionally produced recordings of master therapists (such as those that may be purchased via the American Psychological Association, and via well-established CBT training websites such as www.padesky.com and www.beckinstitute.org, as well as through DVDs that accompany volumes such as Wright et al., 2006, or by showing their *own* work with clients in CBT to their trainees either via video, or via one-way mirror). When supervisors show their own videos of doing CBT, they have a number of choices. They may show exemplars of their best work (serving as mastery models). Alternatively, they may show segments of video in which they struggled but persevered (serving as coping models). In both cases, the supervisors can pause the recordings and add "color commentary" for their trainees (e.g., "Here is what I would do differently if I could do this intervention again"), and/or ask questions ("What do you hypothesize the client will say next in response to my feedback, based on what you know about the case conceptualization?"). Further, supervisors can ask their trainees to supervise *them* based on what is transpiring on the recording (hypothetically so, given that the case may no longer be active), a method which works especially well in a group supervision format.

The Supervisor as Chief Consultant for Critical Situations

Effective supervisors are mindful of the balancing act they must navigate between promoting and encouraging their trainees to act and make decisions independently, and being willing to help the trainees deal with complicated, difficult, perhaps high-risk situations more directly (see Ladany et al., 2005). When supervisees express concerns about a given case (e.g., the client is at increased risk for suicide), the supervisor may choose to spend extra time reviewing the case, and perhaps institute additional "check-in" communications, such as when the trainee calls (or visits the office of) the supervisor immediately following the next therapy session so as to report on what transpired, and to determine whether any further interventions are warranted. In doing so, the competent supervisor promotes the trainee's autonomy by leaving him or her to deal with the direct tasks of managing the high-risk client, while increasing his or her own availability for consultation as the professional in charge.

While a full discussion of the competent management of potentially dangerous clinical situations goes beyond the scope of a handbook on core competencies (see Dattilio & Freeman, 2007; Wenzel et al., 2009 for CBT approaches to the competent treatment of clients in crisis), the following summary points can be made. First, effective supervisors are willing to address the difficult topics, such as clients' high-risk behaviors (e.g., suicidality; crossing the therapist's boundaries), ethical dilemmas (e.g., whether or not there is suspected child abuse that must be reported; handling inadvertent, unavoidable dual relationships), cross-cultural issues in treatment, and trainees' skills deficits, while creating a safe enough supervisory atmosphere to allow for highly sensitive discussions on questions such as, "What should trainees do when they experience sexual attraction toward a client?" (Ladany et al., 2005). Second, supervisors need to be ready to take the *initiative* to discuss and manage the above situations, rather than depend on the trainees to take the lead. Third, there are times when it is appropriate (and perhaps indicated) for a supervisor to speak or meet with a trainee's client directly, especially in a high-risk situation. Yes, competent supervisors allow their trainees to grow by gaining direct exposures to challenging, anxiety-provoking clinical situations, but they are also ready and willing to take charge when concerns about safety and/ or ethics are significantly elevated.

CLOSING THOUGHTS

The following is a very short list of important messages for supervisors to impart to their CBT trainees, some of whom may be uncertain of their professional skills:

1. When your clients at first do not respond well in treatment, do not fret. Remember that hopefulness begins with the therapist. Be a role model for perseverance and optimism.
2. At times you may question your effectiveness as a therapist. To a certain degree this is good, because it means that you are trying to evaluate objectively how well you are performing in your role as a therapist, and how well your clients are doing. Nevertheless, this self-questioning needs to be in the service of *problem-solving*, rather than negatively judging yourself.
3. Clients do not always respond optimally, even to evidence-based treatments such as CBT. Thus, you are going to experience some failures along the way. Learn from them, and your future clients will benefit, including some of the ones who "failed" but later came back!

Becoming a competent CBT practitioner and supervisor does not require perfection. As efficacious as CBT has been shown to be, it is still an inexact science, and it will continue to develop and advance. Being competent means that we accept the responsibilities that come with being in a helping profession, that we have a desire to learn and grow, and that we are motivated to develop, practice, and teach the best methods available to improve the lives of others.

KEY POINTS TO REMEMBER

- The path from novice therapist to competent CBT clinician requires many repetitions and simulations of CBT procedures, assisted by role-playing, seeing as many clients as possible, viewing session videos, and being receptive to the attitudes and value systems imparted by dedicated, competent CBT supervisors.
- Being an avid reader of the literature in CBT heightens a therapist's learning curve, as does participating as a protocol CBT therapist in clinical trials.
- Maintaining competency in CBT requires keeping up one's energy and enthusiasm via good self-care and meaningful outside activities, and preventing lapsing into "safety behaviors" based on an excessive concern that clients will not be ready for CBT procedures.
- A measure of high competency is the CBT practitioner's ability to make the lessons of therapy inspirational and memorable. This process is facilitated by the therapist's having funds of knowledge within and outside of the field of psychotherapy, the insight and motivation to teach CBT self-monitoring and self-help methods via metaphors, analogies, and stories that have significance for the clients, and by delivering treatment with unflagging encouragement and hope.
- Self-reflection may be one of the most important practices of the competent CBT clinician. It produces better self-correction in the face of roadblocks in treatment, and enables the therapist to be a better role-model for adaptive, constructive functioning.
- Competent CBT supervision requires an investment of time in directly observing the work of supervisees (e.g., via session recordings), as well as giving constructive feedback, modeling and teaching techniques, asking questions that stimulate the supervisees' conceptualization skills, explicitly addressing cross-cultural and ethical issues, and offering kind, hopeful words of encouragement when the trainees' confidence may be low.

KEY TERMS

- Competence
- Supervision
- Self-reflection
- Knowledge
- Attitudes
- Values
- Therapeutic relationship
- Culture
- Termination
- Assessment

- Conceptualization
- Interventions
- Homework
- Role-play
- Socratic method
- Cognitive Therapy Scale
- Drop-out
- Self-report
- Skill acquisition

REFERENCES

Alloy, L. B., Peterson, C., Abramson, L. Y., & Seligman, M. E. P. (1984). Attributional style and the generality of learned helplessness. *Journal of Personality and Social Psychology, 46*, 681–687.

American Psychiatric Association (1980). *Diagnostic and statistical manual of the mental disorders* (3rd ed.). Washington, DC: American Psychiatric Association.

American Psychiatric Association (2000). *Diagnostic and statistical manual of the mental disorders (DSM-IV-TR fourth edition [text revision])*. Washington, DC: American Psychiatric Association.

American Psychological Association (2002). Ethical principles of psychologists and code of conduct. *American Psychologist, 57*, 1060–1073.

Anderson, S., Khowaja, M., Rosales, A., Schroth, E., & Street, J. (2011). Unique perspectives on diversity: Experiencing intersecting roles of students in clinical training. *Psychotherapy Bulletin, 45*, 8–10.

Antony, M. M., Orsillo, S. M., & Roemer, L. (Eds.). (2001). *Practitioner's guide to empirically based measures of anxiety* (1st ed.). New York, NY: Springer-Verlag.

Antony, M. M., & Roemer, L. (2011). *Behavior therapy*. Washington, DC: American Psychological Association.

Antony, M. M., & Rowa, K. (2008). *Social anxiety disorder*. Ashland, OH: Hogrefe & Huber.

Arntz, A., Klokman, J., & Sieswerda, S. (2005). An experimental test of the schema mode model of borderline personality disorder. *Journal of Behavior Therapy and Experimental Psychiatry: Special Issue: Cognition and Emotion in Borderline Personality Disorder, 36*, 226–239.

Barber, J. P., & DeRubeis, R. J. (1992). The Ways of Responding: A scale to assess compensatory skills taught in cognitive therapy. *Behavioural Assessment, 14*, 93–115.

Barlow, D. H., Allen, L. B., & Choate, M. L. (2004). Toward a unified treatment of emotional disorders. *Behavior Therapy, 35*, 205–230.

Barlow, D. H., Farchione, T. J., Fairholm, C. P., Ellard, K. K., Boisseau, C. L., Allen, L. B., & Ehrenreich-May, J. (2011). *The unified protocol for transdiagnostic treatment of emotional disorders: Therapist guide*. New York, NY: Oxford University Press.

Barrett, M. S., Chua, W., Crits-Christoph, P., Gibbons, M. B., & Thompson, D. (2008). Early withdrawal from mental health treatment: Implications for psychotherapy practice. *Psychotherapy: Theory, Research, Practice, Training, 45*, 247–267.

Beck, A. T. (1976). *Cognitive therapy and the emotional disorders*. New York: International Universities Press.

Beck, A. T., Brown, G. K., & Steer, R. A. (1997). Psychometric properties of the scale for suicide ideation with psychiatric outpatients. *Behaviour Research and Therapy, 35,* 1039–1046.

Beck, A. T., Butler, A. C., Brown, G. K., Dahlsgaard, K. K., Newman, C. F., & Beck, J. S. (2001). Dysfunctional beliefs discriminate personality disorders. *Behaviour Research and Therapy, 39,* 1213–1225.

Beck, A. T., Epstein, N., Brown, G., & Steer, R. A. (1988). An inventory for measuring clinical anxiety: Psychometric properties. *Journal of Consulting and Clinical Psychology, 56,* 893–897.

Beck, A. T., Freeman, A., Davis, D., & Associates (2004). *Cognitive therapy of personality disorders* (2nd ed.). New York, NY: Guilford.

Beck, A. T., Rush, A. J., Shaw, B., & Emery, G. (1979). *Cognitive therapy of depression.* New York: Guilford.

Beck, A. T., Steer, R. A., Beck, J. S., & Newman, C. F. (1993). Hopelessness, depression, suicidal ideation, and clinical diagnosis of depression. *Suicide and Life-Threatening Behavior, 23,* 139–145.

Beck, A. T., Steer, R. A., & Brown G. K. (1996). *Manual for the Beck Depression Inventory II.* San Antonio, TX: Psychological Corporation.

Beck, A. T., Weissman, A., Lester, D., & Trexler, L. (1974). The measurement of pessimism: The Hopelessness Scale. *Journal of Consulting and Clinical Psychology, 42,* 499–505.

Beck, A. T., Wenzel, A., Riskind, J. H., Brown, G., & Steer, R. A. (2006). Specificity of hopelessness about resolving life problems: Another test of the cognitive model of depression. *Cognitive Therapy and Research, 30,* 773–781.

Beck, J. S. (1995). *Cognitive therapy: Basics and beyond.* New York, NY: Guilford.

Beck, J. S. (2011). *Cognitive behavior therapy: Basics and beyond* (2nd ed.). New York, NY: Guilford.

Bellack, A. S., & Hersen, M. (1977). *Behavior modification: An introductory textbook.* Baltimore, MD: Williams & Wilkins.

Bennett-Levy, J. (2006). Therapist skills: A cognitive model of their acquisition and refinement. *Behavioural and Cognitive Psychotherapy, 34,* 57–78.

Bennett-Levy, J., Butler, G., Fennell, M., Hackmann, A., Mueller, M., & Westbrook, D. (2004). *The Oxford guide to behavioural experiments in cognitive therapy.* Oxford, UK: Oxford University Press.

Bennett-Levy, J., & Thwaites, R. (2007). Self and self-reflection in the therapeutic relationship: A conceptual map and practical strategies for the training, supervision, and self-supervision of interpersonal skills. In R. L. Leahy & P. Gilbert (Eds.), *The therapeutic relationship in the cognitive behavioral psychotherapies* (pp. 255–281). London: Routledge/Taylor & Francis.

Blatt, S. J. (1995). The destructiveness of perfectionism: Implications for the treatment of depression. *American Psychologist, 50,* 1003–1020.

Blenkiron, P. (2010). *Stories and analogies in cognitive behavior therapy.* New York, NY: Wiley.

Bongar, B., Berman, A., Maris, R., Silverman, M., Harris, E., & Packman, W. (Eds.). (1998). *Risk management with suicidal patients*. New York, NY: Guilford.

Bordin, E. S. (1979). The generalizability of the psychoanalytic concept of the working alliance. *Psychotherapy: Theory, Research, Practice, Training, 16,* 252–260.

Burns, D. D., & Spangler, D. L. (2000). Does psychotherapy homework lead to improvements in depression in cognitive-behavioral therapy or does improvement lead to increased homework compliance? *Journal of Consulting and Clinical Psychology, 68,* 46–56.

Cardemil, E. V., Moreno, O., & Sanchez, M. (2011). One size does not fit all: Cultural considerations in evidence-based practice for depression. In D. W. Springer, A. Rubin, & C. G. Beevers (Eds.), *Clinician's guide to evidence-based practice: Treatment of depression in adolescents and adults* (pp. 221–243). Hoboken, NJ: Wiley.

Castonguay, L. G., & Beutler, L. E. (2006). *Principles of therapeutic change that work.* New York, NY: Oxford University Press.

Chen, S. W., & Davenport, D. S. (2005). Cognitive-behavioral therapy with Chinese-American clients: Cautions and modifications. *Psychotherapy: Theory, Research, Practice, Training, 42,* 101–110.

Clark, D. A., & Beck, A. T. (2010). *Cognitive therapy of anxiety disorders: Science and practice.* New York, NY: Guilford.

Crits-Christoph, P., Gibbons, M. B. C., Hamilton, J., Ring-Kurtz, S., & Gallop, R. (2011). The dependability of alliance assessments: The alliance–outcome correlation is larger than you might think. *Journal of Consulting and Clinical Psychology, 79,* 267–278.

Dahlsgaard, K. K., Beck, A. T., & Brown, G. K. (1998). Inadequate response to therapy as a predictor of suicide. *Suicide and Life-Threatening Behavior, 28,* 197–204.

Dattilio, F. M., & Freeman, A. (Eds.). (2007). *Cognitive-behavioral strategies in crisis intervention* (3rd ed.). New York, NY: Guilford.

Davis, D. D. (2008). *Terminating therapy: A professional guide to ending therapy on a positive note.* Hoboken, NJ: Wiley.

Davis, D. M., & Hayes, J. A. (2011). What are the benefits of mindfulness? A practice review of psychotherapy-related research. *Psychotherapy, 48,* 198–208.

Deblinger, E., & Heflin, A. H. (1996). *Treating sexually abused children and their nonoffending parents: A cognitive behavioral approach.* Thousand Oaks, CA: Sage.

DeRubeis, R. J., Brotman, M. A., & Gibbons, C. J. (2005). A conceptual and methodological analysis of the nonspecifics argument. *Clinical Psychology: Science and Practice, 12,* 174–183.

Detweiler-Bedell, J. B., & Whisman, M. A. (2005). A lesson in assigning homework: Therapist, client, and task characteristics in cognitive therapy for depression. *Professional Psychology: Research & Practice, 36,* 219–223.

Dobson, D., & Dobson, K. S. (2009). *Evidence-based practice of cognitive-behavioral therapy.* New York, NY: Guilford.

Duncan, B., Miller, S., Sparks, J., Claud, D., Reynolds, L., Brown, J., & Johnson, D. (2003). The Session Rating Scale: Preliminary psychometric properties of a "working" alliance measure. *Journal of Brief Therapy, 3,* 312.

Eells, T. D. (2011). What is an evidence-based psychotherapy case formulation? *Psychotherapy Bulletin, 46,* 17-21.

Elliott, R., Bohart, A. C., Watson, J. C., & Greenberg, L. S. (2011). Empathy. *Psychotherapy, 48,* 43–49.

Ellis, T. E. (Ed.). (2006). *Cognition and suicide: Theory, research, & therapy.* Washington, DC: American Psychological Association.

Ellis, T. E., & Newman, C.F. (1996). *Choosing to live: How to defeat suicide through cognitive therapy.* Oakland, CA: New Harbinger.

Evans, J., Williams, J. M., O'Loughlin, S., & Howells, K. (1992). Autobiographical memory and problem-solving strategies of parasuicide clients. *Psychological Medicine: A Journal of Research in Psychiatry and the Allied Sciences, 22,* 399–405.

Evans, M. D., Hollon, S. D., DeRubeis, R. J., Piasecki, J. M., Grove, W. M., Garvey, M. J., & Tuason, V. B. (1992). Differential relapse following cognitive therapy and pharmacology for depression. *Archives of General Psychiatry, 49,* 802–808.

Falender, C. A., & Shafranske, E. P. (2004). *Clinical supervision: A competency-based approach.* Washington, DC: American Psychological Association.

Feeley, M., DeRubeis, R. J., & Gelfand, L. A. (1999). The temporal relation of adherence and alliance to symptom change in cognitive therapy for depression. *Journal of Consulting and Clinical Psychology, 67,* 578–582.

First, M. B., Spitzer, R. L., Gibbon, M., & Williams, J. W. (2002). *Structured Clinical Interview for DSM-IV-TR Axis-I Disorders, research version, patient edition (SCID-I/P).* Washington, DC: American Psychiatric Association Press.

Freeman, A., Felgoise, S. H., Nezu, A. M., Nezu, C. M., & Reinecke, M. A. (Eds.). (2005). *Encyclopedia of Cognitive Behavior Therapy.* New York, NY: Springer.

Gibbs, B. R., & Rude, S. S. (2004). Overgeneral autobiographical memory as depression vulnerability. *Cognitive Therapy and Research, 28,* 511–526.

Giesen-Bloo, J., van Dyck, R., Spinhoven, P., van Tilburg, W., Dirksen, C., van Asselt, T., Kremers, I., Nadert, M., & Arntz, A. (2006). Outpatient psychotherapy for borderline personality disorder: A randomized trial of schema-focused vs. transference-focused psychotherapy. *Archives of General Psychiatry, 63,* 649–658.

Gilbert, P. (2007). Evolved minds and compassion in the therapeutic relationship. In P. Gilbert & R. L. Leahy (Eds.), *The therapeutic relationship in the cognitive-behavioral psychotherapies* (pp. 106–142). New York, NY: Routledge/Taylor & Francis.

Gilbert, P. & Leahy, R. L. (Eds.). (2007). *The therapeutic relationship in the cognitive-behavioral psychotherapies.* New York, NY: Routledge/Taylor & Francis.

Goldfried, M. R., & Davison, G. C. (1976). *Clinical behavior therapy*. New York, NY: Wiley.

Goodman, W. K., Price, L. H., Rasmussen, S. A., Mazure, C., Fleischmann, R. L., Hill, C. L., Heninger, G. R., & Charney, D. S. (1989). The Yale–Brown Obsessive Compulsive Scale. 1. Development, use, and reliability. *Archives of General Psychiatry, 46*, 1006–1011.

Greenberger, D., & Padesky, C. A. (1995). *Mind over mood*. New York, NY: Guilford.

Hardy, G., Cahill, J., & Barkham, M. (2007). Active ingredients of the therapeutic relationship that promote client change: A research perspective. In P. Gilbert & R. L. Leahy (Eds.), *The therapeutic relationship in the cognitive behavioral psychotherapies* (pp. 24–42). New York, NY: Routledge/Taylor & Francis.

Hayes, S. C., Strosahl, K. D., & Wilson, K. G. (1999). *Acceptance and commitment therapy: An experiential approach to behavior change*. New York, NY: Guilford.

Haynes, S. N. (1978). *Principles of behavioral assessment*. Oxford, UK: Gardner.

Hays, P. A., & Iwamasa, G. Y. (Eds.). (2006). *Culturally responsive cognitive-behavioral therapy: Assessment, practice, and supervision*. Washington, DC: American Psychological Association.

Hersen, M. (2002). *Clinical behavior therapy: Adults and children*. Hoboken, NJ: Wiley.

Hewitt, P. L., Flett, G. L., & Weber, C. (1994). Dimensions of perfectionism and suicidal ideation. *Cognitive Therapy and Research, 10*, 439–460.

Hollon, S. D., DeRubeis, R. J., & Seligman, M. E. P. (1992). Cognitive therapy and the prevention of depression. *Applied and Preventive Psychiatry, 95*, 52–59.

Hollon, S., Stewart, M., & Strunk, D. (2006). Enduring effects of cognitive behavior therapy in the treatment of depression and anxiety. *Annual Review of Psychology, 57*, 285–315.

Horvath, A. O., Del Re, A. C., Flückiger, C., & Symonds, D. (2011). Alliance in individual psychotherapy. *Psychotherapy, 48*, 9–16.

Howard, R. C. (1999). Treatment of anxiety disorders: Does specialty training help? *Professional Psychology: Research and Practice, 30*, 470–473.

Huppert, J. D., & Siev, J. (2010). Treating scrupulosity in religious individuals using cognitive-behavioral therapy. *Cognitive and Behavioral Practice, 17*, 382–392.

Iwamasa, G. Y., Pai, S. M., & Sorocco, K. H. (2006). Multicultural cognitive-behavioral therapy supervision. In P. A. Hays & G. Y. Iwamasa (Eds.), *Culturally responsive cognitive-behavioral therapy: Assessment, practice, and supervision* (pp. 267–281). Washington, DC: American Psychological Association.

Jarrett, R. B., Vittengl, J. R., Clark, L. A., & Thase, M. E. (2011). Skills of Cognitive Therapy (SoCT): A new measure of patients' comprehension and use. *Psychological Assessment, 23*, 578–586.

Kaslow, N. J. (2004). Competencies in professional psychology. *American Psychologist, 59*, 774–781.

Kazantzis, N., Deane, F. P., Ronan, K. R., & L'Abate, L. (Eds.). (2005). *Using homework assignments in cognitive behavioral therapy*. New York, NY: Routledge.

Kazantzis, N., Whittington, C., & Dattilio, F. (2010). Meta-analysis of homework effects in cognitive and behavior therapy: A replication and extension. *Clinical Psychology: Science and Practice, 17,* 144–156.

Kinzie, J. D., & Leung, P. K. (2004). Culture and outpatient psychiatry. In W. S. Tseng & J. Streltzer (Eds.), *Cultural competency in clinical psychiatry* (pp. 37–51). Washington, DC: American Psychiatric Publishing.

Knapp, S. J., & VandeCreek, L. D. (2006). *Practical ethics for psychologists: A positive approach.* Washington, DC: American Psychological Association.

Kohlenberg, R. J., & Tsai, M. (1991). *Functional analytic psychotherapy: Creating intense and curative therapeutic relationships.* New York, NY: Plenum Press.

Kroenke, K., Spitzer, R. L., & Williams, J. B. W. (2001). The PHQ-9: Validity of a brief depression severity measure. *Journal of General Internal Medicine, 16,* 606–613.

Kuyken, W. (2006). Evidence-based case formulation: Is the emperor clothed? In N. Tarrier (Ed.), *Case formulation in cognitive-behavioral therapy: The treatment of challenging and complex cases* (pp. 12–35). New York, NY: Routledge/Taylor & Francis.

Kuyken, W., Padesky, C. A., & Dudley, R. (2009). *Collaborative case conceptualization: Working effectively with clients in cognitive-behavioral therapy.* New York, NY: Guilford.

Ladany, N., Friedlander, M. L., & Nelson, M. L. (2005). *Critical events in psychotherapy supervision: An interpersonal approach.* Washington, DC: American Psychological Association.

Lam, D. H., Hayward, P., Watkins, E., Wright, K., & Sham, P. (2005). Relapse prevention in patients with bipolar disorder: Cognitive therapy outcome after two years. *American Journal of Psychiatry, 162,* 324–329.

Lambert, M. J., Morton, J., Hatfield, D., Harmon, C., Hamilton, S., & Reid, R. (2004). *Administration and scoring manual for the Outcome Questionnaire-45.* Orem, UT: American Professional Credentialing Services.

Layden, M. A., Newman, C. F., Freeman, A., & Morse, S. B. (1993). *Cognitive therapy of borderline personality disorder.* Boston, MA: Allyn & Bacon.

Leahy, R. L. (2001). *Overcoming resistance in cognitive therapy.* New York: Guilford.

Leahy, R. L. (2003). *Cognitive therapy techniques: A practitioner's guide.* New York: Guilford.

Leahy, R. L., Holland, S. J., & McGinn, L. K. (2011). *Treatment plans and interventions for depression and anxiety disorders* (2nd ed). New York, NY: Guilford.

Ledley, D. R., Marx, B. P., & Heimberg, R. H. (2010). *Making cognitive-behavioral therapy work: Clinical process for new practitioners* (2nd ed.). New York, NY: Guilford.

Liese, B. S., & Beck, J. S. (1997). Cognitive therapy supervision. In C. E. Watkins (Ed.), *Handbook of psychotherapy supervision* (pp. 114–133). New York, NY: Wiley.

Linehan, M. M. (1993). *Cognitive-behavioral treatment of borderline personality disorder.* New York, NY: Guilford.

López, S. R. (1997). Cultural competence in psychotherapy: A guide for clinicians and their supervisors. In C. E. Watkins (Ed.), *Handbook of psychotherapy supervision* (pp. 570–588). New York, NY: Wiley.

Martell, C. R., Dimidjian, S., & Herman-Dunn, R. (2010). *Behavioral activation for depression: A clinician's guide.* New York, NY: Guilford.

Martell, C. R., Safran, S. A., & Prince, S. E. (2003). *Cognitive-behavioral therapies with lesbian, gay, and bisexual clients.* New York, NY: Guilford.

Mayo, J. A. (2004). Psychotherapy with African American populations: Modifications of traditional approaches. *Annals of the American Psychotherapy Association, 7*, 10–13.

McCullough, J. P. (2000). *Treatment for chronic depression: Cognitive Behavioral Analysis System of Psychotherapy (CBASP).* New York, NY: Guilford.

McCullough, L., Bhatia, M., Ulvenes, P., Berggraf, L., & Osborn, K. (2011). Learning how to rate video-recorded therapy sessions: A practical guide for trainees and advanced clinicians. *Psychotherapy, 48*, 127–137.

McIntyre, K. M., Norton, J. R., & McIntyre, J. S. (2009). Psychiatric interview, history, and mental status examination. In B. J. Sadock, V. A. Sadock, & P. Ruiz (Eds.), *Kaplan & Sadock's comprehensive textbook of psychiatry* (9th ed., pp. 886–907). Baltimore, MD: Lippincott, Williams, & Wilkins.

Meehl, P. E. (1954). *Clinical vs. statistical prediction: A theoretical analysis and a review of the evidence.* Minneapolis, MN: University of Minnesota Press.

Miller, S., & Duncan, B. (2000). *The Outcome Rating Scale.* Chicago, IL: Author.

Milne, D. (2009). *Evidence-based clinical supervision: Principles and practice.* Leicester, UK: BPS Blackwell.

Milne, D., & Reiser, R. (2008). *Supervision: Adherence and Guidance Evaluation (SAGE).* Unpublished instrument, available from the first author.

Milne, D., Reiser, R., Aylott, H., Dunkerley, C., Fitzpatrick, H., & Wharton, S. (2010). The systematic review as an empirical approach to improving CBT supervision. *International Journal of Cognitive Therapy, 3*, 278–294.

Moffic, H. S., & Kinzie, J. D. (1996). The history and future of cross-cultural psychiatric service. *Community Mental Health Journal, 32*, 581–592.

Needleman, L. (1999). *Cognitive case conceptualization: A guide for practitioners.* Mahwah, NJ: Lawrence Erlbaum Associates.

Neenan, M. & Dryden, W. (2004). *Cognitive therapy: 100 key points and techniques.* New York, NY: Brunner-Routledge.

Neimeyer, R. A., & Mahoney, M. J. (Eds.). (1995). *Constructivism in psychotherapy.* Washington, DC: American Psychological Association.

Newman, C. F. (1994). Understanding client resistance: Methods for enhancing motivation to change. *Cognitive and Behavioral Practice, 1*, 47–69.

Newman, C. F. (1998). The therapeutic relationship and supervisory relationship in cognitive-behavioral therapy: similarities and differences. *Journal of Cognitive Psychotherapy: An International Quarterly, 12*, 95–108.

Newman, C. F. (2000). Hypotheticals in cognitive psychotherapy: Creative questions, novel answers, and therapeutic change. *Journal of Cognitive Psychotherapy: An International Quarterly, 14,* 135–147.

Newman, C. F. (2002). A cognitive perspective on resistance in psychotherapy. *Journal of Clinical Psychology, 58,* 165–174.

Newman, C. F. (2005). Reducing the risk of suicide in clients with bipolar disorder: Interventions and safeguards. *Cognitive and Behavioral Practice, 12,* 76–88.

Newman, C. F. (2007). The therapeutic relationship in cognitive therapy with difficult-to-engage clients. In P. Gilbert & R. L. Leahy (Eds.), *The therapeutic relationship in the cognitive-behavioral psychotherapies* (pp. 165–184). New York, NY: Routledge/Taylor & Francis.

Newman, C. F. (2010). Competency in conducting cognitive-behavioral therapy: Foundational, functional, and supervisory aspects. *Psychotherapy: Theory, Research, Practice, Training, 47,* 12–19.

Newman, C. F. (2011a). Cognitive behavior therapy for depressed adults. In D. W. Springer, A. Rubin, & C. G. Beevers (Eds.), *Clinician's guide to evidence-based practice: Treatment of depression in adolescents and adults* (pp. 69–111). Hoboken, NJ: Wiley.

Newman, C. F. (2011b). When clients' morbid avoidance and chronic anger impede their response to cognitive-behavioral therapy for depression. *Cognitive and Behavioral Practice, 18,* 350–361.

Newman, C. F. (in press). Training CBT supervisors: Didactics, simulated practice, and "meta-supervision." *Journal of Cognitive Psychotherapy.*

Newman, C. F., & Beck, J. S. (2008). Selecting, training, and supervising therapists in randomized, controlled trials. In A. M. Nezu & C. M. Nezu (Eds.), *Evidence-based outcome research: A practical guide to conducting randomized controlled trials for psychosocial interventions* (pp. 245–262). Oxford, UK: Oxford University Press.

Newman, C. F., Leahy, R. L., Beck, A. T., Reilly-Harrington, N., & Gyulai, L. (2001). *Bipolar disorder: A cognitive therapy approach.* Washington, DC: The American Psychological Association.

Newman, C. F., & Strauss, J. S. (2003). When clients are untruthful: Implications for the therapeutic alliance, case conceptualization, and intervention. *Journal of Cognitive Psychotherapy: An International Quarterly, 17,* 241–252.

Nezu, A. M., Nezu, C. M., & Lombardo, E. (2004). *Cognitive-behavioral case formulation and treatment design: A problem-solving approach.* New York, NY: Springer.

Nezu, A. M., Nezu, C. M., & Perri, M. G. (1989). *Problem-solving therapy for depression: Theory, research, and clinical guidelines.* New York, NY: Wiley.

Nezu, A. M., Ronan, G. F., Meadows, E., & McClure, K. S. (Eds.). (2000). *Practitioner's guide to empirically based measures of depression.* New York, NY: Springer-Verlag.

Nisbett, R.E. (2003). *The geography of thought: How Asians and Westerners think differently...and why.* New York, NY: Free Press.

Norcross, J. C., & Goldfried, M. R. (Eds.). (2005). *Handbook of psychotherapy integration* (2nd ed.). New York, NY: Oxford University Press.

Norcross, J. C., & Lambert, M. J. (2011). Psychotherapy relationships that work II. *Psychotherapy, 48*, 4–8.

O'Donohue, W. T. (1998). *Learning and behavior therapy*: Needham Heights, MA: Allyn & Bacon.

O'Donohue, W. T., & Fisher, J. E. (Eds.). (2009). *General principles and empirically supported techniques of cognitive behavior therapy*. Hoboken, NJ: Wiley.

Organista, K. C. (2000). Latinos. In J. R. White & A. S. Freeman (Eds.), *Cognitive-behavioral group therapy for specific problems and populations* (pp. 281–303). Washington, DC: American Psychological Association.

Organista, K. C., & Muñoz, R. F. (1996). Cognitive behavioral therapy with Latinos. *Cognitive and Behavioral Practice, 3*, 255–270.

Overholser, J. C. (2010). Psychotherapy according to the Socratic method: Integrating ancient philosophy with contemporary cognitive therapy. *Journal of Cognitive Psychotherapy: An International Quarterly, 24*, 354–363.

Padesky, C. A. (1996). Developing cognitive therapist competency: Teaching and supervision models. In P. M. Salkovskis (Ed.), *Frontiers of cognitive therapy* (pp. 266–292). New York, NY: Guilford.

Paris, J. (2007). *Half in love with death: Managing the chronically suicidal patient*. Mahwah, NJ: Lawrence Erlbaum Associates.

Parks, C. W., Jr., & Hollon, S. D. (1988). Cognitive assessment. In A. S. Bellack & M. Hersen (Eds.), *Behavioral assessment: A practical handbook* (3rd ed., pp. 161–212). Elmsford, NY: Pergamon Press.

Persons, J. (2008). *The case formulation approach to cognitive-behavior therapy*. New York, NY: Guilford.

Prochaska, J. O., DiClemente, C. C., & Norcross, J. P. (1992). In search of how people change: Applications to addictive behaviors. *American Psychologist, 47*, 1102–1114.

Ramseyer, F., & Tschacher, W. (2011). Non-verbal synchrony in psychotherapy: Coordinated body movement reflects relationship quality and outcome. *Journal of Consulting and Clinical Psychology, 79*, 284–295.

Rees, C. S., McEvoy, P., & Nathan, P. R. (2005). Relationship between homework completion and outcome in cognitive behaviour therapy. *Cognitive Behaviour Therapy, 34*, 242–247.

Resick, P. A., & Schnicke, M. K. (1993). *Cognitive processing therapy for rape victims: A treatment manual*. London: Sage.

Riso, L. P., du Toit, P. L., Stein, D. J., & Young, J. E. (2007). *Cognitive schemas and core beliefs in psychological problems: A scientist-practitioner guide*. Washington, DC: American Psychological Association.

Rodolfa, E., Bent, R., Eisman, E., Nelson, P., Rehm, L., & Ritchie, P. (2005). A cube model for competency development: Implications for psychology educators and regulators. *Professional Psychology: Research and Practice, 36*, 347–354.

Roth, A. D. & Pilling, S. (2007). *The competences required to deliver competent cognitive and behavioural therapy for people with depression and with anxiety disorders.* Manual prepared for the Department of Health, United Kingdom.

Safran, J. D., & Muran, J. C. (2000). *Negotiating the therapeutic alliance: A relational treatment guide.* New York, NY: Guilford.

Safran, J. D., Muran, J. C., & Eubanks-Carter, C. (2011). Repairing alliance ruptures. *Psychotherapy, 48,* 80–87.

Safran, J. D., Muran, J. C., Samstag, L. W., & Stevens, C. (2001). Repairing alliance ruptures. *Psychotherapy: Theory, Research, Practice, Training, 38,* 406–412.

Safran, J. D. & Segal, Z. V. (1990). *Interpersonal process in cognitive therapy.* Lanham, MD: Jason Aronson.

Schmidt, N. B., Joiner, T. E., Jr., Young, J. E., & Telch, M. J. (1995). The Schema Questionnaire: Investigation of psychometric properties and the hierarchical structure of a measure of maladaptive schemata. *Cognitive Therapy and Research, 19,* 295–321.

Schotte, D., & Clum, G. (1987). Problem-solving skills in suicidal psychiatric clients. *Journal of Consulting and Clinical Psychology, 55,* 49–54.

Scott, J., Paykel, E., Morriss, R., Bentall, R., Kinderman, P., Johnson, T., Abbott, R., & Hayhurst, H. (2006). Cognitive-behavioural therapy for severe and recurrent bipolar disorders: Randomised controlled trial. *British Journal of Psychiatry, 188,* 313–320.

Sperry, L. T. (2010). *Core competencies in counseling and psychotherapy: Becoming a highly competent and effective therapist.* New York, NY: Routledge/Taylor & Francis.

Spielberger, C. D. (1983). *Manual for the State-Trait Anxiety Inventory STAI (Form Y).* Palo Alto, CA: Consulting Psychologists Press.

Spielberger, C. D. (1999). *STAXI-2: The state-trait anger expression inventory professional manual.* Odessa, FL: Psychological Assessment Resources.

Spinhoven, P., Bockting, C. L. H., Kremers, I. P., Schene, A. H., & Williams, J. M. G. (2007). The endorsement of dysfunctional attitudes is associated with an impaired retrieval of specific autobiographical memories in response to matching cues. *Memory, 15,* 324–338.

Strauss, J. L., Hayes, A. M., Johnson, S. L., Newman, C. F., Barber, J. P., Brown, G. K., Laurenceau, J. P., & Beck, A. T. (2006). Early alliance, alliance ruptures, and symptom change in cognitive therapy for avoidant and obsessive-compulsive personality disorders. *Journal of Consulting and Clinical Psychology, 74,* 337–345.

Strunk, D. R., Brotman, M., & DeRubeis, R. J. (2010). The process of change in cognitive therapy for depression: Predictors of early inter-session symptom gains. *Behaviour Research and Therapy, 48,* 599–606.

Strunk, D. R., DeRubeis, R. J., Chiu, A. W., & Alvarez, J. (2007). Patients' competence in and performance of cognitive therapy skills: Relation to the reduction of relapse risk following treatment for depression. *Journal of Consulting and Clinical Psychology, 75,* 523–530.

Sturmey, P. (Ed.). (2009). *Clinical case formulation: Varieties of approaches.* London: Wiley-Blackwell.

Sudak, D. (2011). *Combining CBT and medication: An evidence-based approach.* Hoboken, NJ: Wiley.

Sue, S. (1998). In search of cultural competence in psychotherapy and counseling. *American Psychologist, 53,* 440–448.

Tang, T. Z., Beberman, R., DeRubeis, R. J., & Pham, T. (2005). Cognitive changes, critical sessions, and sudden gains in cognitive-behavioral therapy for depression. *Journal of Consulting and Clinical Psychology, 73,* 168–172.

Tang, T. Z., & DeRubeis, R. J. (1999). Sudden gains and critical sessions in cognitive-behavioral therapy for depression. *Journal of Consulting and Clinical Psychology, 67,* 894–904.

Tarrier, N. (Ed.). (2006). *Case formulation in cognitive-behavioral therapy: The treatment of challenging and complex cases.* New York, NY: Routledge/Taylor & Francis.

Tee, J., & Kazantzis, N. (2010). Collaborative empiricism in cognitive therapy: A definition and theory for the relationship construct. *Clinical Psychology: Science and Practice, 18,* 47–61.

Trepka, C., Rees, A., Shapiro, D. A., Hardy, G. E., & Barkham, M. (2004). Therapist competence and outcome of cognitive therapy for depression. *Cognitive Therapy and Research, 28,* 143–157.

Tseng, W. S., & Streltzer, J. (Eds.). (2004). *Cultural competence in clinical psychiatry.* Washington, DC: American Psychiatric Publishing.

Waller, G. (2009). Evidence-based treatment and therapist drift. *Behaviour Research and Therapy, 47,* 119–127.

Webb, C. A., DeRubeis, R. J., Amsterdam, J. D., Shelton, R. C., Hollon, S. D., & Dimidjian, S. (2011). Two aspects of the therapeutic alliance: Differential relations with depressive symptom change. *Journal of Consulting and Clinical Psychology, 79,* 279–283.

Weishaar, M. E. (1996). Cognitive risk factors in suicide. In P. M. Salkovskis (Ed.), *Frontiers of cognitive therapy* (pp. 226–249). New York, NY: Guilford.

Weissman, A. N., & Beck, A. T. (1978). Development and validation of the Dysfunctional Attitudes Scale: A preliminary investigation. Paper presented at the Annual Meeting of the American Educational Research Association, Toronto, Canada.

Wells, A. (2009). *Metacognitive therapy for anxiety and depression.* New York, NY: Guilford.

Wenzel, A., Brown, G. K., & Beck, A. T. (2009). *Cognitive therapy for suicidal clients: Scientific and clinical applications.* Washington, DC: American Psychological Association.

Whaley, A. L., & Davis, K. E. (2007). Cultural competence and evidence-based practice in mental health services: A complementary perspective. *American Psychologist, 62,* 563–574.

Wheeler, H. A., Blankstein, K. R., Antony, M. M., McCabe, R. E., & Bieling, P. J. (2011). Perfectionism in anxiety and depression: Comparisons across disorders, relations with symptom severity, and role of comorbidity. *International Journal of Cognitive Therapy, 4,* 66–91.

Whisman, M. A. (Ed.). (2008). *Adapting cognitive therapy for depression: Managing complexity and comorbidity.* New York, NY: Guilford.

Williams, J. B. (1988). A structured interview guide for the Hamilton Depression Rating Scale. *Journal of Neurology, Neurosurgery, and Psychiatry, 23,* 56–62.

Williams, J. M. G., Teasdale, J. D., & Segal, Z. V. (2007). *The mindful way through depression: Freeing yourself from chronic unhappiness.* New York, NY: Guilford.

Wilson, G. T. (2007). Manual-based treatment: Evolution and evaluation. In T. A. Treat, R. R. Bootzin, & T. B. Baker (Eds.), *Psychological clinical science: Papers in honor of Richard M. McFall* (pp. 105–132). New York, NY: Psychological Press.

Wright, J. H., Basco, M. R., & Thase, M. (2006). *Learning cognitive-behavior therapy: An illustrated guide.* Arlington, VA: American Psychiatric Publishing.

Wright, J. H., Wright, A. S., & Beck, A. T. (2004). *Good days ahead: The multi-media program for cognitive therapy.* Louisville, KY: Mindstreet.

Wright, J. H., Wright, A. S., Salmon, P., Beck, A. T., Kuykendall, J., Goldsmith, L. J., & Zickel, M. B. (2002). Development and initial testing of a multimedia program for computer-assisted cognitive therapy. *American Journal of Psychotherapy, 56,* 76–86.

Young, J, & Beck, A. T. (1980). Cognitive Therapy Rating Scale Manual. Unpublished manuscript. University of Pennsylvania, Philadelphia, PA.

Young, J. E., Klosko, J. S., & Weishaar, M. E. (2003). *Schema therapy: A practitioner's guide.* New York, NY: Guilford.

Young, R. C., Biggs, J. T., Ziegler, V. E., & Meyer, D. A. (1978). A rating scale for mania: Reliability, validity, and sensitivity. *British Journal of Psychiatry, 133,* 429–435.

INDEX